1929 Aviatrix

"Ingalls and the Andes"
Artist conception of the Ingalls crossing of 1934 in an
open cockpit Lockheed Air Express. Story page 116-117.

Artwork © 2007 Sharon Rajnus

"It is my contention that [aviation] will never be the big commercial industry that the automobile industry is until women take it up."

Attributed to Tex Rankin, Walt Bohrer's Black Cats and Outside Loops

STARS OF THE SKY, LEGENDS ALL

ANN LEWIS COOPER and SHARON RAJNUS, Artist

Women in Aviation
INTERNATIONAL

ZENITH PRESS

First published in 2008 by Zenith Press, an imprint of MBI Publishing Company LLC, Galtier Plaza, Suite 200, 380 Jackson Street, St. Paul, MN 55101 USA

© Women in Aviation, International, 2008
Address: 3647 State Route 503 South, West Alexandria, Ohio 45381

www.wai.org

Text: © Ann Lewis Cooper
Paintings: © Sharon Rajnus

Zenith Press titles are also available at discounts in bulk quantity for industrial or sales-promotional use. For details write to Special Sales Manager at MBI Publishing Company, Galtier Plaza, Suite 200, 380 Jackson Street, St. Paul, MN 55101 USA.

To find out more about our books, join us online at www.zenithpress.com.

Library of Congress Cataloging-in-Publication Data

Cooper, Ann L. (Ann Lewis)
  Stars of the sky, legends all : illustrated histories of women aviation pioneers / by Ann Lewis Cooper ; artwork by Sharon Rajnus.
     p. cm.
  ISBN-13: 978-0-7603-3374-7 (softbound)
  ISBN-10: 0-7603-3374-2 (softbound)
  ISBN-13: 978-0-7603-3375-4 (softbound, WAI ed.)
  ISBN-10: 0-7603-3375-0 (softbound, WAI ed.) 1. Women air pilots--Biography. 2. Women air pilots--Portraits. I. Title.
TL539.C645 2008
629.13092'2--dc22
                                        2007043018

Printed in Singapore

Cover design: Sharon Rajnus

On the frontispiece:
"1929 Aviatrix" Sharon Rajnus

On the title page:
"Ingalls and Andes" Sharon Rajnus

Table of Contents

ABOUT THE AUTHOR

I've watched with pleasure the rapid progress that **Ann Lewis Cooper** has made in the field of aviation writing, from her earliest efforts to her current status as one of the top ranked members in the field.

No book could be more appropriate to Ann's skills than this one, STARS OF THE SKY, Legends All, for she has her finger on both the pulse of the nation and the steady heartbeat of aviation history. Ann combines an understanding of aviation with a deeply felt empathy for those women who have made real contributions to the discipline.

This book marks a new level in Ann's creative process, for in it she combines her familiar writing skill with a level of personal research that is remarkable. Further, she has the wisdom to look outside the realm of record setters and extend her vision into other important fields, such as education. The result is a comprehensive survey of women who, on the basis of their contributions, should be as well known as Amelia Earhart; but, because of the vagaries of the media, are not.

Ann Cooper's knowledge of aviation history is matched in this book by her knowledge of aviation art. She has chosen the spectacular aviation art of Sharon Rajnus to illuminate the stories of her heroines in a way that the best photography cannot do.

This is a book by a woman, about women, for everyone, for no man could read the accounts of these remarkable aviation greats without a sense of wonder. Flying is a tough game; these women have made it to the top in that game. And Ann Cooper has made it to a new level in her swift rising career with this excellent combination of personality, writing and art.

—Walter J. Boyne
Author, Historian,
Former Director National Air
& Space Museum, Smithsonian

ABOUT THE ARTIST

Sharon Rajnus is the perfect choice for the creation of art documenting stories of "Women in Aviation". Sharon is not only an accomplished artist and a superb watercolorist with long experience painting aviation subjects, she has been both pilot and artist for over thirty years. A resident of Oregon with her pilot husband Donald, Sharon is a member of the Crater Lake Ninety-Nines. Sharon personally lives the life of a woman in aviation.

Her love of aviation stems from her father who was an engineer and P-38 project administrator with Lockheed Aircraft during World War II. Her aviation education included working alongside an A&P mechanic in rebuilding a Stinson 108-2 which joined a Cessna 120, a Stinson 108-3, a Maule and a Helio Courier in making possible the personal aerial visits to the wonderful places to be seen in so many of her paintings. Sharon is particularly adept at creating stunning life-like watercolor images of glaciers and ice and snow covered mountains, the grandeur of which can normally be viewed closely only from the air.

Sharon's award winning aviation, wildlife and landscape art has been exhibited nation-wide from Washington, Oregon, and California, to Wisconsin, New Mexico, Missouri, and New York. She is a [former] member of the Board of Trustees of the American Society of Aviation Artists and has won numerous awards in ASAA exhibitions, including her painting of Charles and Anne Morrow Lindbergh skirting a Greenland glacier in their Lockheed Sirius. This art was selected for the cover of the Aviation Week & Space Technology Annual Photography and Art special issue for 2000.

—Keith Ferris,
ASAA Founder
American Society of
Aviation Artists

Prologue

COURAGE – to react positively in challenging situations

CONVICTION – to hold a belief and to act accordingly and morally

COMMUNICATION – to impart and exchange ideas

COMPASSION – with awareness, to put another above self

COMPETENCE – to be qualified and to exhibit capability

COMMITMENT – to follow a course of action to which bound

CHARACTER – ethical strength, moral attributes

COMPETITION – to test ability and skills, to contest

CURIOSITY – a quest for greater knowledge

CONQUEST – to seek a victory

THE ENERGY OF DREAMS

Where do we find motivation for the direction and conduct of our lives? What lies within that spurs us to commit to paths that ultimately will offer the satisfaction of a life well lived? Is it a matter of environment, attributed to the parents who brought us into the world, the households, communities and nations in which we were raised, the teachers to whom our education was entrusted and those who have affected our decisions? Can motivation be traced to our heredity, our inherent characteristics – intelligence, sense of humor, talent, ambition; the personality with which we are blessed?

Or, are there mitigating factors that arrive unbidden? Do surprising events introduce options we'd never before considered and challenge us with new directions and new choice? Those are the stuff of our dreams, the hopes to which we aspire, despite any real or imagined limitations. Encouraged to "Follow our Dreams," we must carefully select those to which we will respond.

It takes courage to make good choices, even to realize that the choice is ours. We can dismiss a dream on the grounds that it might be unattainable or we can be open to new ideas and receptive to taking our futures into our own hands. Those conscious decisions to dare to dream and to reach beyond our limits are the first steps toward mastery of our inheritance and our environment. If we can harness the energy of our dreams and hold tightly to their motivational magnetism, we can take them to the realm of reality.

Consider the women whose stories grace these pages. Bound by the shared passion for aviation, they are exemplary of the motivation, execution and dedication that lead to satisfaction. They are alike in the qualities chosen as chapter headings and they are alike in that, having set admirable goals, they have all demonstrated the enviable and essential characteristic of persistence. They are role models and they are outstanding successes in their chosen endeavors.

Their dreams, their choices and their pathways to success differed. Each one has faced and overcome obstacles that might have been insurmountable without perseverance and determination; yet no single one would acknowledge having done anything extraordinary. In that self-deprecation is a message for us all. In living life, in grasping opportunities as they arose, in working diligently to shape a skill, in exhibiting tenacity, every one has followed her dreams and brought success to her life.

Each woman has contributed to the history and the enrichment of aviation. Simultaneously, each has been enhanced by her experiences and achievements. As she has exerted a vibrant influence on her chosen career and has positively affected this discipline; she has, in turn, profited by the dynamics of aviation's rewarding field of endeavor.

These "Stars" were not chosen simply because they are women; they were selected because they display the attributes with which each chapter is headed. Intriguingly, each woman embodies all ten qualities while simultaneously exhibiting unique individuality. Their admirable personality characteristics are enviable and praiseworthy; but, they are not outside of your realm of possibility. You can follow your dreams. You can profit from the stories of each of these women and make worthwhile choices in your sphere of influence, your field of endeavor.

Anthropologist Margaret Mead wrote, in her autobiography *Blackberry Winter:*

"Because of their age-long training in human relations – for that is what feminine intuition really is – women have a special contribution to make to any ...enterprise."

Mead's words could refer to aviation's women of accomplishment whose stories are the subjects of this book. They are a select group and there are hundreds like them who are equally deserving of attention and appreciation. That the author has had the opportunity to meet and interview the majority of the modern women in these pages has been her good fortune. She cherishes their friendship and considers precious their trust.

Enjoy the following episodes in remarkable women's lives. Some were frightening, some were life-threatening, some included fatalities, and all were pivotal. Identify with these successful women and recognize the choices made that turned their opportunities into achievements.

Artwork ©2007 Sharon Rajnus

The Curtiss Jenny biplane, one of the world's best-known early trainers, was used by 95% of all training pilots in WWI. Equipped with an OX-5 piston engine, it held a crew of two and had an endurance period of 2 hours. Over 6800 of the JN-4 version were built, and after the war many were sold on the civilian market. Charles Lindbergh's first aircraft was a Jenny. The slow speed and natural stability of this biplane made it perfect for stunt flying and aerobatic displays in the 1920s and 1930s.

Dedication

No illustrated book covering the first century of powered flight has been more lovingly created than this. The author and the artist are grateful for the outstanding support and cooperation they received. We especially thank our husbands, Charlie Cooper and Donald Rajnus. We appreciate the willingness of those women who have given generously to ensure the integrity of their stories. We both acknowledge the encouragement of Dr. Peggy Chabrian of Women in Aviation, International, and Steve Gansen, Steve Daubenspeck and Mary La Barre of Zenith Press, and would like to express thanks to Ronald C. Howard for his digital expertise. We have relished the chance to work with a subject we love in hopes that the achievements of remarkable women will surprise and inspire. Their stories should not be lost.

See additonal artwork at RajnusArt.com

CHAPTER ONE

COURAGE AND CONVICTION

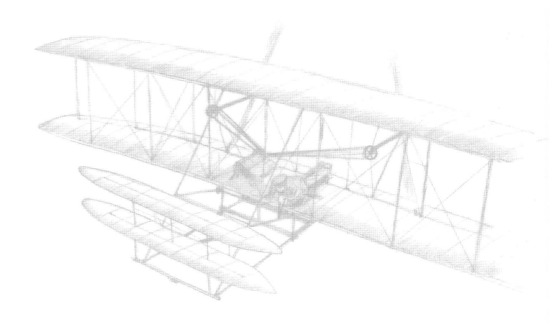

WRIGHT FLYER
Artwork © 2007 Sharon Rajnus

CONVICTION

"I would have done anything, or very nearly, to fly in a new plane. I feel so happy when I'm flying! Why? It's not easy to explain. Perhaps it is the feeling of power, the pleasure of dominating a machine as beautiful and as sensitive as a thoroughbred horse. Today, I fly jet planes that are far swifter, far more powerful. Mingled with these basic joys is another less primitive feeling, that of a mission accomplished. Each time I set foot on an airfield, I sense with fresh excitement that this is where I belong."

Jacqueline Auriol, I LIVE TO FLY

WRIGHT FLYER

Artwork © 2007 Sharon Rajnus

COURAGE

"I don't feel particularly daring. To me, real courage is metaphysical and has to do with keeping one's passion for life intact, one's curiosity at full stretch, when one is daily hemmed in by death, disease, and lesser mayhems of the heart. Still, I am compulsively drawn to pastimes most people would find frightening. Some women consciously pursue danger, as a way of touching the fabric of their mortality."

Diane Ackerman, ON EXTENDED WINGS

CHAPTER 1

Katharine Wright

Selflessness Personified

In this, the young 21st Century, it is difficult to grasp the humility and altruism that characterized Dayton, Ohio's Katharine Wright at the turn of the 20th. Surely, there are young women today upon whose shoulders fall the duties left with an untimely passing of their mothers. Undoubtedly, there are those who affectionately and kindly accept the role of hostess, homemaker, companion, nurse – devoting countless hours to the cares and concerns of home and hearth. Like them, Katharine Wright accepted her roles and cheerfully fulfilled the needs of all closest to her. Yet, because of her father's piety and rigid expectations and in light of her brothers' fame and achievements, much exacted of Katharine was extraordinary.

Born in August 1874, Katharine was six when the yoke of responsibility fell upon her shoulders and, to a lesser extent, on those of her four brothers. From 1880, tuberculosis started wreaking its havoc upon their mother, Susan Wright. Within six years, Susan was confined to her bed and Katharine accepted her homemaking position without complaint. When her mother passed away, Katharine was fifteen; she was zealously devoted to her family.

Her father, Bishop Milton Wright, had already written, "Be good. Learn all you can about housework. . . .Take especially good care of yourself. You have a good mind and good heart and, being my only daughter, you are my only hope of love and care if I live to be old."

As a leader in the United Brethren Church, Bishop Wright was often away from home serving the large and far-flung church membership. During his sons' dramatic forays into the science of flight, Bishop Wright was embroiled in a bitter conflict in his church. His stoic adherence to his beliefs was admirable; but, his rigidity extended to his parenting and Katharine acquiesced, honoring him as she had honored her mother.

Katharine's two oldest brothers, Reuchlin and Lorin, married and started their families and her brothers, Wilbur and Orville, left high school to devote themselves to creating a craft capable of carrying a man in powered flight. Katharine, too, dropped out of high school. She put family first to help Reuchlin's and Lorin's wives when they were delivering babies, to care for Wilbur when he'd sickened with appendicitis, to tend to her nephew who was stricken with typhoid fever, and to see to the secretarial, financial and social needs of her father.

Dawne Dewey, archivist at The Libraries of Wright State University, said, "The more I learn about Katharine Wright, the more fascinating she becomes. Born into a family with conservative values, but forward thinking beliefs about women's rights and education, she lived a life full of contradiction between the reality of the role of women in the age in which she lived and the life she might have entered under different circumstances."

Katharine gracefully made peace with contradiction. From personal experience, she knew of the inequities in salaries and positions between male and female teachers. She passionately threw her energies into the Suffragette movement to gain women the right to vote and her father, somewhat ironically in light of his expectation and treatment of Katharine, preached in favor of women's rights from his pulpit. In 1914, Orville and their father marched with her in a Suffrage protest march through downtown Dayton. Her father expected her to be the family hostess and he simultaneously believed that, for her to realize independence after his death, she should be trained for a career. At a time when relatively few women pursued a college education, Milton sent his daughter to Oberlin College. Lacking a high school diploma, she first invested a year in preparatory study prior to matriculation as a student.

At Oberlin, Katharine was a popular student and she formed lasting friendships with a host of women and a few men. For a short time, she was engaged to be married to Arthur Cunningham; but, she admitted that the union wasn't to be. She noted, "He was evidently relieved when I pretended I thought we had better give it up. I was horribly unhappy for several years, all the time glad I had done what I had, but brokenhearted over the failure of a great ideal with me."

A second fellow student, Harry Haskell, shared Katharine's love of books and, as an excellent mathematician, was a willing tutor to

Katharine. After their graduation in 1898, he married a friend of Katharine's and went on to become a respected newspaperman. Through letters and occasional visits, he and Katharine maintained a cordial friendship. Katharine returned to Dayton with hope of landing a teaching position at the same time that her brothers hoped to conquer the air.

Katharine was drawn ever closer to the same fire that drew her brothers to flight. As Wilbur and Orville met with success, Katharine willingly became crucial to their activities as correspondent, publicist and financial recorder.

In 1908, Wilbur demonstrated the Wright Flyer for sale to interested European governments and Orville exhibited a craft to the U.S. Army Signal Corps in Fort Myer, Virginia. An ensuing crash was fatal to the Signal Corps' representative, Lt. Thomas Selfridge, and seriously injurious to Orville. Katharine immediately left her teaching position to nurse Orville back to health. She devoted over a month to daily care; dealing with the nurses and doctors, bathing him, reading to him and tirelessly administering to his needs.

After his recuperation, Katharine accompanied him to Europe to join Wilbur and, as both brothers were reticent about public speaking, Katharine interceded in their behalf. Orville increasingly depended upon her social skills and her gregariousness, attributes that were even more obvious in Europe. There, Katharine mingled freely with royalty, heads of state and those whose interest in flying machines and aeronautics was growing with each new Wright Brothers' success.

Her position, however, was impressed upon her in the following telegraph wire she received after having flown in a balloon with Wilbur in France. Her father wrote, "It does not make much difference about you, but Wilbur ought to keep out of all balloon rides. Success seems to hang on him."

Her growth as a woman of the world was obvious and her enjoyment of meeting at the White House with William Howard Taft, President of the United States, indicated just how essential she had become to her brothers' achievements. In jest she was called, "The Third Wright Brother"; yet, she received many of the same awards as did her brothers.

KATHARINE 1874 - WRIGHT - 1929

Artwork © 2007 Sharon Rajnus

Katharine tirelessly supported her brothers Orville and Wilbur during their exploration into powered flight. She was secretary, counselor, hostess and advisor, indispensable to their success.

But, tragedy took its toll. In 1912, Wilbur died prematurely due to typhoid fever contracted from oysters taken from polluted waters near Boston, Massachusetts. Five years later, Bishop Milton Wright passed away. The daughter and sister who had proven so completely indispensable became even more essential to Orville.

When, at age 50, Katharine was approached by her Oberlin College friend, Harry Haskell, romance, so long repressed, was the furthest thing from her mind. Harry's wife, Isabel, had died of cancer in 1923 and, in her generous and giving way, Katharine had written to encourage Harry in his grief. The correspondence had flourished and, when Harry dared to speak to Katharine of marriage, suggesting that love was possible for the two of them, she was speechless. She was also frightened by what she knew would be a blow to Orville. She knew that, as sister and brother, they had worked out a comfortable and mutually satisfying, supportive and successful life. She, who had given so selflessly of herself to her immediate family for her entire life, tried to deny her own latent desires and what had been, as she'd said so long before about her first engagement, her "great ideal."

In letters and telegrams to Katharine, Harry was ardent and expressive. She weakened in response to her long-denied and compelling urges. By summer 1925, the lovers decided to be married and Katharine, the one to whom Orville had always turned when hurt or angered or troubled, agreed that she would tell her brother as soon as she could find a way.

It was May 1926 before Harry was the one to break the news to Orville. As Katharine had feared, Orville fell into a deep and silent brooding. Katharine was depressed with his reaction and torn between familial ties and an opportunity for true love. Harry simply asked Katharine to respond to the feelings of her heart.

Orville was adamant. He opposed the marriage, refused to attend, refused to allow the ceremony at the Wright mansion, Hawthorn Hill, and objected to every attempt at reconciliation from either of their older brothers or from Katharine. Nonetheless, Katharine became

Mrs. Harry Haskell on 20 November 1926 in the home of friends in Oberlin, Ohio, the scene of their original meeting and the college they both continued to serve. Katharine was only the second woman to sit on Oberlin's Board of Trustees.

The newlyweds traveled immediately to Kansas City, never to return to the Wright home again. Ten weeks later, Katharine wrote, to a Dayton friend, "I hadn't supposed any one could be so good to me as Harry has been. He is so concerned over having brought me away from all my family and friends."

Deplorably, Katharine developed pneumonia in 1929. She and Harry had been married just over two years and Katharine was fifty-four. When it was obvious that she was on her deathbed, Lorin brought Orville to see Katharine for the last time. They arrived the day before her death on 2 March 1929.

Were she to be able to comment on her life from beyond the grave, one suspects she would fall back upon her giving, loving disposition and proclaim that she couldn't have orchestrated a better life for herself than the one she was given. She would brush aside any admonitions by those who make strident demands of their "rights and privileges." One imagines that Katharine would challenge such effrontery with, "How many women have the chance to follow adventure into the skies, to follow their father and mother into piety, and are given opportunities to meet royalty, heads of state, and Presidents of the United States? At the summit, I had the love of a

Katharine, second from right, played a major supportive role in the first powered heavier-than-air flight.
A college graduate, she enjoyed bicycling with friends from Dayton and Oberlin College, her alma mater.

In France, February 1909, Katharine flew with Wilbur. For the seven minute, four second flight, Katharine's skirt was tied tightly and her hat wrapped securely.

good man. What more could I have asked?"

Through the generosity of Harry Haskell, a memorial dedicated to Katharine Wright Haskell was erected a few years after her death. The memorial, which replicates a renowned fountain in Florence, Italy, is a marble fountain topped with a bronze sculpture. The sculpture is fittingly shaped in the form of a winged cupid. It graces the campus of Oberlin College, where Katharine, who supported her brothers' wings, found love.

The Wright flyer of 1903 launched not only the careers of Wilber and Orville Wright, but Katharine Wright as well. She became crucial to their activities as correspondent, publicist, financial recorder, and social organizer.

Geraldine "Jerrie" Mock

Intrepid Explorer

Petite, 38-year-old Geraldine "Jerrie" Mock glanced from the cockpit to the sea of faces surrounding her. She wrote, later, "Don't they know I'm scared? I looked at the huge metal gas tanks and other exotic equipment that had changed my once-familiar family four-seater into a weird science-fiction-type machine. . . . I wanted to shout to everyone to go away – let me think. . . . My husband Russ, gave me one last kiss – one last smile – and reminded me, as he pushed the cockpit door closed, 'You're off now – remember the stories.'"

Remember the stories! Jerrie was about to embark on an arduous adventure, to successfully complete what no woman had accomplished. But, his reference to his stories created the perfect spark to ignite her already eager motivation. Jerrie enriched the mixture, engaged the master switch and pushed the starter. She heard the strong response of ignition pulse from her taildragger's single engine. Because her beloved *Three Eight Charlie* was overweight with fuel, she radioed for taxi clearance to the longest runway at the Columbus, Ohio, airport, one that her craft had never before required. She almost hoped that someone would waken her from this dream and that she could forget she'd ever thought of soloing around the world. And in a single-engine, eleven-year-old Cessna 180!

She noted, "I was even more scared of what my husband would say if I taxied back . . . than I was of the miles ahead." And ahead lay 23,000 miles of wind, weather, oceans, deserts, jungles and exotic lands and peoples – 23,000 miles of the unknown!

Inspired in 1962 to "add a bit of fun" to her life, Jerrie Mock took her husband Russell's jocular remark, "Why don't you fly around the world?" and ran with it. Twenty-five years before, Amelia Earhart and Fred Noonan's Lockheed Electra disappeared in their fatal attempt. Jerrie was convinced that another woman must have circled the globe in the ensuing quarter century. But, when she contacted the National Aeronautic Association (NAA), she discovered no woman had soloed around the world. The historic first was Jerrie's – if she could pull it off; if she could survive.

A mother of three – the youngest still a toddler – Jerrie didn't lack for confidence. Nor did she let a logbook limited to a Private Pilot certificate and 700 flying hours dissuade her. She obtained her Instrument Rating to prepare her for inclement weather and, boldly, Jerrie aimed high.

Expertise came from two brothers, John Peck, who served as personal mechanic to Eddie Rickenbacker, and Robert Peck, an engineer at Purdue University. Advice came from Air Force Brigadier General O.F. Lassiter of the Strategic Air Command, and sponsorship came from her husband's employer, the newspaper *The Columbus Dispatch*.

Like Amelia, Jerrie was pushing wide her envelope to fully experience life. Like Amelia, she had a publicist husband eager to promote her. *Unlike* Amelia, Jerrie had made all of her preparations herself and she was the sole occupant of the aircraft.

In 1929, Amelia had been sought by publisher G.P. Putnam to write her book, *20 Hrs. 40 Min.: Our Flight in the Friendship*, after her ride across the Atlantic Ocean. Putnam wanted to capitalize with a "Lady Lindy" on the success of his 1927 publication, *WE*, by Charles Lindbergh. Russ Mock intended to publish a front-page story of his wife's adventures and depended upon her to wire stories after each landing.

There Jerrie's and Amelia's stories meshed: both women were supported and goaded by their men's ambitions. Russ and Gippy were encouraging; both loved their wives and were loved in return, both followed the extraordinary flights avidly; yet, both held expectations for their wives that provoked and inspired.

In 1962 in Columbus, Ohio, Jerrie's adventurous attempt provided the scoop that every newspaperman covets. She dove into

With curiosity and tenacity, Jerrie explored the world as no one had previously succeeded in doing. Again, in 1969, she crossed the Pacific and set a flight record between California and Rabaul, New Britain.

a spate of meticulous preparation: completing reams of paperwork, measuring and studying charts and personally visiting the embassies of each country along her route of flight, either to obtain permission or to modify the route if permission was refused. She calculated best power settings, figured the best routes, studied weather forecasts and weather patterns and undertook equipping the aircraft.

As her departure neared and the dream was about to become reality, Jerrie discovered she wasn't the only woman interested in circling the globe. Joan Merriman Smith of Long Beach, California, departed two days prior to Jerrie's 19 March 1964 date and piloted a faster twin-engine Piper Apache. Fortunately for Jerrie, NAA rules mandated that

only one record attempt at a time could be flown and Jerrie's had been the first application; yet, it would be a Pyrrhic victory were another woman to be the first to reach the United States. Russ exacerbated the rivalry and, although she truly circled the world to visit scenes few had ever seen, Jerrie made the best of the competition.

Modifications to her Cessna 180 included installing a new engine, long-range fuel tanks, an airline-type compass, twin radio direction finders, two short-range radios and, an essential item Amelia had left behind, a long-range high-frequency radio with a trailing antenna. Amelia left hers because it was troublesome to manually-operate the reel. Jerrie benefited from this highly-publicized information and

FLIGHT-AROUND-THE-WORLD

1964

In 1964, Jerrie Mock flew where few dared fly. She made history — the first woman to successfully solo around the world and to cross both major oceans — and in a single-engine Cessna.

augmented her fixed antenna, which transmitted and received over a couple of hundred miles, with a long-range antenna operated by motorized pump.

It well may be the antenna proved Amelia's undoing, as communications failed with those waiting for her arrival at Howland Island. Jerrie's long-range antenna could have proved her undoing as well. Having flown from Ohio to Bermuda, on to Santa Maria in the Azores, to Casablanca in Morocco, to Tangier and on to Bône in Algeria, she was over the desolate, sun-drenched desert stretch between Algeria and Tripoli, Libya, when smoke permeated the cockpit. Inadvertently, she'd toggled the switch for retraction of the long-range antenna and failed to turn the motor off.

"The pump was trying to pull in a wire that was already taut," she wrote. "Were there sparks behind the tank [filled with high-octane gas and even more volatile fumes]? Was the wiring burning? . . . What should I do? What could I do?"

Fortunately, her calmer self prevailed and her initial panic gave way to sane reasoning. Having turned off the switch, she gave the scorching metal time to cool and, as the engine purred, the reality of having no long-range radio paled in comparison to the possibility of having a disastrous blaze.

Yet, insistence from Russ produced fiery responses from the

woman braving the challenges. His first telephone call reached her in Bermuda, telling her, "Well, Joan's left San Juan, on her way to South America, so get going."

Winds were forecast to be over 70 mph and storms lashed Bermuda and raged in the Atlantic. With 2,255 statute miles of ocean between Bermuda and the Azores, she exercised her "no-go" decision. She wanted to accommodate Russ, but respected the fury of wind, water and waves and wisely held off.

His next call included, "Look, weather can't be that bad for that long. Woman, you have to fly. That's why you got an instrument rating, so you could fly through fronts. Joan's leaky gas tanks are supposed to be fixed now, and the wire services say she's ready to go on. She'll get way ahead. Remember your sponsors and take a few chances."

Those "chances" included filing her first Instrument Flight Plan for Actual IFR over the ocean while experiencing a rapid build-up of structural icing in clouds at night. Only by the light of her hand-held flashlight could she see the ice forming and recognize the reasons her aircraft was sluggish. They included battling the turbulence of wind- and sand-storms, which played havoc with visibility, flying longer curving headings because of the winds and direction finding radios, and remaining clear of clouds so as not to endanger any other pilot who might be legally flying on instruments. Her "chances" included avoiding purple-black thunderheads, dark sheets of rain and bolts of lightning as well as walking alone on darkened streets trying to find a restaurant that would serve a single woman, bareheaded at that, before finally getting the chance to fall into an exhausted sleep. When her husband caught up with her in Tunisia, he asked, "What are you doing in Bône?"

She answered that she was just trying to get some sleep to which he replied, "Give me some stuff for a story. The papers say that Joan's covering two thousand miles a day. You have to go farther."

Jerrie's response was effusive, "Look, after the horrible day I just put in, I wish I never had to see an airplane again. And I don't care where Joan is. She can be all the way back home for all I care. I don't want to hear about her again. . . . If you call me again to talk about Joan, I'll come home on an airliner!" And she slammed the receiver into its cradle.

"Chances" also included, when she was headed for Cairo, an unintentional landing in Inchas, a Soviet missile base, approximately 50 kilometers away. Immediately she was surrounded by three truckloads of soldiers. They refused to tell her where she was, ordered her to follow and, speaking a hurried Arabic, fielded several telephone calls. When they discovered that she could fly at night they decided she could depart under the cover of darkness. Still uninformed as to where she'd landed, she and her aircraft were rolled into position on a dark runway. The commanding officer told her to take off, to climb to 1,000 feet and to ignore the lights of an airport on her left – a military field. She was advised to look to the right, find the lights of another airport and make a landing at Cairo's International Airport, the second busiest airport on the continent of Africa.

Her daring courage took her from Cairo to Dhahran, Saudi Arabia; to Karachi, Pakistan; Delhi, India; Bangkok, Thailand to Manila, Philippines. It was between Bangkok and Manila that she was beset with fear. She had been navigating as well as her limited radio equipment allowed when suddenly the engine roughened. She wrote, "It wasn't the 'automatic rough' pilots joke about when they talk about single-engine flight over water. Something was wrong. . . . The middle of the South China Sea was no place for an emergency landing."

She applied carburetor heat and the roughness eased, but began anew as soon as she replaced the knob. Flight with carb heat on meant flight with a less efficient engine and the threat of insufficient fuel. Her anticipated fuel reserve of five flight hours had already been halved by added distance and winds and, she wrote, "When the sun went down, it was terribly black over the water and Manila seemed far away. And what if headwinds were stronger than forecast?"

Jerrie knew she had to pump the two cabin tanks dry, transferring the gas into a wing tank. With both transfer pumps on, she had to wait until the fuel-starved engine quit and then turn off the pumps until the engine re-engaged. She'd practiced with an instructor and experienced the sound of silence at the moment the tanks drew down. "But," she noted, "that was over nice, flat, friendly Kansas . . . Over the shark-infested ocean was a different matter. . . . It must have been overcast as I could see no stars and there wasn't a moon either. . . . I felt terribly alone."

Yet, to accomplish the fuel transfer, she let the engine die – twice – before its throaty growl reminded Jerrie that she was in normal and comfortable cruise. Clawing on through the dark sky, she followed the lights of another aircraft – the first she'd seen – and found Lubang, Philippines. From Lubang, she pressed on to the Islands of Guam, Wake and Hawaii, to landfall in Oakland, California; then on to Tucson, Arizona; El Paso, Texas; Bowling Green, Kentucky; and – 29 days, 11 hours and 59 minutes later – home.

Jerrie's record-setting flight ended with a safe landing in Columbus on 17 April 1964. She became the first woman to fly solo around the world, an intrepid aviator who knew well that the ocean waves churning beneath her wings had claimed the lives of several before and could easily have swallowed one more small craft. Joan Smith, a commercial pilot with 9,000 hours of flight time, flew a longer route, landing in the U.S. on 12 May 1964. She was named first woman to solo along the equator. Tragically, Joan perished the following year after an aircraft accident in California.

Jerrie deserved enormous credit for her fantastic accomplishments and her complete success. Her husband was her greatest champion. Yet, undeniably, the pressure he exerted proved further catalyst for success. It brought a positive response that steeled her backbone and added to the courage and determination with which she was already blessed.

First woman and first from the U.S. to receive the Louis Blériot Silver Medal for Aviation, Jerrie also received the FAA's Gold Medal for Exceptional Service from Vice President Lyndon Johnson.

Artwork © 2007 Sharon Rajnus

Phoebe Fairgrave Omlie

"A Woman Taught You to Walk, She Can Teach You to Fly"

Phoebe Fairgrave Omlie spent her lifetime devoted to aviation. In one of her letters, written to Edna Gardner Whyte, she wrote, "All of the pioneers are greatly disturbed over the 'myths' that are being circulated about aviation. No doubt, the 'true' history should be written. So, I am trying to double-check, where I can, events that play some part concerning people who crossed my path."

In a rare footnote to Phoebe's search for accuracy, a researcher, Betsy Kidd, recently uncovered a truth Phoebe was undoubtedly trying to preserve. In delving into the history of the Aerol Trophy, donated by Louis Greve and named for his shock absorber used with aircraft landing gear, Kidd determined that Phoebe, winner of the 1929 Aerol Trophy, was the overall winner of the 1929 All Women's Air Derby. Perhaps it is little-known that the race finalists received points of merit based on a formula that divided the average speed in miles per hour times 2.5 by the cubic-inch piston displacement of the engine.

Kidd wrote, "The point formula gave all entrants a chance to win the race and the class divisions gave all a chance to win a cash prize. . . . Ms. Omlie, who had a total of 289.3 points of merit, has not been historically recognized as the overall winner. She has been credited as the CW- light division winner and Louise Thaden has generally been credited as the victor. Ms. Thaden was first into Cleveland and was

Phoebe, photographed in 1929, the year she was overall winner of the All Women's Air Derby and two years after she earned Transport License No. 199. She was, according to the FAA, "the first woman to obtain the license from a civilian agency of the U.S. Government."

Courtesy of Sharon Rajnus

first in the DW - heavy class; but, upon final calculation, received 273.2 points of merit, which placed her second overall."

Regardless of the official outcome, both women continued to be outstanding leaders in aviation. By 1933, Phoebe was appointed by President Franklin Delano Roosevelt to be Special Assistant for Air Intelligence on the National Advisory Committee for Aeronautics – the first woman to be named to an official U.S. governmental position in aviation. A year later, she instigated, planned and directed the National Air Marking Program for the Bureau of Air Commerce. These were huge departures for the young woman who had starred in her own air circus and stunted as a double for Pearl White in the movie matinee series, *The Perils of Pauline* – wing walking, hanging below aircraft by her teeth, performing the aircraft-to-aircraft switch in midair, jumping with exhibition parachutes and mastering numerous antics few others dared to try.

With her husband Vernon Omlie, a more mature Phoebe worked tirelessly to bring valued aviation to Tennessee – operating its first airport and establishing an early flying school. The Omlies demonstrated the value of aviation by spending hours of flying time in rescue operations following forest fires and floods.

And Phoebe tirelessly promoted aviation education to be included in the curricula of public schools. In 1972, she wrote to Edna Gardner Whyte, "As you probably know, I have always believed that aviation training was and is the basic foundation for [aviation's] development. Many of the 'big-shots' fought me, tooth and toe nail, when I tried to get aviation training into the public schools when I was in Washington in the 1930s. So, I resigned and went back to Nashville and helped write and get enacted the 1937 Aviation Act of Tennessee, which first provided for ground-school training in our free-enterprise system. This program was the forerunner of the Federal Civilian Pilot Training Program (CPTP), later the War Training Program. It was two years ahead of the federal program."

She later wrote, "You know as well as I do that many women and men, not just pilots, had much to do with the development of aviation. . . . You spoke of the 'WASP.' No mention is ever made about the Women's Training Program for Instructors held at Nashville, Tennessee, when there was such a shortage of instructors after Pearl Harbor. Those ten 'gals' came out of training with flight instructor tickets along with five ground-school instructor tickets. . . . On graduation, they immediately began instructing at various places. Of course, there was little glamour to this, just a lot of hard work and constant study for six months. With civilians charged to train and cull two million trainees for the military, they were really needed."

When Phoebe headed this women's research flight instructor school in Nashville, she brought convincing arguments in favor of women's abilities to be excellent instructors and her deeply held beliefs in aerial transportation in time of peace and of war. Phoebe demonstrated her beliefs by putting ten carefully selected women pilots through a challenging curriculum and vigorous daily regimen.

Janene Leonhirth wrote, in the *Tennessee Historical Quarterly*, "Omlie had fought for more than a decade to promote the serious practicality of aviation. . . . The women slept on wooden sportsmen's cots and covered themselves with state penitentiary blankets that Omlie had procured with the help of [Tennessee's] Governor Prentice Cooper. Their daily schedule, six days a week, began at 6:45 a.m. and included calisthenics, ground courses and flight instruction before 10 p.m. lights out. The regimen was comparable to that of regular Army cadets. Omlie designed it so intentionally."

Heavily hanging over their heads was the admonition, "Whether

or not you succeed or fail in this course may prove the turning point for women in aviation in the United States." As it evolved, time was against the furtherance of Phoebe's brilliant scheme. As increasing numbers of male pilots returned from World War II, the dire need for instructors dissipated. Although each of the ten was exemplary, the global push for women to return to home and children was even more successful.

Dot Swain Lewis, one of her ten outstanding trainees, quoted Phoebe as having said, "A woman taught you to walk; a woman can teach you to fly." Embodied in that positive statement are the images of the ten women she guided so successfully. Thousands of women have followed those role models and have found pleasure and success in teaching others to fly.

Phoebe, herself, is such a model. In 1927, soon after the federal government started issuing certificates to airmen and women, Phoebe was the first woman to obtain a Transport License, #199, and the first to receive an airplane mechanic license, #422. She also noted, in her itemized list of achievements, "Entered and won the CW class Women's National Air Derby from Santa Monica, California to Cleveland."

Thanks to Phoebe for her efforts in helping to bring aviation to the level of importance it has achieved in its century of flight. Phoebe went from barnstormer and air circus performer to sales and demonstration of the snappy little single-engine personal aircraft, the Monocoupe, and to an enviable position in aviation history. As to the factual outcome of the 1929 Women's Air Derby, one suspects that she was happy to be the CW-division winner. It certainly motivated her. One year later, in 1930, she entered the Women's Dixie Derby, a 2,000-mile air race from Washington, D.C., to Chicago, Illinois. She took home two-thousand dollars in winnings.

Artwork © 2007 Sharon Rajnus

In 1927, Phoebe joined forces with Monocoupe in sales and demonstrations. She was the only woman in the 1928 National Reliability Tour and a record-setter in this Warner-powered Monocoupe in the All-Women's Air Derby of 1929.

Hanna Reitsch
For the Love of Flying

As test pilot for the Third Reich, the incredible Hanna Reitsch coolly controlled unique, varied, and demanding aircraft. If she, as close confidant of Adolf Hitler and recipient of two Iron Crosses, knew of the horrors being perpetrated during the pogrom known as the Holocaust and World War II, she dismissed them as propaganda from the mouths of Nazi Germany's enemies. She distanced herself from the unsavory aspects of Nazism. She was totally devoted to the sky and grateful for the opportunities that came her way. Having found acceptance among proud wartime pilots, she delighted in being master of whatever craft she touched.

During WWII, whether flying for Nazi or for Allied air forces, pilots generally admired one another's capabilities. Stories abound in which committed enemies have recognized one another's valor, saluted that bravery and pulled away, allowing the enemy to live to fly another day. In this brotherhood, Hanna, more than a mere woman, was esteemed. She controlled the Grunau Baby glider and Klemm Sport Plane, demonstrated the Focke Wulf Fw 61 helicopter and flight tested the Messerschmitt Me 328 as a Suicide Bomber. Hanna found her place and left aviation better for her excellence.

Her greatest challenge came in flying the Messerschmitt Me 163 Komet. This rocket-powered craft, the only operational reaction-engine fighter of its time, came close to becoming the last aircraft she would ever fly.

She was among a select three to flight test Germany's Lippisch / Messerschmitt extremely high performance Me 163 – only nineteen-feet long, with a thirty-foot wingspan. Equipped with two cannons in the wing root, the Komet was meant to sear through the sky using its special fuel – highly flammable hydrogen peroxide and hydrazine methanol – in exceedingly short, powerful flight, blasting to high altitudes above enemy bomber formations. At this crucial moment, the pilot, like a raptor diving toward its prey, talons extended, closed the power and, guns blazing, scorched into what the Nazi command hoped would be sitting ducks. Reigniting the rocket, the fantastic performance could be repeated only once or twice before the fuel would be expended.

As the Komet had no room for gear retraction, the undercarriage was to be jettisoned on takeoff and the craft landed as a glider. Heini Dittmar, the first to flight test the plane, exceeded 625 miles per hour, but he sustained a spinal injury upon landing.

In her biography, *Flying Is My Life*, Hanna wrote, "To fly the rocket plane was to live through a fantasy. One took off with a roar and a sheet of flame, then shot steeply upward to find oneself the next moment in the heart of the Empyrean. To sit in the machine when it was anchored to the ground, and be surrounded suddenly with that hellish, flame-spewing din, was an experience unreal enough. ...it was all I could do to hold on as the machine rocked under a ceaseless succession of explosions. I had to do this until I was no longer frightened by it and could think and make decisions clearly and coolly without a second's delay; for once I had taken off, the smallest error of judgment might mean the loss of the machine and my own death."

As takeoffs and landings were crucial, the takeoff had to be practiced under tow without the use of the engine. At approximately 30 feet of altitude, the undercarriage was to be released. In her fifth test flight of the miniature beast, death came close, too close. During that still powerless test flight in October 1942, a twin-engine Messerschmitt 110 towed her from the field. At the prescribed 30 feet, she moved the release lever governing the gear.

"Immediately, the whole plane began to shudder violently as if in strong turbulence," she wrote. Red flares curved up toward her from the ground: Danger!

Failing in her attempts to communicate with the Me 110 pilot and jostled roughly in the turbulence, she glanced toward the gun-turret and saw an observer frantically waving a white cloth. The Me 110 pilot recycled his gear several times.

"So that was what it was," Hanna noted. "My undercarriage had stuck! Meanwhile, the Me-110 was towing me 'round the ring' over the airfield while I had only one desire – to reach safe height where I could cast off the tow and see if my plane would respond to the controls."

Hanna was tossed and shaken until her tow pilot recognized her need and initiated a climb. She cast off from her mother ship at 10,500

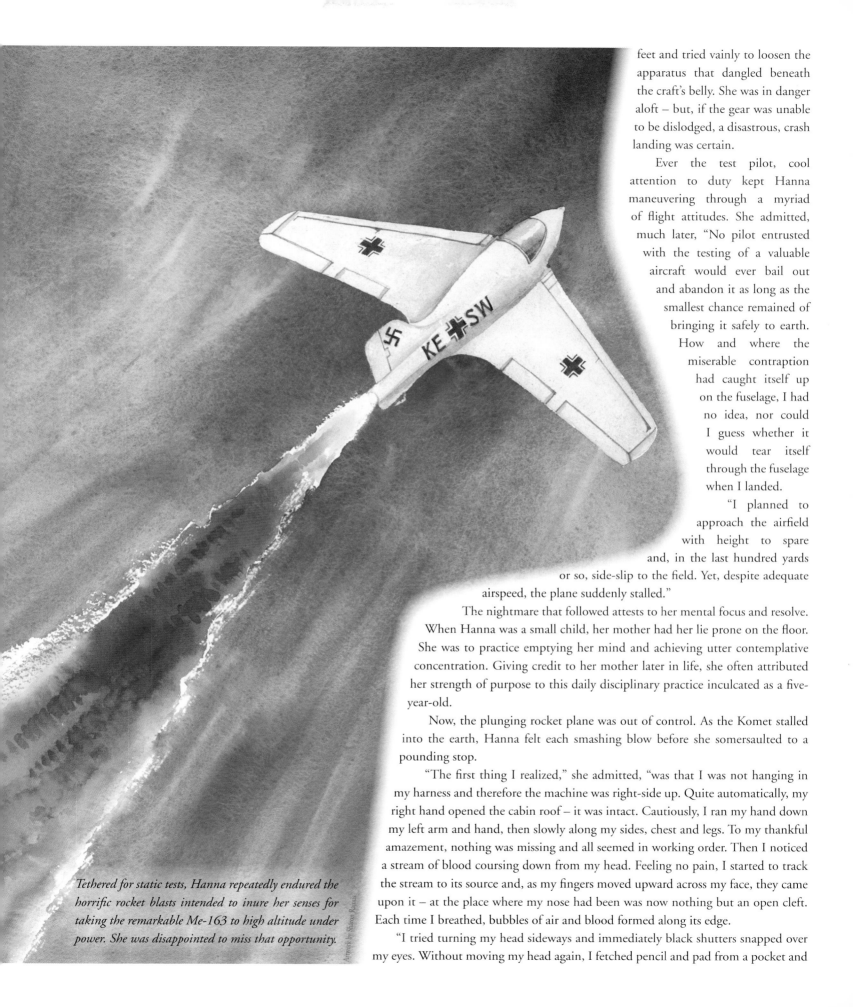

feet and tried vainly to loosen the apparatus that dangled beneath the craft's belly. She was in danger aloft – but, if the gear was unable to be dislodged, a disastrous, crash landing was certain.

Ever the test pilot, cool attention to duty kept Hanna maneuvering through a myriad of flight attitudes. She admitted, much later, "No pilot entrusted with the testing of a valuable aircraft would ever bail out and abandon it as long as the smallest chance remained of bringing it safely to earth. How and where the miserable contraption had caught itself up on the fuselage, I had no idea, nor could I guess whether it would tear itself through the fuselage when I landed.

"I planned to approach the airfield with height to spare and, in the last hundred yards or so, side-slip to the field. Yet, despite adequate airspeed, the plane suddenly stalled."

The nightmare that followed attests to her mental focus and resolve. When Hanna was a small child, her mother had her lie prone on the floor. She was to practice emptying her mind and achieving utter contemplative concentration. Giving credit to her mother later in life, she often attributed her strength of purpose to this daily disciplinary practice inculcated as a five-year-old.

Now, the plunging rocket plane was out of control. As the Komet stalled into the earth, Hanna felt each smashing blow before she somersaulted to a pounding stop.

"The first thing I realized," she admitted, "was that I was not hanging in my harness and therefore the machine was right-side up. Quite automatically, my right hand opened the cabin roof – it was intact. Cautiously, I ran my hand down my left arm and hand, then slowly along my sides, chest and legs. To my thankful amazement, nothing was missing and all seemed in working order. Then I noticed a stream of blood coursing down from my head. Feeling no pain, I started to track the stream to its source and, as my fingers moved upward across my face, they came upon it – at the place where my nose had been was now nothing but an open cleft. Each time I breathed, bubbles of air and blood formed along its edge.

"I tried turning my head sideways and immediately black shutters snapped over my eyes. Without moving my head again, I fetched pencil and pad from a pocket and

Tethered for static tests, Hanna repeatedly endured the horrific rocket blasts intended to inure her senses for taking the remarkable Me-163 to high altitude under power. She was disappointed to miss that opportunity.

Artwork by Sharon Rajnus

Courtesy of Women in Aviation, International

drew a sketch showing the course of events leading to the crash. I took out a handkerchief and tied it round my face at nose level so that, when they arrived, the rescue party would be spared the shock of seeing my condition. Then darkness closed over me."

Hanna recorded events to ensure the validity of the testing and apprise future pilots of what they might expect. Banged mercilessly in the crash, her cranium was fractured in four areas. Her brain was compressed, her jaw bones displaced and her nose was separated from her face. Her condition was extremely serious, yet she attended to the expectations of others and completed her test flight with her own form of debriefing.

Having entered the hospital in Regensburg, Hanna requested the services of a good friend, a Berlin surgeon named Edelgard vom Berg. Edelgard called from Leipzig to say she was en route, but she never arrived. Vom Berg died in a car crash as she rushed to attend Hanna. Hanna fainted when given the grim news and clung even more desperately to her mother, who never left her side. Fortunately, she was treated by an exceptionally good team of physicians.

Yet, she wrote, "Soon I was to be harrowed ceaselessly ...by anxious, fear-ridden thoughts that chased through my badly injured brain. My mother, and she alone, finally persuaded me to abandon thought and lay my mind at rest, placing it in God's hand."

Five long months later, in March 1943, Hanna was well enough to be discharged from the hospital. She was given the chance to convalesce in a sanatorium; but, she elected to retreat to an empty summer home of a friend in Saalburg, halfway up the slopes of the Riesengebirge, the mountain range between the Czech Republic and Poland. "Only I knew how ill I still was," she admitted. "None could guess that my head still ached incessantly or that the shortest car or train ride made me feel sick and giddy. Once in . . . the utter quiet of my new

Hanna, shown in one of the many gliders in which she trained, was Germany's leading female test pilot. For her daring flights in a wide variety of aircraft, she was awarded the Iron Cross Second Class in 1941 and the Iron Cross First Class in 1942 – the only woman so honored.

Artwork © 2007 Sharon Rajnus

abode, however, I hoped gradually to recover my health."

She was determined to conquer her dizziness. She tackled climbing the steeply-pitched, gabled roof of the house, driving herself upward along a narrow flight of steps from the ground to a chimney. Gingerly, she climbed to sit astride the ridge and cling to the chimney, her eyes closed to maintain balance. Carefully, she opened her eyes and focused on each row of tiles to the verge of the roof and from there to the ground. She repeated the exercise on the other side of the roof.

Initially, these climbs left her exhausted, but she continued. Flying was her life and she was determined to return to the sky. With incredible discipline, she subsequently ventured farther from the chimney. By the end of a month she was able to push along the whole length of the roof's ridge

HANNA REITSCH—Me 163

Artwork © 2007 Sharon Rajnus

Following her near-fatal crash in the Messerschmitt Me-163, Hanna retreated to the mountains alone to overcome fierce headaches through sheer determination. Her perseverance returned her to flying status and bordered on the miraculous.

Renowned historian Walter Boyne had the opportunity to meet Hanna, whose attitude toward Nazi Germany's atrocities still seemed coolly detached. He noted, "She felt that the evil of the Third Reich had been exaggerated and that many good people had labored in its cause. She was a formidable woman and the steel of her character showed in her eyes and voice." He added, "She was a hell of a pilot!"

without becoming dizzy.

As a child, Hanna climbed trees, sometimes doing her school work in the highest crevice of the branches. Now, she varied scaling the roof with trees, having to overcome the agony of despair that tree climbing was, like the roof, exhausting. To build strength, she took daily walks along paths leading to the mountain slopes, often turning back because of exhaustion and ferocious headaches. But, these, too, subsided very gradually. Eventually, only through tireless concentration could she contact the commander of the School of Aerial Warfare at Breslau, Schöngarten, for permission to fly.

Returning to the gliding at which she had been so successful, she gradually advanced to power planes, diving, executing steep turns, spins and aerobatics to see whether her head could tolerate rapid changes. Within weeks, she was viewed as a medical miracle woman. She wrote, "All that mattered to me was – I was fit to fly again."

Exceedingly grateful for opportunities to pilot so many complicated and powerful machines, Hanna demonstrated unremitting courage. Her remarkable achievements evoke an admiration bordering on heroine worship from those who know her story. She offers us all a demonstration of the true meaning of pushing one's envelope to accomplish the extraordinary.

Courtesy of Women in Aviation, International

Peggy Russell Baty
Incomparable Vision

In front of Jerry Chabrian's Piper Arrow on the runway adjacent to world headquarters, Women in Aviation, International, Dr. Peggy Chabrian symbolizes one woman's achievements on behalf of thousands who benefit from her foresight and acumen.

Who is Peggy Russell? As a youngster in the early 1960s, Peggy must have asked herself that question repeatedly. Her name wasn't the same as her mother's or stepfather's, Margaret June and Bill Jackson, or her half-sister's, Teresa Jackson. Nor did it match her maternal grandparents' name, the Czykoskis. As a name is significant, her identity must have been perplexing.

By the late 1980s, Peggy Russell Baty, Ph.D., had married Bruce Baty and was Dean of Academic Support and an instructor at Prescott, Arizona's campus of Embry-Riddle Aeronautical University (ERAU). En route in a commercial airliner to Phoenix, the stranger seated next to her asked about her reason for travel. When she mentioned teaching at an aeronautical university, he commented, "Oh, you must teach flight attendants."

She answered, "No. I teach pilots to fly," and she recognized by the question how little most people knew of women's accomplishments in aerospace. The stranger would never know the seed of an idea he had planted. He was seated by a visionary; great things would come from his idle question.

Peggy envisioned a conference that would bring together women in every aspect of aviation – pilots, navigators, engineers, mechanics, airport managers, teachers, air traffic controllers, flight attendants and members of hundreds of other aeronautical fields. Knowing that women could pursue numerous aviation careers, she knew that networking could work wonders in connecting those seeking women as employees with the women who could fulfill varied positions. She was certain that all women could benefit from the camaraderie of a mutually-supportive conference.

The stranger's assumption was one catalyst for Peggy's future successes. Her response startled him and, had she continued, he would have been astounded by the litany of her accomplishments. Peggy attended Tennessee Temple College, obtained her Bachelor's and Master's degrees from Middle Tennessee State University and her Doctorate in Education from the University of Tennessee, Knoxville. She served as Chair of the Department of Aviation Management, Georgia State University; and Director of the Center of Excellence for Aviation Education, Daytona Beach, Florida. She held her Commercial Pilot License; single- and multi-engine land; Flight Instructor,

Chabrian, Ph.D.

single-engine land; an Instrument Rating, Ground Instructor Ratings and was certified Private Pilot, helicopter. Later, she would hold the position of Academic Dean and Associate Vice President at Parks College of Saint Louis University.

Was Peggy the first in her family to be so highly educated, the first to achieve such lofty goals in her chosen field? She didn't know. Her mother and step-sister had not pursued advanced college degrees. As far as she knew, no other in her family pursued a career in aerospace. Her academic credits highlight the outstanding woman that she is; but, her character, her indomitable spirit, her determination, incredible energy and business acumen have been couched partly in mystery. Peggy had never met her father. She knew nothing about him and that mystery was another catalyst in shaping her future.

Her childhood was happy. When she was six years old, her mother gave birth to her half-sister, Teresa. The girls got along well and Peggy's formative years were simple and uncomplicated. Her life was rooted in such positive Christian heritage that, as she entered her teens, she joined a Christian Social Group. Through that group she heard of Tennessee Temple College and was encouraged to form the worthwhile goal of a college education and to apply for scholarship aid. Her persistence was being honed.

Peggy made a fortuitous choice for it was at college that she met and fell in love with Bruce Baty. Bruce taught her to fly and helped her develop the self-confidence that mastering flight can produce. Bruce was further impetus to Peggy's success and, after they were married, he helped her with the mystery of her past.

Peggy recalled having found a birth announcement among memorabilia in her grandmother's house when she was about twelve years old. That announcement welcomed a baby named Linda Russell. Peggy had no memory of a baby; but, she remembered well her Grandmother Czykoski's abrupt reaction when Peggy showed her the announcement. Her grandmother took the card, saying, "You weren't meant to see that!"

When she discovered a picture of a baby propped against pillows in the corner of what she recognized to be their family couch, a nagging suspicion grew that somewhere she had a sister named Linda Russell whom she'd never known. Did Linda know about her? Why had they been separated and why couldn't they be privileged to know one another now? Bruce and Peggy visited a host of governmental locations to shed light on the puzzle. Did Linda Russell exist? Could she be found? Would she even want to be found?

Where to start? With her mother? June Jackson didn't want to talk about it.

With her grandmother? Grandma Czykoski admitted that she wasn't allowed to talk about it.

Pursuing every possible lead – missing persons' venues, searches of various telephone books and other public records – proved fruitful. Peggy found Linda and the timing was incredible. Linda was engaged to be married. In just a matter of months, she would have taken her husband's name and no longer would have been listed as a Russell. Linda would have been lost to Peggy forever.

Emotions ran high as Peggy dialed the telephone for their first

The Robinson R-22 Helicopter, one of the aircraft in a succession of many that Peggy flew, is renown for its classic design, and exceptional in its class for speed and reliability.

Artwork © 2007 Sharon Rajnus

conversation. The two chatted, laughed and cried. They grew eager to get together and arrangements were worked out. The long-estranged sisters prepared for their first and eagerly anticipated meeting. Here was their opportunity to piece together their life stories.

In 1956, Gale Thomas "Tom" Russell and Margaret "June" Czykoski Russell, started their family with Peggy's birth. Tom and June were young parents and the marriage proved to be less than a happy one. Soon after their second child, Linda, was born, the marriage ended in a divorce that blamed Tom with alcoholism. June took Peggy and the infant Linda remained with Tom. Each parent agreed to construct a wall of separation.

Now that the girls had met, it was time to destroy that wall. But, much had occurred in the intervening years. In finding her sister, wasn't it crucial that Peggy also faced the meaning of her own existence? Could the unknown in her own life have been part of the reason that she found it compelling to create a networking society among hundreds of thousands of women of achievement in her chosen field – aviation?

It was thanks to finding Linda that Peggy realized the incredible

opportunity of meeting her father. Tom Russell was not a healthy man and he did not live a long time after he and Peggy became reacquainted; but, he was the father she had never known. How very special that Peggy ever met him at all.

She had always remained in close contact with her mother; but, it was crucial that she bring Linda and their mother together. A subsequent meeting also included their half-sister, Teresa, and their Grandma Czykoski. It was painful when Linda asked her mother, "I was just a tiny baby. How could you leave me with a man you knew to be an alcoholic?" It was joyful when Teresa brought her own newborn and four generations cemented their relationships. It was meaningful that the husbands of Linda, Peggy and Teresa could meet one another. Peggy could never have known that Bruce would succumb to illness not long thereafter; his was a tragic and untimely death in 1998.

Now, two years later, in West Alexandria, Ohio, in June 2000, and joyously for the two special people involved, she was marrying her best friend, Jerry Chabrian. Jerry was as involved in aviation as she. She served on the board of directors of the Experimental Aircraft

Association. He served on the board of directors of EAA, Sun 'n Fun and both served on the board for Women in Aviation, International.

The wedding day was anticipated to be bright and beautiful. The church ceremony was followed with a garden reception under an elegantly appointed white tent. The sun shone, candles mirrored the sun's light and flickered behind hurricane glass. Ribbons, flowers, and greenery created a resplendent area and, across the green cultivated fields, aircraft were visible in the hangars adjacent to the grass runway. Guests, some of whom had flown in for the ceremony, surrounded the bride and groom; family members clustered and the day seemed one of perfection.

The next day as Peggy and Jerry prepared to depart for their honeymoon, they were interrupted with an urgent message. There had been an accident not far from the private field on which most of the guests still lingered. A bright red biplane, a Marquart Charger, had crashed and the pilot and his passenger were badly injured.

"No! This can't be happening!" Rushed to the hospital with the pilot was Peggy's sister, Linda. Peggy was devastated to hear that Linda had been injured; but, only the closest of Peggy's friends knew the depths of despair to which she would have been subjected had the news been worse. Few knew how difficult it had been in the first place for Peggy to discover her sister's existence and to find her. The two young women had only known one another's for a few short years. Those years were blessed with the thrill and amazement of becoming friends, opening the lines of communication, strengthening the ability to exchange and to discuss fears, strengths, interests and experiences. Linda shared her love of horses with Peggy, who, in turn, gave Linda her first flight lesson. Linda earned her private pilot certificate.

Now, however, after the disastrous airplane crash, Linda was in the hospital fighting for her life. All other aspects of their lives fell into perspective. They knew one another; they liked one another and they both suffered terribly that one of them was

hurt. Fortunately, prompt and proper treatment, good care, time and having been healthy in the first place brought Linda through. It took time, but she recovered to regain her strength and her abilities. In cherishing their mutual discovery, the two go on with their lives with renewed appreciation of the challenges and the joys of living.

Dr. Peggy Chabrian can be justifiably proud of her creation of Women in Aviation, International. It began with the first conference she organized in 1990 in Prescott, Arizona, which 150 men and women attended. Under her tireless guidance, ensuing conferences have surged in growth and popularity every year. As a networking center for aviation enthusiasts and vocational opportunists, the event has spotlighted and promoted countless career fields and become a venue for leaders and students alike. In bringing together dynamic attendees of all ages, Peggy has created an annual conference that is increasingly valuable in emboldening and educating tomorrow's aviation participants. It is an important, even essential, organization.

By the year 2006, WAI reached a total of 17,000 members, the annual WAI Conference welcomed upwards of 3,000 attendees and an astounding half-million dollars in scholarships were awarded to worthy young people. Thanks to Peggy's vision and leadership, networking was pushed to its highest levels yet. Through WAI, representatives of numerous career fields have been given the venue to reach potential employees and countless individuals have been introduced to careers they previously would not have considered possible.

Peggy knows personally the value of interrelationships and the importance they represent in a family, in an organization and in a cohesive society. With Peggy at the helm, the sky is no limit.

Courtesy of Women In Aviation, International

In locating her sister Linda, Peggy dramatically exhibited the value of networking. Here she signs one of the myriad of contracts through which her organization also thrives and grows.

The founding of a convention for women that rocketed into a vast global organization required a visionary with tireless energy and amazing capability. Peggy Chabrian recognized a need and more than fulfilled it with Women in Aviation, International. A membership of thousands is her legacy.

Kitty Banner Seemann

Alaska Glacier Pilot

Kitty Banner admits that her love of flight began at an early age and was fostered by her father and brothers – pilots all. In 1974, she graduated from Western Washington State College in Bellingham, Washington, having worked at Bellingham Airport while she pursued her Bachelor's degree in aviation. There she had the good fortune to meet and fly with an outstanding pilot – her college professor and mentor, Dave Rahm, a geologist and a master of aerobatics. Rahm more than flew; he became one with his swept-wing biplane, a Bücker Jungmann, thrilling countless air show fans with his aerial artistry. In her book, *A Writer's Life*, his flying inspired these words from author Annie Dillard:

"I saw a rugged man dressed in brown leather, all begoggled, climb into a black biplane's open cockpit. . . . He climbed high over the airport, very high until he was barely visible as a mote, and then seemed to fall down the air, diving headlong and streaming beauty in spirals behind him. . . . The plane moved every way a line can move, and it controlled three dimensions, so the line carved massive and subtle slits in the air like sculptures."

How fortunate for Kitty to be introduced to aerobatics by Dave Rahm. He also treated her to an unforgettable trip in that very Jungmann the year she graduated from college. Kitty said, "It was as if we'd flown backward in time, back to aviation's Golden Era with open cockpit, helmets, goggles, and even the rudimentary communication system that worked for us as it had for pioneers. Dave and I passed written notes back and forth to one another. We wore parachutes and, for warmth at altitude, I cocooned myself into a sleeping bag. It was incredible to slide over the sharp and rugged Bitterroot Mountains of Montana and Idaho and to have Dave whip into inverted flight and then into a series of crisp rolls. He could make his airplane do everything but speak."

For her own flight training, Kitty worked for and took flight instruction from Carolyn L. Cullen, a member of Class 44-W-6 of the World War II Women Airforce Service Pilots, the WASP. Cullen earned her own wings in PT-17s, BT-13s and Cessna UC-78s and taught Kitty in her Piper Cub. It was invaluable for Kitty to gain taildragger experience from the start and Cullen was an excellent mentor; she stressed excellence in flight basics and strengthened Kitty's resolve to be competitive in commercial aviation. The combination was perfect for developing a future glacier pilot – a woman in a man's world.

Kitty earned the money to fly while adding flight hours and gaining experience. She took classes in aircraft mechanics and pumped gas for transient pilots. An energy company hired her as an expediter – one who ensured the efficient movement of goods or supplies. She oversaw deliveries of supplies to five camps in Alaska and two in British Columbia and, with determination, honed her talents for ownership of her own glacier operation. She worked for Talkeetna Air Taxi for three years and firmly believed that, for someone truly interested in taking aviation to its most demanding edges, "Alaska is the place to be."

Few states boast the air-minded attitudes shown by Alaskans; it is virtually impossible to get along in Alaska without being a pilot or having access to air transportation. Many areas are inaccessible except by air and even those pose challenges to pilots. According to the Alaskan Department of Transportation, "Dead-end box canyons are common; icing conditions

Kitty Banner and her Super Cub rested momentarily on the snow covered glacier beneath the awesome peaks of the challenging Alaskan Range.

can be encountered year round; most of the runways are gravel, many are unlighted, and there are stringent requirements for equipment. Minimum equipment during the summer months is: a week's supply of food for each occupant, one axe or hatchet, one first aid kit, an assortment of fishing tackle, one knife, fire starter, one mosquito headnet for each occupant, and two signaling devices such as colored smoke bombs, pistol shells, etc. sealed in metal containers. Winter flying requires the addition of a pair of snowshoes, sleeping bag and wool blanket for each occupant over four years old."

While working for bush and glacier operations, Kitty put in a few tough seasons flying climbers, handling fuel drums, learning the intricacies of mountain weather, respecting the challenges of ski-equipped landings and ensuring the safety of aircraft and clients. She came to believe that flying in Alaska was, "the ultimate in single-engine flying." She fully earned the respect of the male pilots and developed self-confidence through experience.

She admitted, "Every trip was different – from the weather, the people I flew, the snow conditions, the landing sites. You never knew what you were going to get."

In 1979, Kitty and a partner, Kimball Forrest, bought an air service in Talkeetna, naming it with their two first names – K2. Competition in Talkeetna was fierce, so the success of K2 required tireless effort. Bruce McAllister, in his photographic history of Denali National Park, *Wings Over Denali*, wrote, "Banner had the total inability to look anything but feminine, whether she was wrestling fuel drums . . . or loading a pickup. [She] was intimidating to some of the more chauvinistic climbers – but only because she was so professional." Soon K2 was not only competitive, it was prospering.

Kitty was asked to teach floatplane flying to singer John Denver; in 1982, after having married Bob Seemann, whom she met on a chairlift while on a ski vacation in Colorado, she also assisted Sir Edmund Hillary with a documentary on float flying for the *Discovery Channel*.

Kitty noted, "We were being filmed as we flew and a bald eagle hooked up with us. We'd

Artwork © 2007 Sharon Rajnus

Kitty Banner stated, "Flying in Alaska is no cakewalk. You have to deal with all sorts of unusual circumstances, some of which exist nowhere else in the world." She flourished with every challenge.

turn right and he'd turn right, then we'd circle and the eagle would circle. We made our point turns around a mother black bear and her cubs. The experience was incredible."

But, Kitty's most terrifying experience was more than incredible. She was the one elected to retrieve equipment left behind by an evacuated mountaineer and she landed her Super Cub on the West Fork of the Ruth Glacier in Denali National Park. The equipment was all that remained in a survival site on the lofty snow-covered mountain – the highest peak on the North American continent, renamed from Mt. McKinley to its Athabascan name, Mt. Denali. Mountaineer Charlie Porter and Mike Fisher, the pilot sent to evacuate him, had scooped out the snow shelter after Fisher's Cessna 185 became stuck in the snow. The two men existed for six days with very limited supplies and, when rescued by Jim Sharp, owner of Talkeetna Air Taxi, the equipment, now heavier with its accrual of ice and snow, was left behind.

Mike Fisher had given Kitty a map, hastily scrawled on a restaurant napkin. It warned her away from the site on the glacier he'd chosen and suggested a new landing spot. "His sketch," she said, "marked a crater on the original runway where the first plane had been buried, the location of the stashed gear and noted some crevasses and other hazards to avoid. He warned me that the weather was deteriorating and told me to hurry.

"As I circled above the glacier, Fisher's drawing didn't feel right. It was tricky. There was a dangerous double fall line caused by sliding side ridges merging with the glacier. This created two side cuts and could mean an uneven landing surface that might lead to stubbing a ski and flipping the Cub. Also, the area was completely shadowed, which added depth perception problems. It was essential that I land where I could turn the Cub and be in position to fly out."

Cloud formations thickened and blackened as Kitty trimmed for a landing, skimmed to the surface, reduced power, spun the nose around and shimmied to a stop beside a crater. As Porter's gear was illuminated by flares, she easily found his cache and hurried to collect the first of his belongings onto an orange plastic sled. The glacier moved under her boots, but glacial vibrations weren't unusual, especially in the summer, so gentle tremors were easily overlooked. She pulled out a length of climbing rope, knotted one end around her waist and another to the airplane's strut.

She worked quickly, loading Porter's frozen equipment onto the sled and then hauling it to load into the Cub. Suddenly, she was startled by a thunderous clap. She looked up and faced the horror of an avalanche! Snow frothed as if being plowed; a frigid river plummeted down the Alaskan mountainside toward her. There was no time to escape, nowhere to hide. What had started out as a routine pickup for twenty-four-year-old Kitty Banner had turned badly sour. A monstrous wall of snow from Mt. Huntington started with a lurch as if bulldozed from above. The white wall, like the black Bücker Jungmann, "fell down the air," obscured by blowing snow rising before its blunt prow.

Dave Rahm was quoted as having said, "[Y]ou know, you can get a better feel for a mountain's power flying around it, flying all around it, than you can from climbing it tied to its side like a flea." At that intense and terrifying moment, Kitty Banner felt as insignificant as that flea and as powerless. The ground heaved beneath her feet and the crushing wall swept downward. She checked to see that her lifeline to the airplane was taut.

"Holding tightly to the rope, I said a silent prayer."

Kitty was certain the avalanche would bury her. Almost leaning into what would surely be like being struck by a runaway freight train, she waited, horrified. Seconds later, the Cub disappeared in a puff of blinding mist and the rush of whiteness enveloped her completely. The frigid cold was piercing and bitter. But, as suddenly as the thunderous movement had started, it stopped. Vibrations ceased, the thunderous rattling ended and she gasped, gulping mouthfuls of the thin air.

"Everything was eerily quiet," Kitty said. "I stood stock still. When the slide stopped and the mists settled, there was the Super Cub, untouched. My body was still rigid. Miraculously, the avalanche ended just short of us!"

Avalanches are known to trigger subsequent slides and the

Kitty's professionalism extended to the requirements of pre- and post-flight duties. As an Alaskan charter pilot, she recognized more than most pilots in the Lower 48 the essentials of safe practices and attention to details.

experienced glacier pilot in Kitty came to the fore. She tossed the last of Porter's load into the Cub and took a shovel to hack away the snow barricading the plane. She shoved thick snow dust from the wings, tail surfaces and fuselage and turned to stamp out an escape runway, admitting, "That was the most tiring challenge of all."

Climbing in and holding her breath, she reached for the ignition and, with the answering growl of the Lycoming's engine, breathed a sigh of relief. She ached to get airborne and to clear the area. The Cub was loaded a bit tail-heavy; but, that seemed trivial.

Kitty started the takeoff run and coaxed the Cub into the air, pushing forward on the nose to take advantage of ground effect to gain flying speed. A cloud mass climbed up toward her and she nursed the Cub into shallow-banked, gradual turns to avoid the surrounding mountains.

On the third circling turn, she radioed her position to flight headquarters and rejoiced as she broke out of cloud haze into the clear sky above. She had no trouble returning to land at Talkeetna; but, after she'd shut down the engine and slid out, the other pilots teased her. "We're glad you got it all," they joked. "We didn't want to go up there in this weather."

They didn't know the half of it.

Kitty Banner Seemann and her husband, Bob, live in Vail, Colorado; they are employed by Descente, a ski wear manufacturing company. Kitty is also a representative for Neve Designs, which provides clothing for the U.S. Ski Team and members of bike racing teams. She considers herself more than lucky as she and Bob share their love of the outdoors with their two sons, Mick and Corey. And, gloriously, she is blessed that they are eager to have their mom teach them to fly.

Kitty Banner Seemann made a name for herself among the soaring peaks of the Alaskan Range. Equally adept in the cockpits of the Cessna 185 or Piper Cub on wheels, skis or floats, she flew with confidence and authority. Her clients were hunters, fishermen, mountain climbers, photographers and explorers of the wilderness. Her surroundings were the majesties of Talkeetna Lake, Kahitna Glacier and soaring Mt. McKinley, now renamed Mt. Denali.

All Photos Courtesy of Kitty Banner Seemann

Colonel Eileen Collins

Where Few Have Flown

During final approach, with the Space Shuttle Discovery's nose a few hundred feet directly below the Space Station, Pilot and Commander of NASA's Space Transportation System mission (STS-114) Eileen Collins swept Discovery up in an impressive and unprecedented 360-degree maneuver. She used the Orbiter's reaction control system thrusters to pitch the vehicle into a position that made it possible for Space Station Commander Sergei Krikalev and Flight Engineer John Phillips to photograph Discovery's underbelly.

Airborne in her fourth space flight, Collins carried with her the experience of more than 600 hours in space and more than 6,700 hours flying a variety of aircraft. Her name is carved in the annals of history as the first woman astronaut to serve as pilot in her first mission, STS-63 aboard Discovery in 1995, and Eileen again served as pilot in 1997 on STS-84 in Atlantis during the sixth docking with the Russian Space Station Mir. In her second historic first, Eileen assumed command of 1999 mission STS-93 aboard Columbia. In Discovery's 2005 mission, a two-week, 5.8 million mile space journey in 2005, Eileen repeated her role as Crew Commander.

The purpose of her unique pitching maneuver was born in the aftermath of the tragic loss of the Shuttle Columbia and its crew of seven brave astronauts on 1 February 2003. Columbia's destruction at 207,135 feet in the skies over Texas while traveling at 12,500 miles per hour – an astounding Mach 18.3 – was attributed to a chunk of foam insulation that separated from an external tank and struck a gaping 16-inch hole in the left wing. For two and a half years, NASA focused attention on repairing the external tank to ensure further breakage of foam insulation would not hazard subsequent flights.

Yet, just minutes after Eileen and her crew launched, part of a heat-shield tile ripped away from the edge of a landing gear door. Coolly, she continued to near the Space Station where she pitched Discovery toward the photographers. Using 400- and 800-mm lenses, the duo on the Space Station photographed the underside of the shuttle to allow evaluation of the chipped tile or other damage.

In 1999, under her first command, Columbia suffered electrical problems with the main engine. She recalled, "At five seconds after our launch, we had a caution and warning message, an electrical short and the main engine controllers failed. I immediately went into the 'simulation mode,' meaning that I reverted to training I obtained in the simulator. . . . We just do what we need to do, what we have within our control. Outside of that, we use our judgment."

The mishap that destroyed Columbia and robbed Eileen of her good friends in 2003 recurred during her launch in 2005 in Discovery, yet Eileen had the presence of mind to swing the huge craft for a photographic advantage. The tragedy steeled her resolve. She said, "I'm totally committed: to safe and successful missions, to seeing that my crew has been trained and prepared, ready to fly. But, I can't help but see reminders of the 107 crew, how dedicated they were to their mission, how much they loved exploration and one another, and how well they worked together as a team.

"In 1986 after the Challenger accident, I was in graduate school. The accident, obviously, was just a terrible tragedy; . . . but I wanted to apply to the astronaut program. I wanted to be there. . . . I have a love for this business and I really want to make a contribution. When we have difficult times . . . I see that's where the best in people comes out. . . . If anything, the difficult times increase my sense of commitment."

Eileen, in the classic U.S. Air Force pilot pose, is shown at the time of her graduation in 1979 from U.S. Air Force pilot training, Vance Air Force Base, Enid, Oklahoma.

Photo Courtesy of NASA

Eileen Collins, first woman pilot of a shuttle, first woman to command a shuttle, performed another historic first. To ensure that no foam had shredded from the tank, a potential hazard during the heat of reentry, Eileen performed a maneuver never previously attempted. She pitched the nose upward to enable photography of the protective insulating skin.

When honored at the White House as the first woman Shuttle Commander, Eileen noted, "When I was a child, I dreamed about space - I admired pilots, astronauts, and I've admired explorers of all kinds. It was only a dream that I would someday be one of them. It is my hope that all children, boys and girls, will see this mission and be inspired to reach for their dreams, because dreams do come true!"

Attesting to her cool demeanor, controlled and disciplined behavior and excellent response under pressure, Eileen Collins is a role model for all who recognize the potential of this era of exploration. Not only has she flown where few have flown, but she has performed maneuvers never before attempted. Her capability and indefatigable spirit is demonstrative of the excellence to which humans can aspire.

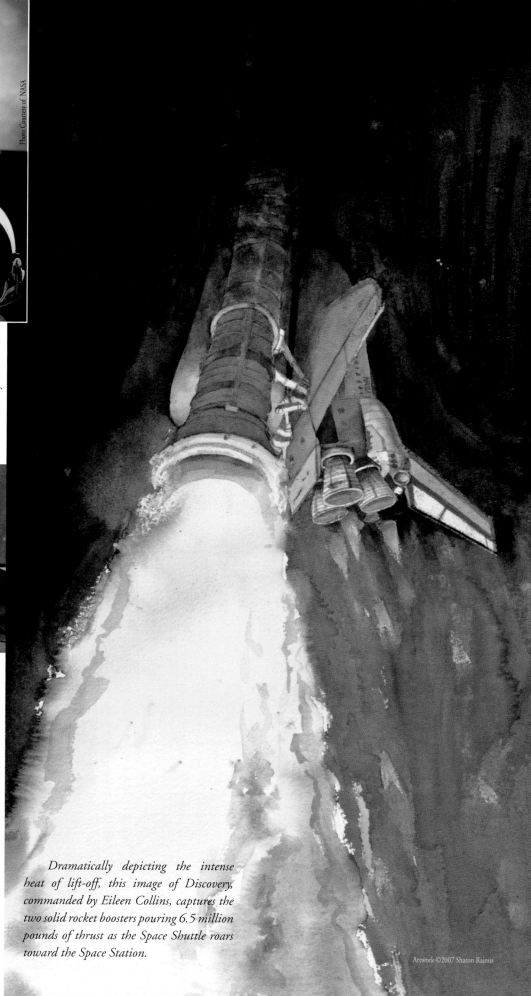

Dramatically depicting the intense heat of lift-off, this image of Discovery, commanded by Eileen Collins, captures the two solid rocket boosters pouring 6.5 million pounds of thrust as the Space Shuttle roars toward the Space Station.

Willa Beatrice Brown

Spirited Wings

When a vibrant, well-educated woman, a successful teacher, Willa Beatrice Brown suffered a disruptive divorce, she harnessed her talent and left her Indiana home to settle in Chicago, Illinois. The move must have required a healthy dose of self-confidence and daring. At the time, she would have faced uncertainty and would have had no idea that her daily routine in the classroom was to be replaced with more adventure than she'd dreamed possible. She couldn't have known that she was about to make history. Yet, all capable women who forge their own destinies are generally too engrossed in daily life to recognize or even be concerned with the possibility of making history. Willa Brown was gutsy; she was involved. She was full of spirit and of life.

Arriving in the early 1930s, Willa searched for a new career into which to invest her prodigious energies. She took a stab at social work, but found little opportunity for advancement for a woman of color. Then she met Cornelius Coffey, a pilot who offered to teach her to fly. The sky, wide and fresh, beckoned. She was introduced to a group of black aviators who had found haven in an airport on the southwest side of Chicago and their excitement with flight was compelling. With Janet Harmon Waterford, who purchased the Curtiss OX-5-powered International F-17 for all to fly, she joined the Challenger Air Pilot's Association and the Chicago Girl's Flight Club. Cornelius Coffey taught her well and, inspired by the freedom of flight, she ignored naysayers who condemned it as a waste of time and money. Willa chose the mastery of her own bit of sky.

Coffey, an auto mechanic who rightfully equated the workings of automobile engines with aircraft engines, had discovered that training as a pilot and as an aircraft mechanic was next to impossible for blacks.

National Archives: 306-PS-D-67-3247 (Box 120)

Proudly, Willa Brown became the first black woman to be an officer in the Civil Air Patrol, CAP Squadron 613. By 1939, Willa was a tireless advocate for pilots and mechanics who had long been barred from opportunities. With Coffey, she co-founded the National Airmen's Association of America and rallied interested blacks to take wing.

Seeking a way around discrimination and without mentioning race, he and a friend, John Robinson, submitted applications for admission to the Curtiss Wright Flying Service. Both were accepted as students, as were their payments toward tuition; however, when it was determined that both were black, the Flying Service tried to return the money and cancel the training. Coffey's employer, Emil Mack, the owner of Elmwood Park Motor Sales, threatened to fund a suit on Coffey's behalf and Flying Service officials relented. Not surprisingly, the highly motivated and ambitious Coffey finished near the top of the class and, although the decision was belated, Curtiss Wright ended its practice of barring blacks. Coffey, who paved the way for others to follow, took his historic position as the first black to hold an Airframe and Engine (A&E) certificate.

In 1937, the vivacious and beautiful Willa earned her Private Pilot license and, in the same year, she obtained her Master's degree from Northwestern University. With Coffey, she co-founded the National Airmen's Association of America (NAAA) and continued to rally talented blacks to become pilots and mechanics.

Involved in planning an all-black Air Derby at Chicago's Harlem Airport, Willa sought newspaper publicity and support. She silenced a room filled with newspaper journalists as she strode purposefully into the office of the nation's most influential black weekly, the Chicago Weekly Defender, wearing her flying outfit – a pair of white jodhpurs, a jacket and tall boots. Editor Enoch Waters became a stalwart supporter of this bold woman and served with her as a board member of the NAAA.

By 1938, she had married Cornelius and they opened the Coffey School of Aeronautics with Willa as a full partner. As a trained and experienced teacher, she was a natural to teach flying; she immediately sought her instructor rating and her aircraft mechanic license.

Within a year, World War II raged in Europe and tongues of flame licked across the Atlantic. The U.S. Government assessed manpower preparedness and called for a program that would provide a cadre of pilots to be rallied in the nation's defense. The Civil Aeronautics Authority (CAA) launched the Civilian Pilot Training Program (CPTP), which offered aviation flight training – wings of opportunity – to qualified civilians. Willa welcomed this news eagerly.

TIME magazine reported, in 1939, "[The CAA] certified 220 U.S. colleges and universities for participation in its pilot training program, prepared to name still more to share $5,675,000 voted by Congress for schooling 11,000 new fliers this year. The trainees are all civilians, most are collegians. They will be taught to fly by commercial air schools, at a cost to the United States of $290 to $310 per student. When they graduate, they will be far from qualified as military pilots, but most of them should rate private pilots' licenses. . . . But CAA's fledglings, with the rudiments of flying, will be far better material for the Army and Navy air corps than total greenhorns."

The Coffey School of Aeronautics became one of those "commercial air schools," thanks in part to Willa's tireless promotion. Initial selections involved colleges and universities whose student bodies were predominantly white; Willa and other black Americans exerted superhuman effort for some colleges and their qualified trainees to be included. Willa lobbied Congress and sought publicity from black newspapers as a tireless advocate for others. She believed wholeheartedly in enabling blacks to join her in welcoming skies.

At their school, she and Cornelius trained pilots and mechanics who had long been barred from such opportunities. Upgrading from the original J-3 Cubs with which Coffey had started to a fleet of WACO

UPF-7 biplanes, approximately 1,500 pilots earned their wings, thanks to Cornelius and Willa. Many of their graduates became participants in the Tuskegee Experiment in Alabama, which led to serving with pride and success as part of the famed Tuskegee Airmen of World War II.

By 1941, Willa Brown was experienced as Federal Training Coordinator of two units of the CPT program and as organizer of the NAAA. She also helped to organize and served as vice-president of the Aeronautical Association of Negro Schools. Despite her successes, Willa constantly struggled against bigotry. In a letter dated December 6, 1941, one day prior to Japan's attacks on the islands of the Pacific Ocean that led to President Roosevelt's outraged, ". . . a date which will live in infamy, . . ." Willa wrote to First Lady, Eleanor Roosevelt. In part, she wrote, "It has been with deep admiration that I have followed your interest in the women of our country . . . During the past three years I have devoted full time to aviation and, for the most part, marked progress has been made. . . . I have, however, encountered several difficulties . . . I would like to talk with you some time when you are passing through Chicago or, if it would please you better, sometime when you are at home in Washington, D.C. I come in and out of Washington quite often. . . . Sincerely yours, Willa B. Brown, President, National Airmen's Association of America."

In 1942, this strong, confident woman of achievement became the first African-American member and an officer of the Civil Air Patrol. She avidly promoted aviation on the radio and taught aviation courses to high school students. By the 1970s, she became a member of the Women's Advisory Committee on Aviation in the Federal Aviation Agency. She was invited to be honored at the Smithsonian's National Air & Space Museum along with other greats of aviation. Through her encouragement of others, she left a lasting and remarkable contribution. Her place in aviation history is assured.

Willa Brown taught flight to men and women of color. With Cornelius Coffey, Willa lobbied for the inclusion of blacks in the Civilian Pilot Training Program. Their school in Chicago launched eager trainees to success as Tuskegee Airmen.

Mabel Hubbard Bell

Soaring Silver Wings

Mabel Hubbard Bell gazed from the porch of her home in Baddeck, Nova Scotia, across the waters of the Bras d'Or Lake. Her calm demeanor belied her energy, her creative intelligence, and managerial acumen – all the more amazing and admirable in light of the fact that Mabel Bell had been deaf since childhood. Her husband, Alexander Graham Bell is renowned; but, Mabel should be held in high esteem for her exciting, pioneering efforts – so vital to Canada's aviation history.

Among those who cherished her qualities was J. A. Douglas McCurdy, whom Mabel and Alexander befriended after Douglas lost his mother. As his father served as secretary and assistant to Alexander, Douglas became part of Bell's family, who helped him receive a degree in engineering. In 1906, Mabel wrote, suggesting that he come to Baddeck and bring a fellow engineer who might also be interested in her husband's latest invention – a flying kite designed to carry a man. Douglas involved Frederick W. "Casey" Baldwin; the two accepted the challenge.

Bell's influence cut a wide swath. Interest in his experimental kites lured the Smithsonian's Samuel P. Langley for a visit in 1894 and, in the summer of 1907, Lieutenant Thomas E. Selfridge arrived in Baddeck, detailed as an observer for the U.S. Army by President Theodore Roosevelt. A search for an appropriate engine to power the kite led to adding Glenn H. Curtiss of Hammondsport, New York. Each man contributed individual talents to the whole and the mutual camaraderie was obvious. Mabel enjoyed the spirited association. She could sense from animated conversations that

ideas fell upon fertile imaginations and each gained inspiration from another.

Mabel participated in the activities, whether towing kites behind motorboats, handling kite wires to measure wind velocity and altitudes reached, testing engines, running propellers or working on construction. It was she who proposed a formal collaboration and, having earned $20,000 from the sale of land inherited from her father, it was Mabel who financed the venture that became the Aerial Experiment Association (AEA).

Glenn H. Curtiss wrote in his autobiographical, *My First Flights*, "[W]hen I first visited [Baddeck] in the summer of 1907, . . . Naturally, there was a wide discussion on the subject of aeronautics, and . . . Mrs. Bell suggested the formation of a scientific organization, to be known as the 'Aerial Experiment Association.' This met with a prompt and hearty agreement . . . Mrs. Bell, who was most enthusiastic and helpful, generously offered to furnish the necessary funds for experimental work, and the object of the Association was officially set forth as 'to build a practical aeroplane which will carry a man and be driven through the air by its own power.'"

Canada's AEA, limited to one year's existence, became an entity on 1 October 1907. Focusing upon the completion of Bell's manned tetrahedral kite, the Cygnet, the group planned for each man to design an aircraft with the assistance of all.

On 6 December 1907, Mabel rode high on the upper deck of the steamer hired to tow a barge carrying the Cygnet, a honeycomb created of hundreds of triangles covered with red silk,

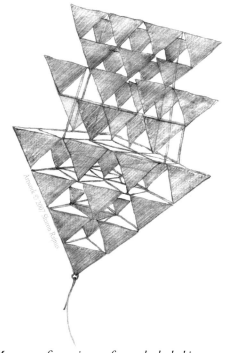

Artwork © 2007 Shonna Raines

Many configurations of tetrahedral kites were created by Alexander Graham Bell and flown with Mabel Bell's assistance. The qualities of flight, strength and lightness proved valuable in creating heavier-than-air, controllable powered aircraft.

for its first flight test. The steamer headed into the wind; Selfridge, chosen as test pilot, boarded the kite, and away he soared to 168 feet to hold steady. When the breeze abated, he dived the kite toward a landing on the surface of the water. Had someone chopped the tow rope immediately, the flight would have been a success. However, as Selfridge splashed to safety, the kite dragged through choppy waters and was destroyed.

During the remainder of the winter, members of the AEA worked in Hammondsport, conducting experiments. As the first to complete a powered craft for testing, Selfridge covered his Red Wing with the same red silk as the Cygnet. However, he had taken ill and Baldwin was chosen to pilot the initial flight.

Red Wing was poised on iron sleigh runners, set to glide over ice-covered Lake Keuka for takeoff. Ice-skate-clad Curtiss, McCurdy and other volunteers readied themselves for Baldwin's historic moment. However, before he boarded and at the start of the engine, the Red Wing surged forward. A flurry of skaters raced after the craft and returned it for a proper start.

This time, Red Wing sped across the ice and rose into the air. Thanks to advance publicity, there was an eager audience to witness aviation history in the making. Casey Baldwin was the first Canadian to make a heavier-than-air powered flight and, as the Wrights had conducted their flights in private, Baldwin's was acclaimed as the first public flight in North America.

Buoyed by the experience, Baldwin completed his White Wing, introducing a tricycle undercarriage, a lighter laminated propeller and controllable hinged surfaces for improved lateral control and Curtiss produced his June Bug. Some test flights were witnessed by Alexander and Mabel, visitors to Hammondsport, and Mabel exalted in their achievements. She wrote, "[T]he air is exhilarating and everywhere they are working and working . . . They are young and their work is the youth of a great new thing in the history of the world."

In July, 1908, Curtiss' June Bug competed for and won the Scientific American Trophy for the first flight of a heavier-than-air powered machine piloted over a measured kilometer. The AEA reveled in its accomplishments. Although the end of the year's term was rapidly approaching, work still beckoned – McCurdy's Silver Dart was yet to be built.

Fate intervened. Lt. Selfridge, whose own design had carried him to success, was fatally injured as a passenger with Orville Wright in Fort Myer, Virginia, on 17 September 1908. Wright was demonstrating the first Wright Military Flyer to the U.S. government and Selfridge was acting as a member of the Army's aeronautical board.

Mabel was distraught; she wrote, "I can't get over Tom being taken. . . . I know he would have said he was having the time of his life, although he must have realized his danger; those last seconds he would still hope to escape and he had no time for unavailing regrets. . . . I am so sorry . . . in this breaking of our beautiful Association. But it was beautiful and the memory of it will endure."

The AEA was extended, completing the Silver Dart in Hammondsport where it took to the sky on 6 December 1908.

Courtesy of the Alexander Graham Bell National Historic Site of Canada

Mabel Bell, deaf from childhood, refused to be handicapped. She, revered and admired, suggested and funded the Aerial Experiment Association and influenced aviation history.

Artwork © 2007 Sharon Rajnus

In sharing her inheritance, Mrs. Alexander Graham Bell made possible Canada's first powered, heavier-than-air flight in 1909 – The Flight of the Silver Dart – a first for Canada, a first for the British Empire. She didn't hear the engine or the shouts of approval, but she knew the historic significance of her contributions.

McCurdy flew it three times on 14 December after which they crated it and shipped it to Baddeck early in 1909 for its first flight on the frozen surface of Bras d'Or Lake.

On 23 February 1909, in the AEA's final success, McCurdy piloted the Silver Dart for a distance of three quarters of a mile. His was the first flight by a British subject of a heavier-than-air, powered, controlled aircraft in Canada – the first in the British Empire. Mabel Bell's dreams soared; her organization was triumphant.

Townspeople of Baddeck gathered for the thrilling occasion – some bundled in horse-drawn sleighs, some ice skating, some playing hockey and all enthralled with the historic powered heavier-than-air flight. Many pleaded for a second flight, but Bell was adamant. He recognized that history was being made and wanted to ensure that no failure dim Canada's first flight success. The next day, McCurdy repeated his triumph; Mabel wrote, "Douglas started about 100 yards from the boathouse, making a glorious sweep. He came back . . . passing close to me purposely as I said I hadn't really seen yesterday's flight."

Mabel Bell heard no sounds of the passing aircraft she helped to create. Deafened by scarlet fever as a child, she was fortunate that her parents hired Alexander Graham Bell as her teacher rather than relegate her to an asylum for deaf mutes as was common at the time. Bell was the third generation of experts in elocution. When hired as a professor

of vocal physiology at Boston University; he referred Helen Keller to her teacher and accepted Mabel Hubbard as his student.

Alexander and Mabel fell in love and married and Mabel, adept at reading lips, learned to speak and became quite successful at communicating. She bore Alexander two daughters, never hearing the sounds of her children's voices. Nor did she hear the shouts of joy that must have erupted from the crowd gathered on the ice of the Bras d'Or Lake as the Silver Dart swept past. Yet, she rose above her affliction and lived life fully. She is due recognition and appreciation for her contributions to the history of flight.

At the dissolution of the AEA on March 31, 1909, Douglas McCurdy read the following resolution: "Whereas the members of the Aeronautical Experiment Association individually and collectively feel that Mrs. Alexander Graham Bell has, by her great personal support and inspiring ideas, contributed very materially to any success that the Association may have attained. Resolved that we place on record our highest appreciation of her loving and sympathetic devotion without which the work of the Association would have come to naught."

On July 25, 1923, the Bell's son-in-law wrote, "Mr. Bell's fame is secure for all ages but few know the quality and genius of his wife, one of the greatest minds and personalities of the times."

CHAPTER TWO

COMMUNICATION & COMPASSION

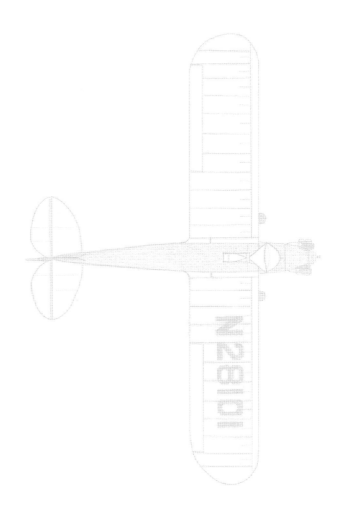

PIPER CUB

COMPASSION

". . . [A writer] must teach himself that the basest of all things is to be afraid; and teaching himself that, forget it forever, leaving no room in his workshop for anything but the old verities and truths of the heart, the old universal truths lacking which any story is ephemeral and doomed – love and honor and pity and pride and compassion and sacrifice. . . . [Man] is immortal, not because he along among creatures has an inexhaustible voice, but because he has a soul, a spirit capable of compassion and sacrifice and endurance."

William Faulkner, speech upon receiving the Nobel Prize, 10 December 1950

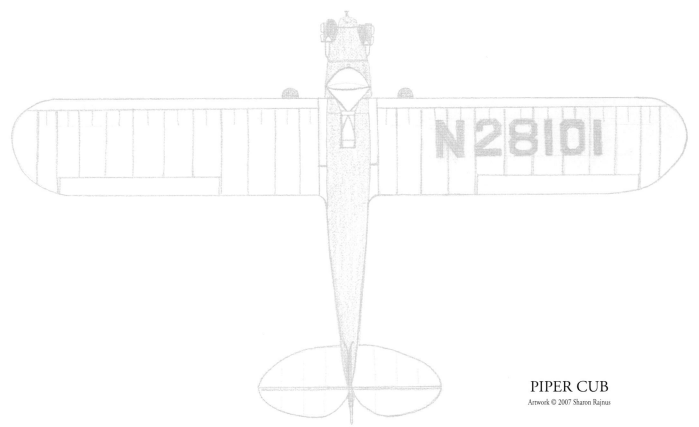

PIPER CUB
Artwork © 2007 Sharon Rajnus

COMMUNICATION

"And yet a few minutes after I finally sat down to read *The Spirit of St. Louis*, I realized that this book wasn't about an airplane, after all. It was about a boy's relationship to the land, where he grew up, and to the sky, where he came of age. It was about agrarian and technological America coming together in this one boy, my father, through a kind of extension of himself that I recognized in his writing, as I had recognized it on those Saturday afternoons when I had flown with him during my own childhood. It was the story of a thrilling and dangerous adventure and a revolutionary transformation of vision. It was a heroic tale, made to order for a storyteller, and it was told by a master storyteller, with a sense of tension and rhythm and romance and craftsmanship. . . ."

Reeve Lindbergh Tripp, UNDER A WING

CHAPTER 2

Patty Wagstaff
Into Africa

Elephants wouldn't be beleaguered if it weren't for their fine ivory tusks and the greed of their greatest predator – man. There is an international ban on the sale of elephant ivory, yet poachers reap more money than any other effort offers. In Africa's Kenya, poaching has reduced the elephant population from nearly 50,000 in 1965 to about 10,600.

Rhinos, too, find man is their worst enemy. They are relatively easy to track and kill; their behavior is predictable as they travel to and from familiar water holes. For thousands of years, man considered the rhino horn magical. It was believed that powdered horn rendered some poisons harmless and that simply positioning an entire horn near a patient would alleviate pain. The rhino's horn has been sought to cure lung and chest illnesses and Asians also covet the skin, blood and urine of the rhino as medical cures. In Yemen, the rhino horn is prized as a dagger handle and considered a symbol of wealth and status. Until the 1970s, few could afford them. But, rising prices for oil have increased the per capita income in Yemen and, to the detriment of the rhino, Yemen has subsequently become the world's largest importer of rhino horn.

The Kenya Wildlife Service (KWS) Airwing, critical in Kenya's campaign to protect both humans and animals, patrols with its airplanes to locate poachers and track elephants and rhinos on the rolling grasslands. One KWS pilot, Captain Mumiah Elijah Anyonyi, was quoted as having said, "You may be called upon to fly to any part of the country on rescue . . . missions, to perform game counts, captures, or animal translocations." For the latter, he carries a veterinarian aboard his helicopter who is prepared to anesthetize an animal with a dart gun.

When she is not airborne in her aerobatic Extra or exhibiting her well-trained horse over jumps, Patty flies a technologically advanced Cirrus SR 22. She said, "The Cirrus is a truly leading-edge airplane. Wonderful to fly."

Personal collection of Patty Wagstaff

He radios a ground team when the animal is sedated and directs the team to the downed animal."

He added, "You may be called to help combat banditry. It means that you require quick planning and quick thinking"

And this is where Patty Wagstaff comes in. Patty, three-time U.S. National Aerobatic Champion, flight instructor, outstanding air show performer and compassionate woman, has thought seriously about living in Africa. She has a genuine love for wild things – animals, birds, even reptiles. While living in Australia, she gained an intimacy with nature that few of us have known. She camped in the bush near the Ord River and felt at one not only with native Australians aborigines, she felt at one with the animals of the river and the subtropical jungle. Her concern for the endangered is sincere. It is no wonder she eagerly accepted the invitation to travel to Kenya to fly with and instruct pilots of the Kenya Wildlife Service.

Adequately trained as pilots, the men were not well-trained in evasive and combat tactics. If they were going to apprehend poachers willing to use automotive weapons to decimate rhinos, elephants and animals sought as bushmeat, they were at risk themselves. Only aerobatic expertise and maneuvering could help them avoid gunfire. Wingovers and other air combat maneuvers could spell the difference between being brought down or living to fly.

Each year since 2001, Patty has journeyed to Kenya to give recurrency, bush piloting and aerobatic flight training. She has learned to love the scenic beauty of Kenya, from its beautiful beaches to the glory of its mountains: Mt. Kenya's 17,000 feet rises at the Equator and Mt. Kilimanjaro towers in the distance, snow-covered and highly visible for miles. She was invited to participate by Dr. Bill Clark, a member of the Israeli Wildlife Service and CITES, the Convention on International Trade on Endangered Species. Dr. Clark, who first envisioned this training program, has contributed significantly to its success.

Patty wrote, "Although the KWS Park Rangers are well-trained and equipped, they are challenged in keeping people safe from potentially dangerous wild animals and in keeping the wild animals safe from poachers. The latter are the more dangerous. Armed and illegal, poachers travel large distances on foot, generally from Somalia and the Sudan, to kill animals that are becoming increasingly more endangered. We are all involved. These animals may live in Kenya, but they are a global treasure and until you've sat on top of a hill and watched a family of elephants saunter into the sunset, you can

Personal collection of Patty Wagstaff

Patty Wagstaff, three-time National Aerobatic Champion and air show star, shares the love of Africa with those who call it home. As the animal population and those who protect it are threatened by poachers, Patty shares her aerobatic experience to teach evasive maneuvers to Kenya Wildlife Service pilots.

only imagine what a loss it would be to humanity and the ecosystem if wild things ceased to exist."

Five hundred young African men were selected to undergo paramilitary training – combat, intelligence and investigations – to protect animals and humans. Equipped with combat gear, vehicles and modern communication and navigational electronics, they formed the core security force for the KWS. The Airwing enlarged the KWS and provides an aircraft for each company. Based at Nairobi Wilson Airport, the Airwing is equipped with Aviat Huskys, Piper Super Cubs, Cessna 180s, Bell Helicopters and others. Their aerial patrols alone are a serious deterrent to poachers; but, no matter how dedicated and brave, KWS pilots fly long hours in extremely remote areas and at low level.

"Their skills need to be extremely sharp for them to do their job well and to survive," said Patty, "so recurrency training - which is important for all pilots - is of the utmost importance to them."

Training initially in a Cessna 152 Aerobat, Patty was glad to see that generous donations later made possible a Super Decathlon. "The field elevation is about 3,000 MSL, the weather is warm and density altitude is always prevalent. The Super Decathlon performs well in such conditions.

"When there has been plentiful rain, everything is beautiful and green and each taxi or takeoff gives us the chance to see different animals: elephants, zebra, impala, eland, giraffe, hippo, crocodile, oryx, kipspringer (a new one for us), baboons, Cape buffalo, lots of bird life and even a huge African Fish Eagle. The diversity and beauty

of the creatures we need to protect is astonishing."

Africa itself suffered with the Hutu-Tutsi Massacres as humans continue inhumanity toward their own. The insanity of human greed includes the animals as well. A friend of Patty's, Safari Guide Mark Ross, survived as a Hutu hostage. In his biographical book, *Dangerous Beauty*, he wrote, "The gentleness and predictability of the bush had not altered; only I had changed, and that occurred through the hand of man, not 'beast.' How ironic the word 'beast.'"

Africa's animal population, especially those in the sights of poachers' AK-47s, is in dire need of intervention and protection. The head of the KWS airwing, Captain Ibrahim A. Ogle, performs evacuation missions for stranded tourists and rescue missions for orphaned infant elephants. In Tsavo East National Park, Ogle has personally been confronted by as many as thirty poachers, all armed with fully automatic military rifles and explosive projectiles. Anyone willing to gun down an elephant has no qualms about killing a human who prevents that destruction and the cost ecologically is cumulative. When a mature female elephant with a suckling infant is killed, unless Ogle or another of the pilots of the airwing can manage a rescue of the baby, future generations of elephants are doomed. The KWS faces a huge challenge.

Patty's contributions to the KWS pilots caught the attention of the photographers and writers of the television program, *Animal Planet*. They accompanied her to film the KWS for their special, *Operation Animal Shield*. Obvious in the film is the pleasure taken by KWS pilots to have her teach them aerobatic techniques; yet, devastatingly poignant is the footage of the carnage wreaked by poaching. A benefit of such coverage is the raising of awareness of all.

Having gone on safari several times and repeatedly flying over the savannas, Patty witnesses the seriousness of the threat time and again. She said, "Taking off from one of the national park airstrips in a Super Cub with the door open and a Jurassic Park-like beauty spread before me, flying over a herd of elephant, giraffe, rhino and hippo bathing in pools of water with eight foot crocodiles lounging nearby, watching Martial eagles soaring overhead with monitor lizards in their talons – well, to say it is 'magical' is just too much of a cliché. But, it is and, more than that, it is soothing to my soul to know that such wild creatures and wild places exist when I'm immersed in the insanity of everyday life in an industrial nation."

Patty Wagstaff, an exciting and accomplished aerobatic pilot, performs with excellence; yet, she is far more than an aerial performer and a National Aerobatic Champion. She gives of herself unselfishly and transfers her aerobatic skills to those whose lives may depend upon them.

Patty said, "We have worked on soloing taildraggers, performing slips to landings, short field landings, short field takeoffs and on general airwork, including some aerobatics. Short field takeoffs were sometimes accomplished over zebra or warthogs and short field landings often turned into go-arounds when giraffe, impala or ostrich were on the runway! The opportunity to fly in Africa is a treasure. It has been incredible to work with this group of pilots and to accomplish a very successful training mission. Kenya is now part of me. Once you have spent time in Africa, you never forget it."

Bush piloting instruction offers a lot of surprises: muddy landings, giraffes on the field, rhino and hippo up to the neck in water and, unfortunately, poachers willing to shoot at the pilots who protect the wildlife.

Patty noted that there are poachers who snare animals, even more of a cruelty as the animals die a slow death or are maimed for life. Annually, she returns to Kenya to teach recurrency and bush piloting training to wildlife pilots, her joy and her privilege.

Beth Settlemyer

A Matter of Identity

Personal collection, Beth Settlemyer

In Africa, Kehinde Adeduji means "second born of twins," a name adopted by Beth Settlemyer as a teenager. Having been the second born twin and having flown in Central Africa meant a great deal in shaping her identity – her tapestry of beliefs, tenets, values, and faith that created her character. Who she is, what she believes, and how she reacts in trying situations exposes the core of her being, which can be sorely tried.

Beth and her twin brother, Roy, were adopted and raised by Charles and Jean Settlemyer as babies. Their home was located so close to Andrews Air Force Base in Maryland that overflying aircraft affected life for the whole family. Captain Settlemyer, a World War II B-17 pilot who returned after 26 missions with the Distinguished Flying Cross and a Letter of Commendation from General Jimmy Doolittle, recognized early that Beth, even more than Roy, shared his love for the sky. He enjoyed her eager enthusiasm.

In her childhood dreams, Beth soared with birds; at air shows, she perched on her dad's shoulders for the "bird's eye view" of aircraft displayed on the ramp and in aerobatic performances overhead. Her father talked often and glowingly of role models who might further inspire her – expounding upon the exploits of many worthy aviation pioneers.

Beth wanted desperately to learn to fly, but her father was strict. He insisted that she first obtain her education and earn at least her Bachelor of Arts or Science before heading into the sky. Dutifully, she entered and graduated from the University of Maryland, pressed on to earn her Masters and beyond that to pursue doctoral research and her thesis at the Universities of Maryland and Dalhousie, Nova Scotia.

Having proven that she was prepared for a variety of occupations, she took a menial job as lineman at a Fixed Base Operation in Albany, New York. Finally, Beth was close to the airplanes that were her source of inspiration. She squeezed flight lessons between pumping fuel and greeting incoming transient aircraft pilots and she soloed in a Cessna 152.

"Then," she admitted, "with an incredible leap of faith, I invested all my savings in a flight school in sunny Florida, away from Albany's wintry weather. When I graduated, my father attended the ceremony and presented me with his most treasured possession, his service wings."

Beth became an instructor and taught flight students while she packed her logbook with hours of experience and earned the Flight Engineer and Air Transport Pilot ratings. Hired to fly the old "piston pounders," DC-6s and DC-7s, on night cargo flights throughout the United States and into Central and South America, she worked toward her A&P certificate when faced with too many O-ring failures that plagued the pistons.

In the 1980s, at a time when few women were in the commercial airline ranks, Beth was hired as a flight engineer aboard Boeing 727s. Originally, she was involved with passenger carrying out of Miami International Airport and she progressed to flying for Worldwide Commercial Aviation, repositioning B-727s throughout the world.

It was in this capacity that, in 1997, a pivotal event changed Beth's life. The International Red Cross (IRC) put out a request for flight assistance in Central Africa. Several nations responded and a resulting airlift was formed to aid thousands of Rwandan refugees, survivors of the devastating Hutu / Tutsi War. Beth volunteered to serve as a Flight Engineer.

Hutus and Tutsis have a long history. The Tutsis, moving from Ethiopia six centuries ago, invaded and conquered the Hutus in their homeland, Burundi. During the Colonial Era and ruled by Belgium, which had gained the area from Germany at the end of World War I, the Hutus and the Tutsis lived together, shared the same language, intermarried and revered a Tutsi king. In the 1960s, following the granting of its independence from Belgium, the region imploded. A coup placed Tutsis in control. Grievances mushroomed into antagonism; antagonism erupted into violence. In 1972, a Hutu rebellion failed and more than 150,000 people died. In 1993, as ethnic violence ravaged the area, more than one million were forced into refugee camps in Zaire and Tanzania. The Hutus overthrew Tutsi rulers and elected a Hutu president. Yet, the bloodshed was far from over.

Safari guide, reporter, photographer and author Mark Ross, in his book *Dangerous Beauty*, wrote, "In April, May and June of 1994, between eight hundred thousand and one million people were murdered in Rwanda in just one hundred days, with the tribal conflict between the Hutus and the Tutsis ultimately spilling into neighboring Congo and Burundi, where both murderers and refugees fled."

Ross knew the brutality personally. He was taken hostage by rebels known as the Interahamwe, Hutus who blamed the United States, Britain, and Uganda for supporting a Tutsi-led government after the slaughter in 1994. Ross lived, but some of his clients, on safari with him, were hacked to death by machete. The horror of man's bestial side lives with him still.

Beth, compassionate and sincerely wanting to help, joined with other volunteers who responded to the IRC pleas for assistance. As a crew member on the Boeing 727, she flew in and out of Burundi during the massive attempt to carry the helpless out of tragic circumstances. They tried to safely load streams of malnourished and distraught people caught in the cross-fire of violence and lawlessness.

She acknowledged, "Everyday for many weeks, hundreds of starving and dying refugees were airlifted from hostile areas inside Burundi and repatriated back to Rwanda. Some flight crews operated B-727s and other large aircraft off dirt strips, often under hostile fire from guerrillas. Sadly, many malnourished refugees failed to survive, despite flight times of only thirty-five minutes."

As gunfire threatened the aircrews, the IRC eventually deemed the missions too dangerous and terminated the airlift. Beth was discouraged, left with the nagging sense of hopelessness and distress that the humanitarian effort couldn't have been more successful. Haunted by the desperation she'd seen in the eyes of those she'd pledged to help, she agonized over good intentions that came to an abortive close. This mission changed how Beth looked at the world; it changed the course of her life.

Back in the United States, she read of a call for 1,000 cyclists to spend six and one-half weeks in a bike ride across the country to raise awareness of those who suffer with diseases of the lung. In the GTE Big Ride Across America and under the auspices of the American Lung Association, she completed 3,000 miles, riding from the Pacific Northwest, across the prairies to the nation's capitol. She had an epiphany during that ride, deciding she would find ways to combine her love of flying and her desire to help others.

Once again, she returned to school. Beth earned her Paramedic credentials and took a position with Dare County (North Carolina) Emergency Medical Services. She became a flight crewmember aboard the Dare Medflight helicopter, the only medic from Dare County to take part in North Carolina's State Medical Assistance Team deployed to help in the devastation following hurricane Katrina.

"Through flight and healing," she explained, "I have found a way to demonstrate the value of a single human being. I am working to make a difference."

This loving woman, known to many as Kehinde or Ky, has returned to her anglicized name after the death of her brother. Secure in her identity, Beth Settlemyer stays busy with Medflight. In planning for the eventuality of, as she puts it, "no longer being able to lift gurneys," she has chosen to pursue her Master's of Divinity and to enter a hospital chaplaincy program. Her sights are set sky high and her compassion has taken wing.

From a Boeing 737 Flight Engineer during the Hutu/Tutsi War in Rwanda to the Messerschmitt-Bolkow-Blohm BK 117 in natural disasters at home, Beth Settlemyer devotes her wings to, "touch those who hurt, from the street to the hospital." Ever caring, she is humbled by strengths shown in those facing utter destruction.

Janet Harmon Bragg

Obstacles Hurdled, Joys Unrestrained

In her autobiography, *Soaring Above Setbacks*, Janet Harmon Bragg admitted, "Memories are like paintings and each one of us has our own gallery." Thinking of barnstorming in Ohio, her painting was bright and colorful. She reminisced, "While flying, my plane was always alive. It responded so beautifully. I could feel the rudder pedals through the soles of my feet . . . I felt comfortable and at ease. I was free in spirit. I could give vent to my feelings through the maneuvers. In all, my plane and I were communicating. I would say, 'Let's try a spin, two to the right,' or 'One to the left. Are you ready?' I'd say, 'Let's go.'"

The memory of her treatment by a federal flight examiner at Tuskegee, Alabama, would have been painted in a darker image. More than well-prepared and qualified to receive her commercial license, Janet flew with a Mr. T. K. Hudson who, at the completion of what appeared to have been a successful flight, drawled to Janet, her instructor and her Tuskegee well-wishers, "Well, . . . she gave me a good flight. I will put her up against any of your flight instructors. But, I've never given a colored girl a commercial license and I don't intend to now."

To Janet, every defeat was a challenge. Born Jane Nettie Harmon in 1907 in Griffin, Georgia, Janet was the youngest of seven children in a loving and supportive family. She experienced the pain and degradation of prejudice and discrimination, but despite

National Archives: 306-PS-D-67-3247 (Box 120)

Janet Bragg became the first black woman pilot to earn a Commercial Certificate. Thanks to her hard work and successful medical career, she obtained the means to finance not just one, but three aircraft and made them available for the flight training of countless black pilots.

every obstacle, she forged a life of which any woman would be proud. She left a legacy of excellence.

Graduating from high school in 1925, a private Episcopal boarding school, Janet enrolled in Spelman College, Atlanta, one of the very best of the historically black women's colleges. She was especially outstanding in math, physics, science and athletics and, thanks to hard work and the training from dedicated teachers at Spelman's MacVicar Hospital, she became a graduate nurse in 1929. Through friends and relatives, she sought and found a lucrative medical career in Illinois. Earning graduate credits in public health, she was hired as a health inspector for an insurance firm. She worked steadily and earned the financial freedom to pursue flight. As Chicago was a beehive of black aviation activity during the 1930s, she soon heard about the activities of Cornelius Coffey and John C. Robinson and their Aeronautical University.

Discrimination, which was more overt in the nation's South, existed in the North as well. It was widely believed that blacks lacked the intelligence to become pilots and, in Janet's Chicago, blacks were denied instruction, aircraft rental, the use of airport facilities and career opportunities. However, the enterprising forged a way. Following the lead of white barnstormers who operated out of pastures and farm fields, the likes of Coffey, Robinson, Willa

Brown, and Janet Bragg found their own paths to the sky.

Coffey and Robinson were licensed aircraft mechanics and licensed pilots. They had fought for the education and certifications they justly deserved. Following suit, when Janet discovered there weren't sufficient tools for everyone in the maintenance class, she purchased her own from Sears, "with a shiny green toolbox to keep them in."

The group, about thirty strong at the time, built an airfield in nearby Robbins and Janet found it necessary to repeat her initiative. Thanks to steady employment and frugal spending habits, she afforded the purchase of an airplane. For $500, she bought a red Curtiss OX-5-powered International biplane. It was a first for the group, which became the Challenger Air Pilots' Association, and it allowed her and others take the flying lessons they craved. Without her contributions to Chicago's black pilots and mechanics, their experiences might have turned out far differently. It was Janet who purchased and provided for herself and others the first airplane for flying lessons, thus paving the way for those from Chicago who entered what became the highly successful Tuskegee Experience, the Tuskegee Airmen of World War II.

Unfortunately, a storm destroyed their hangar and opportunities at Robbins came to an end. Turning still another defeat into challenge, the men and women moved to Harlem Airport on the outskirts of Chicago. As the group grew and the need for more aircraft became obvious, Janet generously purchased a Piper Cub and a Piper Cruiser, which, again, she made available at a low per hour cost to others.

With the outbreak of World War II, Janet applied to the Women Airforce Service Pilots. She received a telegram inviting her to an interview with Ethel Sheehy.

Janet noted the surprised look on Ethel's face when she walked in and wrote that Ethel said, " 'I've never interviewed a colored girl. I'll have to refer your case to Jacqueline Cochran at headquarters.' . . . I was refused because of the color of my skin."

The scene worsened. Still eager to be of service to her country, Janet applied to the nursing corps, hoping to serve in the military. Told that the quota for colored nurses had been met, again her application was refused.

Janet elected to further her flight training at Tuskegee, Alabama.

It was 1942 and Janet attended Tuskegee Institute's Civilian Pilot Training School where, with the help of Charles Alfred "Chief" Anderson, she prepared for the ill-fated commercial pilot test flight with T.K. Hudson. She was honest when she wrote, ". . . every defeat was a challenge from which I profited in one way or another."

Still stinging with the pain of his pitiful dismissal, she returned to Chicago where she was tested by an examiner who cared more about her ability to fly than the color of her skin. She passed as she knew she was capable of doing. Janet pursued the certificate, even though there were few opportunities for black women to fly commercially at the time. In 1943, Janet Bragg received the historic first — her commercial license. She never used the license for gainful employ; but, she cherished the character development that accompanied the training.

Janet was instrumental in developing the first college preparatory Training Flying Program for blacks. This civilian pilot program provided a cadre of intelligent, motivated young people for future demands as military pilots and hundreds profited from her efforts. Janet paved the way for others to learn the determination, confidence and sense of accomplishment that pursuing aviation can teach. When she passed away in 1993, the world lost a woman of character and of great achievement.

In her autobiography, she shared a story that is oft-repeated by other members of the Tuskegee Airmen. "According to recognized aerotechnical principles, because of the shape, weight and size of its body in relation to its total wing area, the bumblebee cannot fly. But, the bumblebee doesn't know this. The bumblebee goes ahead and flies anyway."

Late in her life Janet said, "Although the passport has expired, I always am ready to prove that this bumblebee can fly!"

Janet Harmon Bragg should be well-known in aviation history. Janet may well have been the first black woman in the nation to purchase an aircraft. She was decidedly the first to receive a Commercial pilot's certificate. Her sphere of influence touched countless persons and affected their lives positively.

Artwork ©2007 Sharon Rajnus

> *Janet Bragg purchased a Piper J-3 Cub and a Piper Cruiser to lease to others for flight lessons. The three-seat version of the Cruiser boasted a deeper fuselage and more powerful engine.*

Anne Morrow Lindbergh

Solitude in Silence

Her name alone – Anne Morrow Lindbergh – elicits mental images of a lovely, well-educated lady. Her generous smile brings to mind the grace with which she lived her life and the plethora of beautiful words she offered. Her writings, like the woman, display elegance. Anne's meteoric rise – from the daughter of the Ambassador to Mexico and the wife of a great international hero to receiving, twice, the National Book Award as an author – was timely. In a nation still reeling with the bleak depths of the debilitating crash of the New York Stock Exchange and ensuing Great Depression, citizens responded eagerly to inspiration. The 1929 marriage of Charles and Anne Lindbergh brought a hero and a heroine to all.

Anne never sought the publicity that swirled around her. She simply strove to share with her husband as a full partner and, through their adventures, her fame increased and spread. Anne accompanied Charles as a crewmember on exploratory flights that examined safe air routes for passenger travel. She navigated, used Morse Code, and transmitted and received radio signals that were crucial to their safety.

She was a lover of solitude and privacy; yet, with her intense need to write and to express herself, she drew fame as a candle attracts a moth. Her crowning achievement, in addition to the sons and daughters with whom she was blessed, was her success as an author. Ironically, her literary genius was her refuge as it simultaneously thrust her further into the public eye.

Lesser known is her place in aviation history, which was secured by a singular remarkable feat: Anne Spencer Morrow Lindbergh was the first woman in the United States to obtain a glider pilot license. Where did she find the wellsprings of courage to commit to and revel in such an opportunity, so wildly different from the ordered and even introverted pursuits that characterized her earlier years?

On 27 May 1929, Anne, who had once admitted that she wanted to "marry a hero," did just that and was catapulted into a life of vigorous

Personal Collection of Anne Lewis Cooper

Clothed for the frigid cold of the arctic, Anne navigated and handled the radio for the famed 1933 flight of discovery and research of the North Atlantic.

In this watercolor titled "Greenland and the Lindberghs", Anne was a vital crewmember in the Lockheed Sirius for the 30,000-mile survey flight in 1933. For her important contributions to transoceanic exploration, she was first woman to receive the National Geographic Society Gold Medal named for Gardiner Hubbard, National Geographic's founder and Mabel Hubbard Bell's father.

activity and amazing challenge. In 1930 and in anticipation of flying great circle routes that would carry them west over Canada, Alaska and to the Far East, the Lindberghs ordered a Lockheed Sirius and flew to California to test fly the craft.

While in California, Charles arranged a meeting with one of his friends, W. Hawley Bowlus, the man who had been shop foreman at Ryan Aircraft in San Diego, California, and the supervisor during the building of Charles' famed trans-Atlantic aircraft, "The Spirit of St. Louis."

At the time of their visit, Bowlus, who was the second American citizen to achieve the "C" soaring badge and in a sailplane of his own design and construction, was eager to share soaring with the Lindberghs. Bowlus saw the advantages in using powerless flight to

Personal Collection of Anne Lewis Cooper

Anne flew solo in a powered craft for the first time only months after her marriage in 1929. Whether in a glider launch from the summit of a mountain or climbing into the rear cockpit to perform as crew, Anne Lindbergh exuded courage and daring. Moreover, her eloquent prose brought aviation to millions.

promote greater "airmanship" among aspiring pilots. Every pilot could profit from knowing more about the lift associated with drafts, currents and topography. Gliding offered a preeminent opportunity for pilots to "feel" the aerodynamic forces and it offered rich rewards to those with budgetary constraints – especially student pilots.

Bowlus threw himself wholeheartedly into the design of safe, easily built craft. His Model A glider, which both Charles and Anne flew, had a wingspan that stretched an impressive sixty feet. Under Bowlus' guidance, both Charles and Anne became interested in trying this relatively new realm and being among the earliest U.S. licensed glider pilots. To the reticent Anne, Hawley's enthusiasm was infectious. On the ground, he taught her the basics of handling his craft and, solo in the Model A, this courageous young woman took her place in aviation history.

Adolph "Bud" Perl, a teenager who worked for Hawley at his Bowlus Sailplane Company on Lindbergh Field and who participated in Anne's historic flying, told of the primary training with auto tow – a training glider nicknamed "Tillie" – and subsequent bungee cord launches for her more advanced flights. In his interviews with Joe Streetman, author of *The Lindberghs Soar in San Diego*, Perl noted that Anne and Charles made perhaps 30 or 40 flights in auto tow during their basic training. To experience the lift of the on-shore breezes – more advanced training – she made a couple of flights at Point Loma. But, to establish a flight record, Anne made a bungee cord launch from the summit of La Jolla's nearby 822-foot Mt. Soledad.

Perl said, "[I]t is significant [that] she was the first person to ever launch from there. . . . She took off, made a beautiful flight, just kept gliding down and finally got in a beautiful landing in a field."

Anne wrote, in a letter to her mother, "We are back in Los Angeles after a most exciting day. Gliders! . . . [Charles] has a friend in San Diego, Hawley Bowlus, who has built what he calls a 'sail plane.' It has a tremendous wing span and a small body (no engine, of course) and it looks just like a great gull – perfectly beautiful. It has no wheels but just skids onto the ground, landing on its shiplike keel. Hawley Bowlus has painted the body (fuselage) a deep sea blue and the great tapering wings are silver.

"The pilot sits in the front; there is only room for one, of course. Hawley is very interested in the project from the point of view of teaching young boys and girls to fly, as it is inexpensive to build, needs no gas, etc., to keep it up. Also, it is so much safer than power flying – slower, of course, and you land slowly and lightly in a few feet almost anywhere. And it is wonderful training for the prospective power pilot: knowledge of air currents, landing when his motor has failed; And it is such fun.

"I wanted to try it. So yesterday I was towed behind a car across a field in a training glider. The car goes faster and faster, pulling the glider behind it, and you point the nose up a little, and up you go. Then they cut the rope loose and you glider down.

"I didn't make very good landings with this and bounced lightly like a balloon. It was terribly funny."

Airborne in 1930 in Hawley Bowlus' Model A Albatross after a bungee-cord launch, Anne Lindbergh soared from Mt. Soledad in San Diego, California. Hers was a dramatic and successful first for a woman.

Streetman quoted Anne as having written, "All the men were ready to pull at the elastic cord and shoot me off. Cameramen all set and ready for a show... when I got into the cockpit and all the people stood around, C. said, 'All set?' and Hawley said, 'All set?'. . . I felt like a lamb about to be sacrificed (right on the top of a mountain too!). . . . Then the men started running, pulling the rope. I heard the keel scrape and I was off!

"Oh, the relief of getting off! It was quiet and the ship rose steadily. I was not frightened now; there was plenty of time to think; the ship responded easily to the controls. And it was so delicious, so still. . . . I picked out my route (more or less as C. had instructed): along one hill, across to another, and down into a green field . . . When I was quite near the field I heard a bird singing. Then I turned around the field to face it the long way and skimmed along the ground and it stopped, without any jolt, like a sled plowing into snow with a slight crust."

In her diaries, Anne penned, "The letters I wrote home . . . were not strictly accurate. The accounts were tempered to allay the anxiety of my mother or my mother-in-law . . . Actually, I was frightened to death being pulled off the mountain alone in a glider, but I could not admit fear to my knight. Once in the air, however, it was an ecstatic experience I have never forgotten or regretted."

Omitted from her letters was the fact that Anne was pregnant with her first child – her tragically lost son. Somehow, that makes her achievement even more poignant. She was daring, she was disciplined and she was courageous. Anne Morrow Lindbergh became the first woman and the tenth person in the United States licensed as a first-, second-, and third-class glider pilot. As she was wont to do, she wrote.

She said, in her poem Ascent,
"Plunge deep
Into the sky
O wing
Of the soul.
Reach
Past the last pinnacle
Of speech
Into the vast
Inarticulate face
Of silence. . . ."

And, on great silver, tapering – and silent – wings, she flew.

Lest We Forget
Susan Maule's
"Aerial Blessings"

Captain Susan Maule, with her legacy of a flying family, flies for US Airways. This 737-200 shown in watercolor is emerging from stormy weather into clear air, a metaphor for Susan's story.

Artwork © 2007 Sharon Rajnus

Comfortably seated in the pilot-in-command position of her 737-200 US Airways Metrojet, Flight 2657, Captain Susan Maule felt fortunate to have flown from Baltimore to Chicago in the crisp early dawn, the sun rising from behind and bathing the Windy City with its pale light. Now, at 8:42 a.m., her jet was being pushed away from the gate for its return flight. Perhaps her passengers had completed business appointments and, like her, were headed home. Perhaps some were flying in the early morning calm to visit relatives or friends in the environs of the nation's capital. As in every airliner slated for the skies of this particular September morning, the seats were filled with a wide variety of travelers. Little did they or those in the cockpits know of the unforgettable drama in which they were about to play a part.

One would think Susan had been destined to be an airline captain; she is the daughter of Ray and Rautgunde Maule and granddaughter of June and Belford "B.D." Maule who designed and marketed the highly successful light aircraft that carries their name. When old enough to fly alone at sixteen, and thanks to fellow pilots who brought their planes, she soloed twelve aircraft, land and sea, before dashing to the motor vehicle bureau to obtain her driving license. One year later, she celebrated her seventeenth birthday by taking her private pilot flight test with her dad as examiner in a Maule M4 145 and received her seaplane rating in a Citabria.

From her childhood Susan was intimately involved with the manufacture of Maule Aircraft. Hers has been a path from learning to fly in Michigan, through flight instructor, co-pilot and first officer

positions to the left-seat command of the Boeing 737 Metrojet. Hers has been a lifetime in the aviation industry. As an airline pilot, Susan knows well her responsibility to a planeload of passengers; she is acutely aware of their dependence upon her for the safety of the flight.

But, September 11, 2001, was an extraordinary day with extraordinary demands upon not only Susan in one aircraft, but the entirety of more than 17,000 crew members in 4,500 aircraft in the skies over the United States. It was a day none of us should ever forget.

"Pushed from the gate at 8:42, my 737 departed Chicago and headed for home in Baltimore, Maryland," Susan recounted. "In clear, beautiful weather, we climbed over Lake Michigan. When we reached our cruise altitude, I glanced down and saw the small town of Napoleon, slightly south and west of Ann Arbor, Michigan, where my dad taught me to fly at the airport built by my grandpa. I said to my First Officer Mick Van Rooy, as I pointed to Napoleon's airport, 'Days like this make me want to go up in a small plane.'"

Her reverie was interrupted with a radio transmission. A controller's voice stated, "A plane has struck the World Trade Center in New York City."

She'd been thinking of small taildraggers and her first thought was of an errant small, private aircraft. Susan noted, "When we heard it was an airliner – American Airlines Flight 11 – Mick and I knew the situation was drastic. He was a military reservist and we agreed, 'This has terrorism written all over it.' We proceeded to notify the flight attendants to remain out of the cockpit and to be alert. We said nothing to disturb or rile the passengers."

Within minutes, their flight was over Ohio. "We heard a garbled, foreign-sounding communication over an open microphone." Although air crews had been trained to react passively to hijackings, which generally led to safe landings at a hijacker's chosen air terminal, a new and dreadful reality was occurring. Muslim extremists were prepared for their own deaths as they took with them thousands of innocent men and women. A new and terrible meaning was being ascribed to the word hijack.

They later witnessed sounds that might have been part of the vicious murder of the crew in the cockpit of United Flight 93. Despite the tragedy that all aboard that ill-fated flight lost their lives in Shanksville, Pennsylvania, heroic passengers reacted to their dire plight. Brave men rushed the radicals and took the obviously doomed flight out of the sky before it could strike another target. At the garbled sounds, Susan went off the frequency and tuned into an AM radio station to hear the further horror that the second tower of the World Trade Center had been struck – this time by United Airlines Flight 175. It defied comprehension.

Calling upon their shared decades of aviation experience and honed competence at the controls, Susan and Mick responded quickly to directives from the beleaguered controllers of the nation's aviation system who, at the time, didn't know but what there were a dozen aircraft being taken over. For the first time in U.S. history, starting at 9:03 a.m., the nation's skies had to be cleared of more than 4,500 aircraft.

"We were northwest of Pittsburgh," said Susan, "when we heard, 'Speed to your destination!'" They advanced the throttles and rushed toward a landing at Baltimore. While entering their previously friendly skies of home, smoke was rising from the ashes of the portion of the Pentagon. They were among the more fortunate.

Basking in the beauty seen from the cockpit of the airliners and general aviation aircraft she has captained, Susan Maule considered her view an almost separate realm. In awe, she reacts to dreadful realities of a changed world by sharing her appreciation for the earth.

Personal Collection of Susan Maule

"My first officer said, 'Our lives have changed,' and, although we initially thought of our own lives as pilots, we both came to recognize that change as enormous – culturally, socially and personally."

"Given a straight-in approach to runway one-five right, we landed and were told to evacuate the terminal. We boarded the employee bus – one of the last allowed up to the terminal – and heard that subsequent crews walked two miles to the parking facilities and their cars. I asked a friend to give me a hug, needing to ground myself with the warmth of human contact after the raw intensity of the previous two hours."

Susan's aircraft pushed from the gate at 8:42; the first tower was struck four minutes later.

After only 18 minutes, United Air Lines Flight 175 hit the south tower at 9:03. Thirty five minutes later, at 9:38, American Airlines Flight 77 blasted into the Pentagon, a section of which erupted into exploding fire and debris. In Shanksville, Pennsylvania, at 10:06, brave passengers sacrificed themselves to ensure that another treasured landmark and its people remained unscathed.

Having touched down at 10:11, Susan was witness to it all – from its beginnings in New York City to the smoke billowing skyward from the Pentagon and the terrible reality of the thousands of deaths. She saw the ends to which terrorists would go. After a flight to New York City a few weeks later, her first since 9/11, she saw smoke still rising from the skyline rid of its familiar twin towers. She admitted, "It seems I had to see it all"

Much later, after having seen replay after replay of the televised coverage of the devastation in New York City and Washington, D.C., envisioning the otherwise tranquil and rolling landscape of Pennsylvania, and feeling the angst in the crew room at Baltimore's BWI Airport, Susan took a few days off. "I took time for some essential soul searching," she said. "I needed to analyze my place in this pivotal change to the aviation I had known and loved. I rented a solitary cabin in West Virginia, away from television, telephones and any disruptions. I meditated, trekked for long hours in the mountains and finally chose a direction to follow that would mean healing to me and, hopefully, many others."

Susan, accomplished as a shiatsu practitioner, a flautist and a woman devoted to her own well-being and to that of others, began to compile her thoughts and impressions into a small booklet, *Aerial Blessings*. She wanted readers to rekindle their own appreciation of the beauty and majesty of flying, the freedom and exhilaration of being airborne. With the success of her compilation of poetry, she embarked upon the creation of an instrumental CD – *Celestial Journeys* – which celebrates her joyous hours in the sky by combining flute melodies with her writings and photographs. The world has changed, but each of us can be reawakened to the full appreciation of special, cherished moments.

She wrote, "In a world now changed, I still fly with awe. There is beauty and an allure in flying; an experience that is different from any on earth. There is a music to flying – a dance, an art all its own. From above we are able to see how history relates to geography; how our community's environment is connected to communities hundreds of miles away and where our ancestors traveled on their quest for unseen destinations. The earth's magnificent beauty seen in twists, swirls and colors is the art upon which we live."

Susan Maule's "Blessings" echo and reverberate throughout the vast distances between earth and sky. Like widening circles on a pool disturbed by a tossed stone, they can circle, stretch, reach and touch us all.

Suzanne Asbury Oliver

Vapor Trails Sky High

Teenaged Suzanne Asbury soared into the sky on sailplane wings near her family's Forest Grove, Oregon ,home. Her father had discovered she could solo a glider at age fifteen and, as he was eager to learn to fly, he made arrangements for them to take lessons together. So began Suzanne's love affair with flight that has yet to lose its passion. Suzanne and her dad rushed to the gliderport when cumulus clouds invited them aloft and, flight by flight, she amassed hours in her logbook and was licensed as a sailplane pilot at sixteen. Within a year, having graduated from high school, Suzanne was old enough to legally solo in a powered airplane; she transitioned into taildraggers and tricycle gear aircraft and progressed toward advanced ratings – commercial, instrument and certificated flight instructor (CFI). She pocketed her instructor's license at eighteen and started teaching student pilots from the Hillsboro Airport near Portland. Aviation was lucky to have snared a talented pilot and Suzanne was lucky to have found aviation.

Much earlier, the Pepsi Company chose advertising via skywriting. As early as 1931, Drink Pepsi-Cola graced the sky over New York City.

Courtesy of Oregon Aero, Inc.

Suzanne is unique among women – the best and only woman skywriter in modern skies. She shares the controls of SkyMagic and SkyDancer in which Steve performs aerobatics and she is renowned for painting mile-high messages in an oil based fluid vaporized in the engine's exhaust.

PepsiCo amassed a fleet of fourteen airplanes and hired three pilots, Dave DeBlasio, Andy Stinis, and Cecil Cofren. The trio worked regularly until 1953 when television commercials dominated major advertising and skywriting faded in its appeal. The aerial art languished.

In 1973, when it came time for a celebration of 75 years of soft drink manufacture, the company asked "Smilin' Jack" Strayer, a veteran of more than 40 years in aviation, to search with Pepsi's Alan Pottasch for an old skywriting aircraft. They located the 1929 Travel Air D4D, N434N, with pilot Andy Stinis. From a plan to simply display the craft at Corporate Headquarters, Strayer convinced company officials to refurbish the forty-four-year-old biplane, upgrade the systems and to let him tour as a skywriter. For eight years, giant letters spelled PEPSI overhead as Strayer brought the Travel Air in view of millions of people in more than 200 North American cities.

Then the serendipitous happened: Suzanne Asbury and skywriting discovered one another. She explained, "A friend of mine saw a Pepsi ad for a skywriting pilot and showed it to me. Initially, I dropped the clipping into the trash. Then, as curiosity

Air show stars spend precious flight hours seeing that their aircraft are flown to and from show sites to home base. Having performed for Pepsi for more than 20 years, Suzanne and Steve gained valuable flight experience criss-crossing the country with her Travel Air, the Pepsi SkyWriter and his de Havilland Chipmunk, the Pepsi SkyDancer. Married since 1982, the duo are America's only husband and wife professional skywriting and aerobatic team.

got the best of me, I dug it back out and placed a call."

Jack Strayer was all business when he arrived in Oregon for their interview. He asked Suzanne to provide a Super Cub. As they walked out to fly, Jack asked, "Which seat do you generally choose?" As the Super Cub is generally piloted from the front seat with a solo pilot, Strayer knew that would be Suzanne's choice. Purposefully he crammed his six-foot-two-inch frame into that coveted front seat. Suzanne climbed into the rear seat and fastened her seat belt and shoulder harness.

He said, "I like to see how pilots react when their habits are challenged."

Suzanne admitted, "With his broad back ahead of me, I couldn't see forward at all. I figured out, later, that was exactly what Jack had in mind. I could do S-turns during taxi, but seeing forward during takeoff and climbing flight was impossible. He was giving me a taste of the blind flying that I would get piloting the Pepsi Travel Air."

Suzanne must have met his expectations, as "Smilin' Jack" finally lived up to his name; he grinned as he invited her to join him on the Pepsi Skywriting circuit. It was 1980; Suzanne was 22. With eight years of experience behind her, she was more than capable, but awed and a bit frightened by the prospects.

"I wasn't sure but that I'd bitten off more than I could chew," she admitted.

Her learning curve lay ahead. It began one morning when Jack strapped into the front seat of the Travel Air with Suzanne acting as Pilot-In-Command (PIC) in the rear. She had performed the pre-flight walk-around and was satisfied that the biplane was more than ready for the early morning flight. Glancing around before taxiing for takeoff, she pushed the throttle forward and they sped forward.

"Jack taught me to take off in a three-point attitude," she recalled, "and the stick was fully back at our start. Once we were airborne, things went from bad to worse pretty quickly. The elevator was rigid, the stick was frozen and I couldn't budge it. I tried to press it forward to level the nose, but was horrified to be in an extreme climb attitude with a frozen stick. We were in serious trouble.

"Jack glanced down and discovered that he'd inadvertently included the control stick when he pulled his seat belt snugly around his waist. The controls were wedged into his stomach. He released the belt just in time to prevent a crash and I learned a valuable lesson. I never again took off without rotating the stick fully just before pouring the coals to the engine."

Another lesson was learned when Suzanne was solo. Her biplane suffered a double magneto failure and the engine quit. Luckily, she was close to a tower-operated field and she radioed the controller, "Engine out. Request permission to land!"

Artwork © 2007 Sharon Rajnus

There is romance and beauty in Suzanne's famed PEPSI Skywriter, "Nancy," the 1929 Travel Air D4D. Few aircraft can boast that they were collectively designed by the likes of Lloyd Stearman, Walter Beech, and Clyde Cessna. As for Suzanne, a better pilot couldn't have been found to show this classic beauty at its best. It was as if the two were meant to fly together.

The controller told her, "Stand by. You are Number Two for landing."

Suzanne repeated, "I have no power! I will be landing now!" She only later discovered that the controller mistakenly assumed that she was flying one of the new Beech Travel Air twin-engine aircraft.

"He thought that I'd lost one of my two engines and could safely fly on the one. He was very surprised when my 1929 biplane – I called her 'Nancy' – came in dead stick, touched down on the runway and rolled off onto a taxiway. I learned to describe my biplane more fully for future radio communications."

Initially, Strayer and Suzanne fulfilled the advertising requirements for PepsiCo. With every flight she became more adept at timing and altitude and directional control. She also fell comfortably into greeting fans who gathered at the airport to marvel at the young woman and her biplane. More than 1,200

Courtesy of Suzanne Asbury Oliver

Suzanne is shown in the 1929 D4D Travel Aire which was retired in 2000. Today it is beautifully displayed in the Udvar-Hazy Center, National Air and Space Museum, Smithsonian Institution.

Travel Air open-cockpit aircraft were built and they served more than that number of barnstormer, crop dusting and sport pilots. One of Suzanne's greatest pleasures has been to have nostalgic pilots approach her, eyes bright with tears, and tell her about flying a Travel Air, how it handled and where they flew.

Suddenly, however, within less than a year, Strayer died at age 72. It was early in the spring of 1981 and several scheduled appearances lay ahead. The company decided to cancel the rest of the year's schedule until Suzanne convinced them that she would be able to fulfill the contracts; she was good to her word. On her own, she painted the Pepsi name high in the sky for the rest of the year.

Today, no other woman is a professional skywriting pilot. Suzanne paints vapor trails into mile-high letters across a 10-mile swath of sky. She forms letters – or smiling faces – at altitudes between 7,000 and 14,000 feet, depending upon the temperatures at altitude – the warmer the day, the higher she flies.

"Ideally, it works best in clear skies against a background of brilliantly blue sky," she said. "It is like an aerial dance sequence. I count off seconds just as a dancer counts off steps. Everything is precisely choreographed and timing is essential. Lose count, no matter the cause of the distraction, and your skywriting will fail."

Between performances, Suzanne accrues most of her flight time ferrying "Nancy" across the country. One windy West Texas day, Suzanne headed for the tarmac at El Paso International Airport, Texas. A flight instructor John Paul Jones recalled, "It was one truly blustery day. No one was flying; even geese knew enough to stay on the ground. We were checking the chocks and tiedowns to make sure all the airplanes were safe from the gusts and, suddenly, here comes a bright red, white and blue biplane. This relic of yesteryear came toward the runway, landed as if there was no wind whatsoever, taxied in despite a rugged crosswind and came to a stop. The pilot climbed out, took off a leather helmet and shook loose her long blond-hair. Those of us who had cancelled our flying just dropped our jaws."

Then, in May 1981, as horses' hooves pounded the track below, Suzanne performed for the crowd attending the Kentucky Derby. Towing a banner to advertise over the same crowd was a handsome Stearman pilot, Steve Oliver. Their meeting was meant to be; it was love at first sight. Steve and Suzanne married in 1982 and formed an unbeatable team that flies high.

PepsiCo retired "Nancy," their 1929 Travel Air D4D, in 2000. Suspended in a place of honor in the Steven F. Udvar-Hazy Center of the Smithsonian's National Air & Space Museum, the Travel Air seems about to start the smoke trail to paint PEPSI for admirers below.

Suzanne and Steve pilot a de Havilland Chipmunk, the "SkyDancer." They have endeared themselves to air show fans from coast to coast and are the only husband and wife professional aerobatic and skywriting duo. Still passionate about flying, they have joined in sponsorship with Oregon Aero, a company that specializes in the design and manufacture of products that prevent pain, improve impact

Steve was towing banners behind a 1941 Stearman at the 1981 Kentucky Derby at which Suzanne was performing her classic skywriting. Married a year later, Suzanne and Steve have brought the art of skywriting, pyrotechnic night aerobatics, and skilled aerial performance to thousands of loyal fans.

protection and reduce noise – from the headsets worn by Steve and Suzanne to the liners in helmets worn by our servicemen and women.

They bring boundless energy to air shows. As Steve controls "SkyDancer" from the exotic tango to the boisterous hip hop, he creates snappy aerobatics and explosive night "pyrobatics," an exciting display of aerobatics laced with wild and colorful pyrotechnics. Suzanne changes the pace, taking "SkyDancer" through a different dance, writing vaporous messages against a cerulean sky.

It is difficult to imagine all the factors with which she contends: correct spelling, continuity of line, sizing the letters correctly, timing meticulously, maintaining headings, controlling smoke oil, and monitoring altitude, drift and relationship with the ground. Perhaps most challenging is that she flies upright which means that her letters are backwards; they also are created on the horizontal, though they appear to be vertical or perpendicular to fans on the ground. Suzanne's expertise has been honed and she pays careful attention to detail. Debbie Gary, an air show star and friend of Suzanne's, quoted her as having promised to pass on the secrets of skywriting when she retires as her mentor, Jack Strayer, did for her in 1980.

In 1999, Suzanne and Steve were pleased to be awarded the prestigious Sword of Excellence presented by peer members of the International Council of Air Shows (ICAS). The recognition stated, "The Sword of Excellence is presented each year to one of air show industry's leaders, someone who has worked selflessly for the best interests of the entire air show community. The award was first presented in 1981 and Steve Oliver and Suzanne Asbury-Oliver are the 25th recipients of this high honor."

All of us who look up and thrill to the sight of smoky letters drifting with the movement of the winds are beneficiaries of this incredible woman's love of flight and her talented handling of her aircraft. We are witness to a continuum in sky writing that started well before Suzanne was born and flourishes with each of her performances. When Suzanne draws a smiling face, as it blurs and softens miles overhead, we can't help but return that smile. We can be thankful that this unique aspect of aviation launched this special woman sky-high.

Dr. Barbara "Doc" Gilbertson

Serving the Flight Environment and Flyers

Now that medical doctors have accomplished surgery in the near-weightlessness of simulated space, eyes will focus on Flight Surgeons to learn how medical science has progressed from the earliest days of medical practice to this advanced position. When Dr. Barbara Gilbertson was a young child, such advancements were unknown – as was her own future.

She recalled, "The first thing I ever wanted to be was a doctor. As a kid, I was the one examining frogs and getting medical kits, dissecting kits and a microscope as gifts. In addition to that, I loved flying – huge airliners and small private planes were equally exciting to me."

It seems natural that this talented woman sought to make a career of both. Unable to finance an advanced education and medical school, Barbara joined the United States Air Force in the 1980s. She applied for a scholarship and the Air Force awarded her the chance to attend medical school and, upon her graduation, to receive a commission as a second lieutenant. She studied at the College of Osteopathic Medicine of the Pacific, Pomona, California; went on to an internship in Tucson, Arizona; and then followed that challenging and valuable training with assignment to active duty with the USAF.

After a successful three-month course in aerospace medicine, Barbara was relieved to be assigned to fighter aircraft and the medical care of fighter pilots, flight crewmembers and their families. "I chose fighters because I love speed and love to fly," she said. "It was even more exciting that I was assigned to the 461st Tactical Fighter Training Squadron – the Deadly Jesters that are part of the 405th Tactical Training Wing – at Luke Air Force Base, Arizona, at approximately the same time that the 461st was the first unit to receive the F-15E Strike Eagle."

When Barbara joined the 405th Wing, pilots transitioning into the new aircraft flew several sorties per week and flight surgeons were required to fly at least once a week. These airborne missions were intended to inculcate in a medical doctor the effects of high speed flight, the stresses – mental and physical – on the body, and the realities of aerial combat. In order to properly treat her patients, the experiences were vital.

"Air Force pilots are always in training," Barbara explained. "and many of those training flights involved air combat maneuvers – dogfights. A highly complex dogfight was called a hairball. This was mock conflict with a simulated enemy and it was some of my favorite flying."

She cared for crewmembers whose health was paramount in their demanding roles and treated equally a head cold that precluded flight or a personal matter that could affect performance. In so doing, she learned a great deal about flying and about herself.

She said, "Flight surgeons need to learn the flying environment to better understand what pilots and crew are experiencing. At the controls, I learned initially to fly straight and level and then I progressed to flying formation and holding the jet steady without taking my eyes from lead. We flew in formation to and from the air combat exercise area. In short, a summary of a typical flight would be – exhilaration! One feels so alive and all senses are active.

"But, as I was required to examine an accident site as soon as transportation to the site could be arranged – generally via helicopter – I learned to develop caution. I learned to request being put on the flight schedule for the day following an accident investigation to preclude the natural buildup of fear."

She recalled one particularly difficult day. Two student pilots from another squadron were killed during a dogfight. Called to investigate their fatal crash, "Doc" Gilbertson was flown to the scene. She noted, "An ejection had gone wrong – the canopy didn't release and, when the seat blew, the pilot's head hit the canopy with such force that his spinal column was driven up through the back of his neck. He died instantly, his chin resting on his chest, a peaceful expression on his face; but, the protruding spine told the story of the forceful blow."

The bodies of the two airmen were released to representatives of their own squadron. During this exchange, Doc Gilbertson had a brief moment to speak with that squadron flight surgeon, who commented on having given physicals just two days prior to "two healthy airmen."

It was after such a poignant event that she knew she had to be

scheduled for the next available daily practice. She was trained in a combat casualty care course and she learned to respond to physical wounds as well as any results of nuclear, bacterial, and chemical warfare. She served during the conflicts in Central America and as a member of the Reserve during the Gulf War. She responded as needed at Holloman Air Force Base as well as at Luke. She also knew that it was imperative that she avoid dwelling on the negative, to fly in the next exercise, and to remain focused.

Barbara was prepared to respond in a mission-ready atmosphere. "We practiced all the time," she said, "even in the middle of the night. We never knew if the mission for which we prepared was real or whether it was practice. If deployed, it would have been my responsibility to stabilize a patient in life and death situations."

It was an added benefit of her job for her to have the opportunities to fly in some of the hottest aircraft known. She knew euphoria and, at the opposite end of the spectrum, she knew the grim reality of warfare and combat. She girded herself for the tragedy of death as every good surgeon must do. Her service to her patients and to her country is commendable and priceless.

Coursing through the sky in the fastest of fighter jets commands every sensory response. The excitement in speed is part of what draws pilots and crewmembers in the first place. For a flight surgeon to properly treat fighter crews, experience in their realm is essential. Dr. Gilbertson embraced the exhilaration of speed and flew with the spirit of the eagle.

Patty Wagner
She Spells Aviation ... F-U-N!

To speak to fans during the 1987 EAA Convention and Fly-In, Air Show Stars Bob and Patty Wagner were introduced by the renowned Duane and Judy Cole. Judy said, "I happened to be here at Oshkosh when Patty took her first ride on the wing. I held her Mama, who was in hysterics. She just cried and cried. She'd say, 'Oh, this is my only little girl. Why is she doing this?' She'd sob, then she'd look up at Patty, who was up there just having a ball. Patty's been having a ball at it ever since."

Patty called her mom, LaVerna Walsh, a "worrier." But most with any maternal instincts at all would think twice about a daughter climbing onto the wing of an airplane, leaning against a rigid brace, attaching a harness, and waving goodbye as the pilot takes off and proceeds to rock and roll at up to 150 miles per hour.

Bob Wagner explained, "Patty wears a wide three-inch seat belt around the waist and is snapped into a separate safety harness, which is like a parachute harness that is guy-wired to the front. Normally this is slack until she is inverted and then it takes a little bit of weight on her shoulders. She is still primarily supported by the seat belt, but you have to have the back brace. Despite the tightness of the seat belt, Patty's feet come off the wing unless she really stretches to hold it. All of the available horsepower of the engine is needed to pull a wing rider through the air. And, with my Stearman in an inverted push-up, I get a real funny shudder on the elevator and the rudder."

LaVerna had every right to be a "worrier." But Patty fell in love with aviation early in her life. Immediately after having graduated from high school in 1966, she landed a managerial job at a country club and opted to invest her hard-earned salary in flight lessons. Enrolled in flight lessons in the Moraine, Ohio, airpark, the same airport at which Bob was flight instructing, Patty earned her private pilot certificate in 1966 and her commercial certificate a year later. That Patty and Bob were married in 1968 at 8 a.m. so as to leave the rest of the day for flying is not surprising. Theirs is a marriage that united two joyous souls and they have reveled in the fun of flying ever since.

How did the wing act get started? Bob, who had already flown aerobatics on the air show circuit, said, "I scheduled an air show with a male wing rider knowing our act had to be witnessed by an FAA representative before we were permitted to perform. When the Rep arrived, my male volunteer was too large to fit into the harness. The only person quickly available was Patty. The FAA inspector shuffled his feet, eyed his watch and got fidgety while we prepared."

It was 1970 and, although Bob had never flown with anyone on the wing, he did confer on the phone with Judy, Duane, and Marion Cole. Bob said, "They had wing riding experience and gave us good advice. We had to start somewhere. So, we scurried around, buckled Patty onto the wing and away we went. One trip around the pattern; the airplane handled all right, the landing was okay. We talked it over and agreed, 'Let's go do it.'

"We took off and I did a loop. We came back and landed. Patty was still up there. The FAA inspector told us we needed to do a roll, so up we went to do a roll and that was fine. Then he said, 'How about negative?' We took off again and I flew it upside down the length of the runway. The nose was up a little high and the airplane shuddered a little bit in reaction to the drag of having her on the wing; but, we came on in around the pattern and landed. He signed us off and we were approved."

Bob added, "I did have to promise Patty a steak dinner for riding the wing."

"When we started," Patty recalled, "I was supposed to be the one to be up for a while; then, I was going to fly the plane and Bob was going to get up. He told me this." She grinned and added, "He lied, but I didn't know it at the time."

Her joie de vivre is palpable. Then Patty continued, "Of course, we are interested in antique airplanes, homebuilts,

This "Aviation Gothic" by the celebrated photographer, Dan Patterson, captures Bob and Patty Wagner in front of their hangar at Wagner International Airport, home to the Wagners, their fleet of airplanes, their animals, their friends and where it is FUN to fly.

Courtesy of Dan Patterson - www.flyinghistory.com

and vintage biplanes. Our weekends are spent flying to air meets and shows, hopping rides and hauling passengers. So, it wasn't like shedding your skin with a whole new experience. Being in, around, and involved with airplanes is something we've always done. This is our whole life. We ran an airport, we had a flight school. We lived on the premises. For us to be able to buy a Stearman, to go into business doing something we like and to keep the old planes flying; well, that's why we did it."

And, for more than a quarter of a century, they did it for the fun. A film taken with a camera mounted on the aircraft tail gave a viewer some idea of the pressures felt by Patty. Initially the wind is the major force on the body when thrust through the air at high speed. Then, with the aircraft rolled inverted, a G force is added to the frontal stress. Pull that airplane into curved flight during maneuvers and G forces can increase three or four times. That Patty flies aerobatics and knows about flight forces is a boon.

For added safety and to communicate in case of trouble, Patty and Bob worked out a hand signal. She said, "We agreed that I was to give a 'thumbs-down' signal if something went wrong, if I was really having trouble up there. I've used that three or four times, but each time Bob forgot to look up at me. That was key. He had to look up to see the signal."

One memorable time, Patty and Bob were performing their routine over a boat show – miles from an airport. "We were trying out a new harness," Patty explained, "and it came loose. The wind caught it and it started beating against me. I was taking a whipping and later had the black and blue marks to show for it. I wanted Bob to slow down, to let me try to do something about it. I was giving him the 'thumbs-down' like crazy; but, he never looked up at me. We were flying with another aircraft and an aerial photographer was trying to film us both. The other airplane was faster and we kept going faster and faster to keep up. To top it all off, it started to rain! Each raindrop stung like pins and needles and still Bob didn't look up.

"If I'd had a brick or something, I could have thrown it. I knew he was busy flying, but there was something inside me that said, 'get mad!' Then it said, 'get more mad!' He didn't even know if I was UP there, if he forgot to look. The hand signal was our only communication in the air; but, we did talk about it on the ground later, of course."

Flying together has been a trip. From Patty's first airplane, a Luton Minor, to her Cubette, a 65 horsepower J-3 Piper Cub scaled down to 5/7ths, her Clipped Wing Cub, to her piloting WACO aircraft and entertaining millions from her vantage point atop the Stearman wing, she has not only basked in the joy of flying, she has carried that joy to millions.

By 2003, after over 30 years in air show center, Patty and Bob had performed over the United States and Canada and brought their act to air shows in South America. "There," Patty admitted, "we were known as 'Los Aeros Locos.'"

They retired their act, but kept the fun in their lives. Patty and Bob are pilots, flight instructors, aerobatic instructors, mechanics, WACO Aircraft and Museum volunteers, aircraft restorers and the owners of their own grass strip – Wagner International Airport in Ohio. Their retirement from airplanes is as distant as interplanetary travel.

Never having strayed too far from the Americas, Bob was coaxed

Artwork © 2007 Sharon Rajnus

For more than thirty years Patty Wagner graced the top wing and Bob Wagner ably handled the controls of their red and white Stearman. A favorite among air show fans, they performed in South America where they were dubbed, "Los Aeros Locos."

into taking Patty to England and Scotland where he could look into family roots. The trip was planned for aviation enthusiasts, with stops at air shows and air museums, or he might have been more difficult to persuade. For her part, Patty, an avid volunteer with Women in Aviation, International, has also represented the U.S. at airwomen's gatherings in Moscow and in Italy. She volunteers her time, her piloting, and her valuable experience with children at WACO Summer Camp, at EAA AirVenture and at the growing WACO Museum, Troy, Ohio.

From having flown the opening act for Evel Knievel at Kings Island Amusement Park, having graced the covers of a wide variety of magazines, to hosting a huge party for her Clipped Wing Cub's 50th Birthday, Bob and Patty Wagner have shown others exactly what joy aviation can bring. They were "having a ball" before she took to the wing. Despite a few times when she tried to gesture "thumbs down," to no avail, Patty and Bob Wagner have, more than anyone, epitomized the idea that Flying is FUN!

Dodie Jewett

It's All About Safety, Safety for All

In July of 1982, Delores G. "Dodie" Jewett was given her opportunity to serve her nation as an Auxiliary Member of the United States Coast Guard, now under the Department of Homeland Security. She volunteered her piloting skills and her aircraft to perform as eyes in the skies over Cleveland, Ohio and the waters of Lake Erie. She is from a family of volunteers – her husband Harlan, who also wears the uniform of the Coast Guard Auxiliary, spent forty years with the U.S. Army Corps of Engineers and her daughter Jennifer Syme has served as a career officer with the U.S. Army Nurse Corps. Her son, Bruce, is an airline captain.

Knowing exactly what it means to serve, Dodie fashioned her own niche that not only has been of valuable service to the citizens of her area, but has also been of enormous satisfaction to Dodie. Having joined the Coast Guard Auxiliary in 1979, Dodie was first qualified for boat crew duties. Her progression then led to becoming a courtesy marine examiner, an instructor, and as an aircraft commander in air operations. Holding a multi-engine and single-engine commercial pilot certificate with an instrument rating, Dodie also is an FAA licensed aviation basic ground school instructor. She has risen to lieutenant commander and has spent more than a quarter of a century in the United States Coast Guard Auxiliary.

Initially, Dodie had to join a Coast Guard Auxiliary Flotilla. For standardization, it was mandatory that she review and pass a test in Boating Skills and Safety and then to review and pass the Basic Qualification test after having studied Auxiliary manuals. Having completed the basics, she had to complete the Auxiliary Air Operations course satisfactorily.

The air operations manual stated, "All pilots and observers need to perform a qualifying 50-yard swim while wearing a personal flotation device, receive training in water survival, emergency egress procedures and training in the use of specific survival equipment carried on the Auxiliary aircraft flown. While operating under Coast Guard orders, the appropriate uniform must be worn and can be purchased through military exchanges.

"There are four levels of qualifications in the air operations program: 1) Air Observer, the airplane's crew; 2) Co-Pilot, must hold an FAA pilot certificate, have a minimum of 200 hours of flight time logged of which 100 hours are as Pilot-In-Command (PIC). Co-pilots perform the following missions: cargo and passenger transport flights, aides to navigation and chart updating patrols, pollution and ice patrols, and area familiarization flights; 3) First Pilot, must hold an FAA pilot certificate and have 500 hours of flight time logged as PIC. First pilots perform the following missions; fly all missions as stated for the Co-pilot, fly search and rescue missions (SAR), and to fly any other mission except search and rescue flight procedure flight checks; 4) Aircraft Commander, must hold an FAA pilot license with an instrument rating and have logged 1,000 hours of flight time as PIC. Aircraft Commanders are able to fly all missions and are qualified to perform SAR flight procedures flight checks. The aircraft must meet strict criteria, most of which is met by having been licensed by the FAA. In addition the aircraft must have front seat shoulder harnesses and an exterior antenna for a marine radio."

Dodie took Emergency Egress Training at the Coast Guard Fall Conference in Niagara Falls, New York, undergoing the simulated ditching twice. Using a PVC pipe-constructed frame that simulated a cockpit, with a five point seatbelt attached to flotation devices, she was dumped upside down into a hotel pool. Two coast guard trainers took to the water to determine that she could extricate herself from the seatbelt and the mock-fuselage within the 60-second time limit. She was fully clothed in a flight suit, shoes and a safety helmet, which made the exercise a bit more of a challenge.

These training exercises are annual training events and Dodie has found them to be important and worthwhile. She said, "In September of 1995 we went to Selfridge Air National Guard Base where we were trained on the use of our equipment and survival gear by members of Coast Guard Air Station, Detroit. Once in the water we had to inflate and climb into a life raft. It gave me a good deal of confidence to know that I would be ready to perform in real life what we so carefully practiced."

Some of the hundreds of missions she has flown include Ice Patrols, plotting the movement if ice flows, the types of ice and ice levels. This is to assist the Coast Guard cutter in keeping the shipping lanes open.

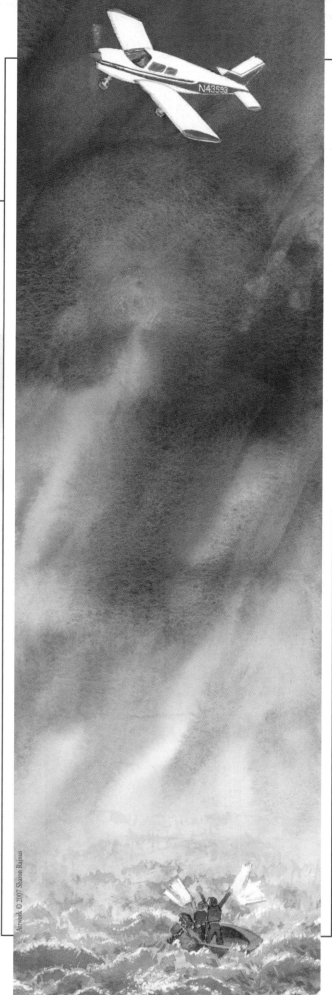

Under threatening clouds, Dodie Jewett circles her Piper Cherokee over a hapless threesome, adrift and out of gas in turbulent Lake Erie. Dodie, a member of the Coast Guard Auxiliary, was their lifeline to a Coast Guard rescue.

She proudly wears the golden wings of the United States Coast Guard Auxiliary.

They include environmental patrols, watching for spills and detecting areas of pollution. And, since September 11, 2001, there has been stepped up activity and marine domain awareness patrols (MDA Pats) have become a primary mission. Dodie said, "After 9/11, our area Auxiliary aircraft were among the first aircraft in the air to do security patrols for the Coast Guard."

Honored several times, Dodie has been awarded the USCG Meritorious Unit Commendation Award in 1990, the USCG Auxiliary Service Award for Instructor in 1993, the USCG Unit Commendation ribbon from the Admiral and, in 1994, was promoted to District Staff Officer – Operations Air for the 9th Eastern Regions, including Ohio, Pennsylvania, and New York.

During the winter of 1994, the Coast Guard and its Auxiliary worked particularly long and arduous hours. It was a record breaking winter in terms of temperatures, the harshest in nearly two decades. With nine ships that were capable of icebreaking, the Ninth District's fleet worked around the clock to assist in the passage of iron ore, coal and petroleum traffic through ice in the Great Lakes. For their labors, Dodie and the men and women of the Ninth District were awarded the Department of Transportation's highest award, the DOT Gold Medal for Outstanding Achievement. In 1994, too, Dodie was named a district staff officer.

Traditionally, the Great Lakes' boating season has been considered to be relatively short because of the harsh winters and ice-plagued waters. Search-and-rescue units, augmented by Reservists and Auxiliary personnel like Dodie, who served generously with their own aircraft and their own skills, manned four Auxiliary Operation Stations and work to handle approximately 7,200 cases per year. Two of the Ninth District's stations are among the Coast Guard's five most active. With more than a third of the recreational boats of the United States located in the Great Lakes, the Auxiliary is also counted upon take a safe boating message directly to the public.

Imagine having the task – the job – of flying your own well-maintained red and white Piper Cherokee through cerulean blue summer skies over Cleveland, Ohio. Imagine wheeling like a white gull out over Lake Erie where the gentle waves crest with white foam

Photo Courtesy of Dodie Jewett

As she has since 1979, Dodie readies for another mission for the U.S. Coast Guard Auxiliary. As a volunteer and in her own Piper Cherokee, Dodie, an aircraft commander, covers the shores of Lake Erie whenever and wherever she is needed.

safety of others first.

She especially remembers a time in the late 1980s when she was on the last leg of a Sunset Patrol, an evening sweep of Lake Erie that is designed to locate any stranded boaters before the darkness of night – or worse, dangerous, stormy weather. She came upon a drifting open boat, its outboard motor stilled and the weather darkening and roiling the skies and the water with wind and threatened rain. Two adults and their young daughter, a toddler, were in trouble. The man and his wife circled towels above their heads, waving frantically as the airplane approached. "The lake was churning and growing rougher by the moment. I could tell by the way they were waving their towels how frantic the man and woman were becoming."

Dodie radioed Coast Guard Station Cleveland Harbor and reported the small craft's location. She said, "I was requested to circle until a surface craft could arrive to rescue the passengers, remaining overhead as a beacon to guide the ship to the helpless boat. In the days prior to the widespread use of GPS (global positioning system), this saved time in managing a rescue."

She must have given vital reassurance by simply being there for the hapless pair hanging onto the gunwales of the boat and clutching their daughter tightly. She felt enormous satisfaction with a successful end to an otherwise dangerous situation.

That's what the U.S. Coast Guard Auxiliary is all about – safety of individuals, safety on our navigable rivers and lakes, and seeing that the safety of our nation is sacrosanct. Dodie said, "I do this for the love of my country, to help people in distress and to support the service whose uniform I'm proud to wear."

and move endlessly with the direction of the breeze and to be able to look down to check on the safety of powerboats, sailboats and trolling fishermen who ply the lake for pleasure and for sport. There must be days in which Dodie Jewett asks herself, "How could I have been so lucky to have such a wonderful opportunity, such a beautiful sky in which to fly?"

Then, be realistic. Most demands upon Coast Guardsmen come in the harshest of weather, the strongest of winds, in torrential downpour or accompanied by drastic inclement weather. Dodie has been airborne when the sky out of the northwest has darkened to a cold, slate gray and clouds have closed low, ominously close to the water and the wind has whipped those gentle whitecaps into a frothing fury. She knows enough to ensure her own safety, but she is often called upon to put the

Artwork © 2007 Sharon Rajnus

Dodie's United States Coast Guard Uniform today displays a proud array of awards and ribbons. Her U.S. Coast Guard hat, with the Auxiliary emblem, repeats the symbol.

CHAPTER THREE
COMPETENCE & COMMITMENT

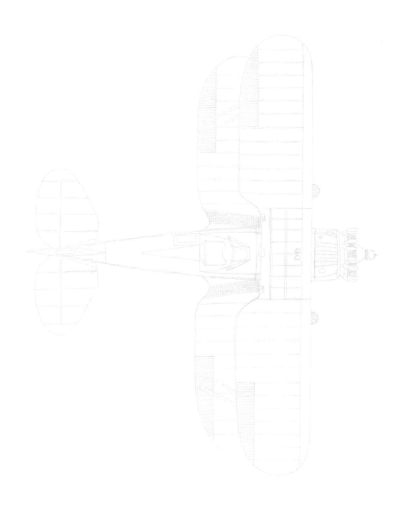

WACO Biplane

Artwork © 2007 Sharon Rajnus

COMPETENCE

"I think someone around 15 or 16 can handle flight training. The actual age isn't the important thing. In my opinion, it's a matter of maturity; and attitude is extremely important. It takes plenty of concentration, and young people often have other pressures to consider. But, I can remember some examples of teenage students who started taking lessons and going to ground school a year or two before their 17th birthdays and then becoming licensed pilots. Those are quite the accomplishments."

Emily Warner, LEARNING HOW TO FLY AN AIRPLANE

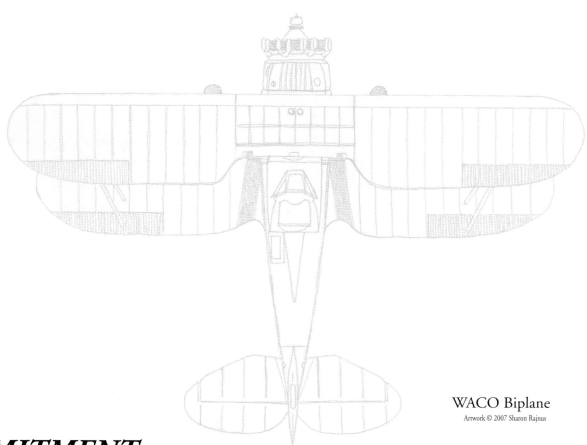

WACO Biplane
Artwork © 2007 Sharon Rajnus

COMMITMENT

"Every individual who gains employment in the field of aviation joins a special group of citizens – those who continue to contribute to one of humankind's greatest achievements, powered flight. The achievements of the aviators of this century – in the military, in civilian aviation, in space, in industry, and in the minds of great thinkers – were born of a determined pursuit. And from this relentless quest for innovation and exploration, we have created a remarkable capability for our nation."

Secretary of the Air Force James G. Roche,
Remarks to the Women in Aviation, International, Reno, Nevada, March 12, 2004

CHAPTER 3

Mary Stan Feik

A Matter of Mastery

The scene was KidVenture adjacent to the EAA AirVenture Museum at the 2005 Experimental Aircraft Association Convention. Denise Waters volunteered in the aircraft mechanic booth, devoting her time to educate and excite kids of all ages. A steady stream of youngsters and their parents trooped past, experiencing hands-on projects designed to fire their imaginations and encourage their participation. But, of utmost gratification to Denise was the question posed by a young man who entered the display, his eyes sweeping the area. He asked, "Do you have anything here about Mary Feik?"

Denise was delighted. Mary Feik had long been one of her mentors, an accomplished woman and an extraordinary and award-winning mechanic, pilot, aircraft restorer. To think that a youngster was astute enough to ask about Mary Feik was gratifying in the least. To be able to help him learn more about this remarkable woman was her distinct honor and pleasure.

Perhaps the child heard about Mary through the Civil Air Patrol (CAP). In 2004, Mary, a Colonel in the CAP, received a Distinguished Service Award for her service between April 1982 and August 2004. It has long been Mary's passion to encourage young people toward goals in aviation and to make them aware of the endless possibilities in technical training. The Civil Air Patrol is the fortunate recipient of Mary's dedication as an instructor and lecturer, for which she has been the three-time recipient of the Frank G. Brewer Civil Air Patrol Memorial Aerospace Award. Mary is an "Eagle" aviation pioneer in the CAP National Congress on aviation and Space Education. In CAP, she joins a prestigious list of aviation notables – Billy Mitchell, Jimmy Doolittle, Eddie Rickenbacker, Charles Lindbergh, and Amelia Earhart, to name a few – who have been recognized with ribbons in their names. Mary's ribbon is awarded to cadets who have successfully completed specific levels of accomplishment. The citation accompanying the ribbon states, "In final review, the Mary Feik Achievement Ribbon commemorates the leadership and pioneering

Mary flew with the Alaska Wing, Civil Air Patrol, in this de Havilland Beaver. In it she experienced the bush piloting and search and rescue missions undertaken by the northernmost members of CAP and participated with the mechanics who keep it flying.

Personal Collection of Mary Feik

contributions Mary Feik has made to the world of aviation."

Or the young man might have heard of Mary's work in rebuilding aircraft through the Paul E. Garber Facility, a restoration arm of the Smithsonian's National Air and Space Museum. Mary was an integral part of the team that restored an exceedingly rare 1910 biplane, the Wiseman-Cooke, based on the most popular aircraft models of 1909 and named for its designer, an automobile racer, Fred Wiseman, and a pilot, Weldon Cooke.

Perhaps the boy read of Mary's help in restoring Smith IV, the fourth Spad XIII assigned to and flown by World War I Ace Arthur Raymond "Ray" Brooks. This historic aircraft was named for Smith College, Brooks' sweetheart's alma mater, and was Brooks' fourth Spad. In Smith IV, Brooks accounted for one enemy downed of his six and other pilots took this particular craft to five more victories. Thanks to workers like Mary, this Spad was saved from falling into complete disrepair and was placed back on exhibit.

Mary also helped to restore ALPHA NC11Y, Northrop's 1930 all-metal, streamlined craft. An ALPHA pilot flew in an open-cockpit while, immediately forward of that position, passengers and cargo were transported in the modern comfort of an enclosed, sleek and aerodynamically clean cabin.

The youngster might have visited the Steven F. Udvar-Hazy Center and seen the results of Mary's help in restoring Curtis Pitts' second aircraft, the Pitts S-1C Little Stinker. The meticulous restoration successfully returned this craft, the smallest Pitts Special in existence, to its heyday of 1949–1950 when it was flown to aerobatic championship at the hands of Betty Skelton.

And Mary's accolades continued. Perhaps the boy heard of her receiving the Charles Taylor "Master Mechanic" Award, the most prestigious award issued by the Federal Aviation Administration (FAA) to persons certificated as Airframe and Powerplant mechanics. The Charles Taylor "Master Mechanic" Award, named in honor of the first aircraft mechanic who labored so well with and for the Wright Brothers, had never before been awarded to a woman. To be eligible to be selected, the candidate must be a U.S. citizen; must have worked for 50 years in an aviation maintenance career and must have been an FAA-certificated mechanic or repairman working on N-registered aircraft for a minimum of thirty of the fifty years required. When Mary received the coveted award in 1996, the certificate stated, in part, ". . . in appreciation for your dedicated service, technical expertise, professionalism, and many outstanding maintenance contributions, to further the cause of aviation safety."

The young boy couldn't have chosen a more inspiring mentor. In seeking information about Mary, he was showing the same initiative that she applied in forging her own career. Following in the shadow of her father, who repaired auto engines while scrabbling to make a living during the Great Depression, Mary overhauled several different models. The confidence she gained encouraged her to feel

Artwork © 2007 Sharon Rajnus

A master mechanic experienced as a flight engineer aboard the Boeing B-29, Mary participated in the restoration of numerous aircraft, including a SPAD XIII, Northrop's ALPHA and Betty Skelton's Pitts S-1C now exhibited at the Smithsonian's Udvar-Hazy Center.

qualified for, and to submit an application to, the U.S. Army Air Forces (USAAF) to perform aircraft engine repair and overhaul. She was hired immediately. Mary was only 18 when she became a teacher, educating USAAF crewchiefs and mechanics. Having felt frustrated with limited to obsolete equipment and inadequate instruction manuals, Mary sought assistance from experts at the Engineering Division of the Air Technical Service Command, Wright Field, Dayton, Ohio. Her talents were recognized and she was invited to transfer to Dayton to work for the USAAF as an engineering aide. It was during these early months and years of World War II that Mary's genius flowered.

Mary was the first woman in Army Air research and development and, when assigned to fighter pilot transition training, she was elevated to flight status. In this capacity, she started accruing time and expertise in fighter, attack, cargo and training aircraft. Her 6,000 hours included time as a flight engineer aboard Boeing B-29 bombers. She was awarded an engineering designation based on ability rather than formal education and, along with having created training and maintenance manuals for a wide variety of military aircraft, she also was entrusted

with actual aircraft for static testing. Charged to return the various models in airworthy condition, she developed the specifications for test stands on which aircraft could be mounted and secured while engine operations could be conducted. She called her anchored aircraft, "Captivair," and these test beds gave pilots, instructors and mechanics the opportunities to conduct operational engine run-ups in P-47s, P-38s and P-51s in "live," but grounded and tightly secured fighters.

Mary's goals have been and continue to be to encourage young people to enrich their lives through involvement in aviation and to learn the value of teamwork in every application of life. The inquisitive young man who sought information about Mary will profit from having chosen his inspiration from exactly the right pilot, mechanic, restorer. Mary Stan Feik learned teamwork from the start – working at her father's side. She has practiced teamwork in everything she has done and her valuable lessons for us all hinge on that attribute. Whether the young man wants to be an aircraft mechanic or has his goals set in other directions, in following in the footsteps of Mary Feik, his first steps are following those of a master.

Martha King
At The Cutting Edge

If anyone had told Martha King in 1974 that she'd complete a 14,000-mile around-the-world flight, hold every possible category and class of FAA pilot and instructor certificate, live the concept of crew coordination, and that she would contribute to training half of the licensed pilots in the United States, she would have been the first to scoff. At the time, although she had graduated as valedictorian of her high school class, with honors from Indiana University and was obviously bright and self-disciplined, she was feeling the angst of having launched a business jointly with her husband, John, and forced to watch that venture fight a losing battle.

She and John had initiated a mobile service that delivered fuel, lubrication, oil, and filter changes to customers who owned vehicle fleets. These enhanced the fleet operations significantly and ought to have resulted in success. Their plan was sound; they later sold franchises, the profits from which financed their first airplane, a Piper Cherokee 140; but, they were victims of circumstance. An oil crisis erupted in 1973 as members of the Organization of Arab Petroleum Exporting Countries (OAPEC) placed an embargo on oil shipments to nations that supported Israel in its confrontations with Syria and Egypt. World oil prices quadrupled and economic activity suffered.

To recoup their losses, the Kings turned toward other opportunities. At that time, Martha suggested, "Let's try our luck at something that will be fun until a real career comes our way."

John remembered vividly his first aviation experience; his father took him flying in an Aeronca Champ, an experience that left an indelible impression. The idea of

Martha and John King happened upon teaching aviation ground schools while searching for pleasurable careers. Through multi-media technology, they have educated half of all U.S. student pilots and created an impressive industry that mirrored their passions.

Personal Collection of Martha and John King

adding some fun to their lives was timely and, as John's enthusiasm for the Champ was contagious, he and Martha looked to the sky for temporary solace. As Martha and John had decided before they were married that whatever they chose to do, they would do together, Martha learned to fly.

Her flight lessons led to one particularly intoxicating flight. On a solo round-trip cross-country from Indianapolis to Richmond on the Indiana-Ohio border, her departure was delayed by rain showers. Inadvertently, day darkened into night during her flight and Martha had no previous night flight training. While her husband and flight instructor worried on the ground, Martha was enchanted by a spectacular view of the afterglow of the setting sun and the sparkling array of Indianapolis' city lights. Flying suddenly became her magic carpet, assuming a priority in her life that has never ebbed. As so often happens to those who seek its challenges, Martha found satisfaction in mastering flight; a satisfaction that translated into mastering life itself.

In preparing for the requisite FAA written test that preceded her private pilot flight test, Martha recognized a niche in flight training into which she and John could throw their prodigious energies and talents – weekend aviation ground schools. In many cases, ground school was as diverse as there were individual flight instructors. It occurred to Martha that practical knowledge should not only be presented to students in an understandable and enjoyable manner; but, that it was critical to safe flight. She and John discovered that most flight training sites were eager for excellence in the ground training of pilots. They chose to pursue their instructor

Martha, who holds certificates and ratings in every category and class of pilot and instructor licensed by the FAA, has flown this airship over the Kentucky Derby and the Super Bowl. Her personal experience is crucial to enhance the education she imparts to so many.

ratings and to work at the fun of preparing students.

"In the early 1970s," Martha explained, "John and I held certificates for aircraft private pilot single- and multi-engine land with instrument ratings. Within a period of two months, we added commercial, flight instructor (CFI), instrument flight instructor (CFI&I), advanced and instrument ground instructor, and multi-engine CFI, and launched our ground school business."

Today, Martha and John King train half of all student pilots in the United States. Via multimedia presentation, they are welcomed into living rooms, offices and airport classrooms. They are as familiar as family members to the millions who have pursued courses of home study via King Videos, CDs and DVDs from the catalogue of their King Schools, Incorporated, of San Diego, California.

But that wasn't always the case. Initially, the Kings personally conducted weekend ground school courses that began with two or three hours of instruction on Friday nights, progressed through Saturday and Sunday to administration of the FAA written test on Monday. The task of preparing to speak for 16 to 20 hours on Meteorology, flight computing, chart usage, flight planning, FAA rules and regulations, navigation, communication, aerodynamics, and flight systems was daunting enough without the aerial commuting they undertook. For ten years, Martha and John flew long round-trip cross country trips to personally conduct instruction. Theirs was a hectic schedule that placed them in fifty different cities each week of each year. Between California and Alaska alone they flew fifty round-trips and shared some challenging experiences. They were as committed to their students and as dedicated to learning for themselves as they were to teaching others and hours of preparation were required for each weekend's presentation. Martha and John experienced the wisdom of the 19th Century French essayist, Joseph Joubert, who stated, "To teach is to learn twice."

"We set an exhausting pace," John admitted, "and began to find it increasingly difficult to enjoy one another's company in our airplane."

Martha and John discovered truths applicable to all who share

Artwork © 2007 Sharon Rajnus

Martha King, type-rated in the Falcon 10, piloted this jet with her husband, John, in an around-the-world flight.
They explored the future of General Aviation in Russia and elsewhere and enhanced their training goals.

cockpit duties. Commensurate with the fun of flying can be the tensions, aggravations and irritations that accompany competition and intimidation. Any of these can cause serious problems in communication, in piloting and in relationships.

"When both are pilots and both are flight instructors," said John, "there is a great tendency for one to teach the other despite who happens to be doing the flying at the moment. We honestly believe that the person in the right seat, not acting as pilot-in-command (PIC), has an I.Q. that is about fifty points higher than the one in the left seat."

"The person in the right seat," added Martha, "can see every

mistake about thirty seconds prior to the person at the controls who is carrying a greater load of responsibility. It can be very frustrating to the PIC."

"With us," explained John, "it was happening both ways. Both of us were correcting each other. Our goal was a fifty-fifty partnership in our business and in our flying, but we often ended our flights with smoke coming out of our ears. We admitted to a friend that sometimes we'd park the airplane and drive home without speaking."

Their friend mentioned having recently obtained a type rating and learning the then-new concept of crew coordination. Martha and John pursued not only one, but three type-ratings – for Lear Jet, Citation 500 and Falcon 10. Invaluable lessons in cockpit resource management (CRM) taught them to practice the use of standardization: standard call-outs, procedures and terminology.

"Whenever Martha was low on the glide slope," John explained, "I used to say, 'Martha, you're too darned low.' Taking the lead from CRM, we established a rule. When addressing the person in the left seat, we consistently use one word first – 'Captain.' Now I say, 'Captain, sink nine hundred feet, below glide path.'"

"Acknowledging the authority of the other person comes first," said Martha. "Then it is time to input facts, not opinions. Facts are accepted as assistance, not as criticism. With advice or opinions, the left-seater becomes focused on the criticism rather than the remedy. With the authority of the pilot-in-command readily acknowledged, a fact can be acted upon with no loss of pride, ego, face or whatever you want to call it."

Crew Resource Management's important ramifications extend to all two-pilot operations. Knowing and practicing its precepts helped to ease shared duties in the Kings' Cessna 340 in their days as commuting ground instructors. Now that their vast array of classes are conducted via the latest in computer-based interactive software and video multimedia products, their continued practice of CRM extends to such as the intricacies of instrument approaches in inclement weather in the Kings' sophisticated Dassault Falcon 10 N10F, which Martha and John flew to ". . . explore the future of general aviation in Russia and throughout the world."

Martha and John piloted over the length of Russia during a 14,000-mile flight that included landings in Moscow, Yekaterinburg, Novosibirsk; Khabarovsk; Magadan; and Anadyr. This adventurous around-the-world flight included dealing with foreign communication, marginal weather, new and different approach charts and airports while navigating with altitudes in meters above the airport, wind speed in meters per second and altimeter settings in hectopascals.

Martha and John rely on personal experience before they introduce their cutting edge training programs. As they embarked on their planned multimedia training series on flying under instrument flight rules (IFR) around the world, they continued to hone their personal approach to Joubert's wise adage. Martha and John live the education

that they impart and they ". . . learn twice."

They are the only husband and wife team to have earned every category and class of FAA pilot and instructor certificates, holding airline transport ratings and commercial privileges in single- and multi-engine land and sea airplane, helicopter, gyroplane, glider, airship and free balloon; certificated flight instructor ratings in single- and multi-engine airplane, instrument airplane and helicopter, helicopter, gyroplane and glider; and advanced and instrument ground instructor. Martha, the first and only woman to have attained all of these achievements, takes these privileges seriously and maintains her currency in such vastly different aircraft as the Robinson R 22 and the Fuji Airship. She has flown the airship, complete with its mechanical rather than hydraulic controls, over crowds at the U.S. Tennis Open, the Kentucky Derby, the Super Bowl, and the annual AirVenture held by the Experimental Aircraft Association at Oshkosh, Wisconsin.

She explained, "It is physically demanding, very grueling; but, lots of fun."

And therein lies the secret of the enormously successful Kings. Martha and John sought something that would be fun while they waited for a career to find them. In truth, they pioneered an entire industry based on their limitless passions – for flight, for sharing, for educating, for stretching beyond apparent limitations, for embracing excellence and for encouraging all with whom they come into contact to capture this contagious spirit. Through the magic of multi-media education, Martha and John have replaced their laborious personal weekend ground school lessons with what Martha terms, "...our kind of personal, intimate contact and impact on half of the pilots in the country. That is truly satisfying."

Whatever the topic – aviation safety, entrepreneurial skills, learning to fly a light sport aircraft, obtaining your type rating; a student can invite Martha and John into the living room and cherish them as personal trainers. Of the students who complete one of their courses, ninety-nine percent pass the FAA exams. It seems that feelings are mutual and that is truly satisfying, too.

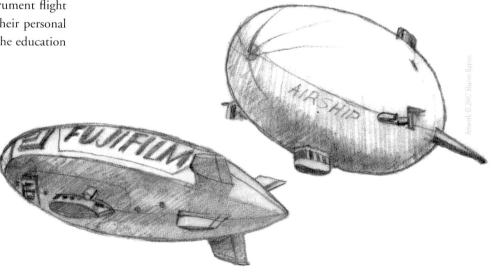

The 200-foot-long helium-filled Fuji Airship travels smoothly and quietly at about 35 mph and at an altitude of 1,000-3,000 feet. Powered by two Porsche engines with rotatable-ducted propellers used to control direction, it can take off and land almost vertically.

Ellen Paneok
If Not for Flying, What Then?

In 1973, fourteen-year-old Inupiaq Ellen Paneok of Kotzebue, Alaska, left her sixth foster home with the same feelings of resignation and hopelessness that plagued the first five and with added defiance born of experience. Ellen had known the anxiety of wondering whether there would be a next meal. After her parents divorced, her mother found it difficult to cope and Ellen had personally experienced the downward spiral to which welfare recipients can be reduced. Prior to having been placed in foster care, she survived four years of abandonment. Now she was headed for a Girls' Home.

Her rebellion increased, her frustration overflowed. The Girls' Home could have proved her undoing had it not been for a curious coincidence. Ellen doesn't recall exactly when it happened; but, by the time she was sixteen, she had picked up an aviation magazine and read it cover to cover.

She was in a great place to be introduced to flying and to flying careers. Of all of the United States, Alaska endures some of the most difficult and challenging weather conditions known to pilots; yet, with so much of its population living and working deep in the bush and far from cities and settlements, Alaska also has more requirements for air transportation than any other state.

The challenges, the dangers, and the lure of flight couldn't have reached a hungrier young woman. Ellen sought a way to climb toward a satisfying career and vowed she would learn to fly. She was the age at which she could legally solo an aircraft and remarkably, under the Alaska Native Claims Settlement Act, the Native Corporation gave her a check for $1,500. Despite scorn from others who thought she was wasting her time and her money, Ellen deposited the entire amount at a flight school. Flying became her salvation.

When her money ran out, Ellen turned to producing works of art, selling portraits of cats and dogs to school children and creating beautiful scrimshaw carvings to support her new passion. By the time she was twenty-three, she had her commercial pilot's certificate, her instrument rating and her flight instructor's license.

Her first flying job was in Kotzebue flying a Cherokee Six. She went on to fly out of Bethel, St. Mary's, Barrow, Aniak, McGrath and Anchorage. She now holds an airline transport pilot certificate and is rated in multi-engine airplane and as an instrument flight instructor. With more than 15,000 hours of commercial flying in thirty adventurous years, Ellen is a role model and an inspiration to all. In addition to bush piloting, she has served as an aviation safety inspector with the Federal Aviation Administration, as a published author and featured speaker, and now donates much of her time and talent to the Alaska Aviation Heritage Museum.

In an article published in Anchorage's Merrill Field newsletter, she wrote in part, "Flying for Jayhawk Air, . . . my main steed is a Cessna 206, equipped with 24-inch 'Gars' (tundra tires) on the mains, an 850-size nose tire with an oversized strut fork, a Robertson STOL kit, and bubble windows. Jayhawk Air specializes in off-airport landings – beaches, sand bars, mountaintops, you name it."

Delivering hunters, fishermen, loggers, miners, and gold exploration workers to various camps and U.S. mail and supplies to widespread villages, Ellen explained that almost all of her flying has been in remote areas. She added, "I have landed on railroad service roads, ocean beaches, and village strips so remote that they aren't even on the charts. I've hauled such strange stuff as dynamite and caps (thankfully not on the same flight), kitchen sinks, and full coolers of food for fishermen whose food was stolen by 10-foot Kodiak brown bears on Kodiak Island. The bears used their teeth to pop the cooler latches."

Personal Collection Ellen Paneok

Ellen Paneok, renowned Inupiaq pilot, author, lecturer, and scrimshaw artist, flies the 1939 Stinson L-1 Vigilant of the Alaska Aviation Heritage Museum – one of two still flying in the world.

Winging over the dramatic and challenging Alaskan countryside, Ellen Paneok, who has flown everything from live wolverines to the U.S. mail, is depicted piloting the Stinson L-1. This observation aircraft of WWII was highly useful as it maintains full controllability at 28 knots and cruises at 105.

Ellen took food to the same fishermen twice. She explained, "The second time that the bears got their food, the fishermen were stuck in a raft on the Karluk River, watching helplessly while the bears ate every last bite."

Recognized as a heroine, Ellen said, "I have had to chase polar bears off the runway before I could land. Then, as I unloaded the airplane, I'd think, 'I just chased a polar bear away; where did he go?' You don't know how fast someone can unload an airplane when they think a polar bear is right around the corner!"

Her love of her homeland is obvious and, with such natural magnificence around her, she also admits to being incurably romantic about flying. Her career in the air over Alaska – in her words a "beautiful state full of wilderness and artistry," has strengthened that romance.

She wrote, "The wilderness envelops me as I fly over countless mountain ridges, each looking enough alike to confuse a neophyte flier. I know each ridge . . . having flown so many hours in the area. I know the wind flows, and I know a favorite creek with its eddies and currents. I know the weather patterns as they come rushing up from Southwest Alaska – weather that could bring the lower forty-eight states to their knees, but normal for Alaska. As I fly, I watch caribou, moose, and bear as they trudge cross the tundra in their relentless search for food."

But there are crucial demands on pilots in Alaska. Ellen nearly died as a result of an unusual mechanical problem during a frigid winter landing at Barrow. Bruce McCallister, photographer and author, wrote in *Wings Above the Arctic*, "Ellen's aircraft muffler failed and lethal gases entered her cockpit. Carbon monoxide is odorless and Ellen was unaware that lethal gas was seeping into her body. However, she began to [lose] feeling in her arms and legs. Her limbs were becoming numb and her breathing was labored and difficult. . . . Nobody realized how serious her condition was until she staggered into a heated hangar and passed out."

"I was close to death," said Ellen. "Fortunately, I was hospitalized in the intensive care unit and I survived blood poisoning and heart palpitations."

During her stint as an aviation safety inspector for the FAA, she lectured widely on safe flying practices. Having lived through this ordeal and others that involved extreme safety issues, Ellen's lessons are even more compelling and memorable.

Ellen will tell you that she has made a darned good living in aviation. Generously, she has also made a career of extending a hand to educate and encourage others.

Anne Bridge Baddour

Winter and the North Atlantic

Between 1977 and 1997, Anne Bridge Baddour carved a niche in aviation history as the first woman pilot to be selected by the Lincoln Laboratories Flight Test Facility, Massachusetts Institute of Technology (MIT). As an Experimental Research Pilot, Anne flew missions for the Department of Defense and the Federal Aviation Administration, including such projects as the early testing of the Traffic Collision Avoidance System (TCAS). Department of Defense projects were classified, the crews cleared for Secret, but even the mission pilots were not told program details.

Having first started flying in 1953, Anne earned her certificates and ratings to airline transport pilot, multiengine. Then, she admitted, "The idea of piloting across the Atlantic Ocean intrigued me. I also wanted to pilot a single-engine aircraft as Charles Lindbergh had done. It was no easy matter; but, an opportunity came my way. In 1985, with Margrit Orlowski, a German citizen and experienced transoceanic ferry pilot, I ferried a single-engine Mooney 252 from Bedford, Massachusetts, to Reykjavik, Iceland, under Instrument Flight Rules (IFR) the whole flight."

Having completed the Application for Sanction and submitted the necessary forms required by the National Aeronautic Association (NAA), Anne's flight set five National and World Speed Records registered under Class C-1c and established over five courses. The records were recognized by the NAA and the Fédération Aéronautique Internationale (FAI).

The two hoped to repeat their experience and, in 1988, Anne and Margrit accepted what would normally have been an enviable task of delivering a pressurized, twin-engine Beechcraft 58P Baron to Genoa, Italy. They anticipated a speedy flight over the ocean, refueling in Iceland, on to Italy and then a quick return by commercial jet. The takeoff was planned for 20 December, 1988 and they hoped to return home to

Vice President Lyndon Johnson presented this Harmon Trophy to Anne in 1989. Part of a set of four honoring an aviator, aviatrix, aeronaut or astronaut, the trophy is given for the most outstanding international achievements in the preceding year, focusing upon the art of flying. It represents just one of Anne's numerous awards and honors.

Courtesy of Anne Baddour

spend Christmas Day with their families.

To protect themselves, they packed winter clothing – windproof long pants, felt-lined boots, down parkas with fur hooded ruffs. They brought survival equipment, food and water. Charts were assembled, courses plotted. Anne prepared the documentation necessary for the NAA with the hope of establishing national and world speed records, this time for twin-engine flight. On 20 December at Hanscom Field, Bedford, Massachusetts, she and Margrit performed a preflight of the Beechcraft.

"Despite a touch of fading to the paint," Anne said, "the Baron looked fine and a thorough inspection revealed no visible hazards. But, trouble lurked underneath that acceptable exterior."

They filed an Instrument Clearance with the Federal Aviation Administration. When the clearance was received, they boarded the Baron ready to depart.

"We took off at 1750 UTC, a coordinated universal time based on atomic time," Anne said, "and headed north toward the Millinocket radio navigation aid in Maine. From Millinocket VOR (very-high frequency omni range), we pressed on for a four-hour and 27-minute non-stop flight, navigating via Mont Joli and Sept-Îles, Quebec, to a landing at Goose Bay, Labrador."

It had been an uneventful flight, but something was clearly wrong. The cabin was frigid and both pilots suffered with the cold. There was no way Anne could have known that, upon departure from Massachusetts, the landing gear retraction had severed the wire that provided power to heat to the cabin; but it was clear that no heat was reaching the cabin or its occupants.

She said, "We had flown at an altitude of nineteen thousand feet with an outside air temperature of minus fifty degrees Fahrenheit. Our supply of fresh drinking water had frozen to solid ice."

Having landed after-hours, there were no mechanics available to make repairs at Goose Bay. Anne and Margrit donned arctic clothing and, having checked the weather, winds and clearances, pressed on. Anne wrote, "It felt good to wear the felt-lined boots, protective trousers and down parkas."

They climbed to 24,000 feet into a clear black night. Below them, the full moon had cast a golden stripe across the water. " We flew through the night with no feeling of motion. We were suspended between sky and water, no earth, towns or trees to mark our passing.

"The Northern Lights waved like a gigantic stage curtain in the sky," recalled Anne, "colors billowing out for miles. I would have loved to have been entranced by the sight; but, the cockpit was frigid. To make matters worse, the instrument air system failed, which caused the loss of a gyro making the autopilot and deicing boots unusable. The Baron had to be hand-flown and the losses, though not disastrous, were certainly debilitating. With known significant problems, we worried that others might crop up."

That unease, which crept into the cockpit with the cold, turned out to be justified. "Several hundred miles off the eastern coast of Greenland," she continued, "first the right engine and then the left engine began to sputter and cough. Flying the North Atlantic is formidable in any season, but it's particularly forbidding with a crippled airplane. The ocean below offers no hospitality and no refuge."

Anne and Margrit took off their heavy clothing and struggled into one-piece hooded survival suits. Anne admitted, "We had to be prepared. If we were forced to ditch in the ocean, at best we might only minutes to live. At our altitude, the outside air temperature was minus sixty-four degrees Farenheit. It was two o'clock in the morning and the night's blackness was interrupted only by the moonlight and reflections of the Northern Lights. Nursing the rough engines, we made a 180-degree turn and radioed Greenland's Narssarssuaq Airport, requesting permission to land."

A man's voice responded, "The field at Narssarssuaq is closed."

Anne radioed, "We have two rough engines, one inoperative pump, the deicer on the right wing isn't working and we have no heat in the cabin."

The man insisted they would have to declare an emergency.

"Yes," Anne promptly replied, "We declare an emergency."

When blue runway lights shone across the miles, her relief was palpable. Their altitude enabled the lights to be visible. Now, if only the wounded airplane could be coaxed through the correct fjord to a safe landing.

"The Greenland Icecap is six thousand feet high," she said. "Surrounding the coast on almost every side are thousands of fjords, all of which are narrow and most of which lead to a blind end. Choosing the wrong fjord, like flying into a box canyon, leaves insufficient space to roll into a turn and reverse course. You perish!"

Having established a descent while the runway lights were still visible, it was imperative that Anne choose the one and only fjord that led to the village of Narssarssuaq, to the runway, and to safety. It was possible at 16,000 feet to see the runway lights ahead, but that view would be obscured at a lower altitude.

"We continued to descend in order to enter the fjord; but, it was not a straight shot. As we entered at three thousand feet, mountains of ice towered above us on both sides and shone with an eerie blue. At the end of the fjord we made a ninety-degree turn to the left which was followed seconds later by another turn to the right. To our joy, there were the runway lights welcoming us to Greenland."

Anne and Margrit flew on to Iceland, maintaining lower altitudes for better engine performance. The delivery of the aircraft was completed and both returned to their homes in time for Christmas Day. As this flight was sanctioned by the NAA, Anne established eleven national and world speed records, Class c-1. Included were five records set between the destination of Goose Bay, Labrador and the time from: Bedford, Massachusetts; Millinocket, Maine; Presque Isle, Maine; Mont Joli, Quebec; and Sept-Îles, Quebec. Also established was one record between Goose Bay, Labrador and Narssarssuaq, Greenland; one between Narssarssuaq and Keflavik, Iceland, one between Narssarssuaq and Reykjavik, Iceland, and three between Bedford, Massachusetts, Millinocket, Maine and Presque Isle Maine to Narssarssuaq.

Nominated for the Harmon Trophy for these achievements, Anne joined the ranks of the greats of aviation when she received this Aviatrix Award for 1988, presented to her by the Vice President of the United States. She said, "I never dreamed a Harmon Trophy would be mine, but hearing the confirmation from General Clifton von Kahn of the NAA was one of the great moments of my life. I am awed and humbled by its beauty and significance."

Anne Baddour, the benefactor for whom the Library at Daniel Webster College is named, has enjoyed a lifetime of aviation achievement and has given of herself to benefit others. To encourage aspiring pilots and mechanics, she founded several scholarships and created an ongoing Aviation Scholarship Program & Scholarship Auction for the Aero Club of New England (ACONE). That ACONE named an Anne Bridge Baddour Scholarship for Advanced Pilot Training is further testimony to her dedication. In return for the opportunities that she has enjoyed, Anne has helped to further the aviation careers of tomorrow's achievers.

In sub-zero temperatures, Anne coaxed the rough-running twin to an emergency landing in icy Greenland. Even brilliant Northern Lights failed to dispel the tension in the cockpit before the wounded bird landed safely.

Commander Trish Beckman

An Officer and a Lady

In an open note addressed, "Dear Women Airforce Service Pilots" (WASP) and published in the WASP Gosport Gazette in 2003, Trish Beckman, then-president of the Women Military Aviators, Inc., and the first woman to qualify as a naval flight officer (NFO) in the F-15E and the F/A-18D, wrote, in part, "We possess our variety of military aircraft experience because you proved during World War II that women can fly military aircraft. Thank you for paving the way for us.

"I see three distinct generations of military women aviators – the WASP of WWII, . . . the military women of the 1970s/1980s, and the military women of the 1990s, post repeal of combat exclusion laws. . . ."

"You persevered through the trials of military aviation, including occasional gender bias in World War II, because you were driven by two strong passions – your love of country and your love of flying. We, second and third generation women, 'inherited' those same two passions. Our advantage, though, has been in our ability to obtain your valued advice during our difficult times. Thank you for being our mentors."

In turn, Commander Patricia Trish Beckman, U.S. Navy, Retired, is due thanks for her role in ensuring that women were not excluded from combat aircraft. Finding advancement in the military stifled by the limiting of women to only non-combat roles, Trish recognized the need for spokespersons. She dealt with then-U.S. Secretary of Defense, Dick Cheney, and she addressed the U.S. Senate on behalf of women's careers and women's opportunities for advancement. She was quoted, in Rosemarie Skaine's *Women at War: Gender Issues of Americans in Combat,* as having said, "Every American citizen is a rugged individualist. He/she should contribute to our nation's defense based on . . . individual capabilities, not on arbitrary assumptions of what is 'average' for each. . . . Women will never be given full rights of citizenship until they accept the full responsibilities."

Directly out of high school, Trish volunteered for the enlisted ranks of the U.S. Navy. Given the opportunity, she obtained a Bachelors degree in Aerospace Engineering and later earned a masters degree in aeronautical engineering. Commissioned as an officer, she was selected for Naval Flight Officer Training and, as one of the first group of women navigators, she later gained the coveted chance to attend Navy Test Pilot School, Patuxent River, Maryland. There, in addition to having flown in over twenty varied military airplanes, she excelled and in a subsequent tour, returned as an instructor.

Later chosen for an engineering role, Trish was the defense plant representative for F/A-18C/D Acceptance Flight Test at the McDonnell-Douglas Aircraft plant. "To do my job best," she noted, "I flew as a weapons systems officer – NFO – in F/A-18D strike aircraft.

"I fought a two year battle for the right to fly in the F-15E, which I finally won in 1992. I became the first woman designated as a crew member in the F-15E (even if it was only for production flights in St. Louis!). I'm taking credit for that, because I had to fight such a hard battle. I wasn't just 'in the right place at the right time' when the option became available. This predated the allowance of women to officially begin training in combat aircraft in 1993."

And Trish enjoyed every acceptance test flight performed in the hottest of fighter aircraft. She said, "I flew the acceptance and delivery flight of every two-seat aircraft that came off the line and, in this capacity, I was responsible for discovering any problems in aircraft performance and remedying them. I loved pulling Gs and testing the G-limits, which pegged at 7.5 Gs for the F/A-18. We'd surpass that in order to ensure the aircraft's capability when stressed during actual combat."

Courtesy of Trish Beckman, Comander, USN Retired

In 1990, Commander Trish Beckman, Navy Flight Officer, became the first U.S. woman to qualify as a crewmember in the F/A-18D. She flew acceptance and operational testing and considered the F/A-18D her "baby" for three years at the McDonnell-Douglas aircraft plant.

Artwork © 2007 Sharon Rajnus

Freshly painted Boeing 737-700 series jets leave the factory for a variety of destinations. These particular aircraft bear the livery of those in which Trish Beckman performed as Flight Navigator for multiple aircraft engineering test and delivery flights.

HEROINE of the HEART

Colleen Barrett was honored with her name and a bright heart painted on the fuselage of the Boeing 737-700 delivered to Southwest Airlines with Commander Trish Beckman, USN Retired, as Acceptance Engineer. As the president of Southwest Airlines, Colleen Barrett is the highest-ranking female executive in the U.S. aviation industry.

As "Heroine of the Heart," she made history as the first woman to receive the Tony Jannus Award. The award is named the adventurous pilot who inaugurated commercial aviation in 1914 with the first scheduled airliner – a Benoist XIV flying boat that plied the waters and shortened the trip in Florida between St. Petersburg and Tampa to 21 miles in 23 minutes. Barrett, the 45th to receive the award, was cited for her leadership in maintaining Southwest's profitability over the past three decades. She received the award in October 2007.

After having retired from the military, Trish accepted a position as flight navigator for multiple aircraft engineering test flights and aircraft ferry flights to customers of Boeing Commercial Airplanes Group, Seattle, Washington. In addition, she is an aircraft dispatcher and a systems operator. In these roles, Trish has ferried B-737s to Shanghai; has participated in two around-the-world trips in a B-777 and a B-737. She was on board when a B-777 flew to the Middle East to participate in the Dubai Air Show. Closer to home, Trish participated in testing the B-737-700 adorned with the red heart and the words "Heroine of the Heart" for Colleen Barrett, president, Southwest Airlines. She flies high.

Raised in Huntsville, Alabama, Trish's schoolmates were the children of an international array of atomic scientists and rocket physicists who had come to the U.S. Space & Rocket Center to aid in the quest for aerospace developments. She acknowledged the powerful influence exerted upon her then and for her important life choices thereafter. Imagine the thrill in June, 2007 when she was invited to return to her hometown as Guest of Honor for a reception during the celebration of the 25th Anniversary of Space Camp and as featured speaker at their graduation ceremonies the following day.

This major accomplishment is because of her generous mentoring of others. She helped open doors of opportunity to all women with hopes of advancing militarily and to enjoy the possibilities of promotion. In addition to Space Camp, she has given generously of herself through Women Military Aviators (WMA), Women in Aviation, International (WAI), the Sino-American Aviation Heritage Foundation (SAAHF) and she has volunteered as a workshop presenter at Sally Ride Science Festivals, which continue to encourage girls to pursue careers in math and science.

From her earliest times, Trish's heroes were the Mercury, Gemini and Apollo astronauts. She would have loved to soar with them all. Although her eyesight kept her from reaching her goal of becoming an astronaut, she still harbors plans to get to space, even if she has to pay to go. Undeterred, Trish found other ways to pursue her dreams and she has generously shared those dreams.

Trish has said, "Military aviation is by far the most exciting facet of aviation. When women strive for success in a military career, they should be accepted for what they can do."

Her admirable career has been one of demonstrated ability, tenacity and determination. Through commendable military service and talent in aerospace engineering, she has left a rich and valuable legacy.

Dr. Mae

Dr. Mae Jemison was inspired by Nichelle Nichols, Lt. Uhura on Star Trek. After Mae flew as Mission Specialist aboard NASA's Endeavor, she was pleased to appear on a segment of Star Trek – the only crewmember of television's Spaceship Enterprise to have actually gone into space.

On 12 September 1992, Mae Jemison, United States astronaut and mission specialist, headed into space and beyond aboard the Space Shuttle Endeavor. It was the zenith of a dream. When she was but five years old, her teacher in Chicago's inner-city elementary school asked the classic question, "What do you want to be when you grow up?" Mae's hand flashed up quickly for she knew. After several children had given conventional responses: fireman, policeman, mailman, the teacher called upon Mae.

Mae said, "I want to be a scientist."

Her teacher questioned, "Don't you mean you want to be a nurse?"

An indignant Mae put her hands on her hips and restated, "No, I mean a scientist."

This intelligent, determined little girl was one year old when the history-making artificial satellite, Sputnik, was launched by the Soviet Union in 1957 and a "space race" was on. Newspapers, magazines and media broadcasts were filled with the competitive excitement, challenge and lure of space exploration. As advancements followed, this very precocious child continued to be influenced by the startling events that captured everyone's imagination.

Mae Jemison enjoyed reading, especially science fiction. She first saw *Star Trek* on television in 1966; it strengthened her determination to travel in space. She admitted in her autobiography, *Find Where The Wind Goes*, "[B]efore seeing *Star Trek*, [I] had a set of encyclopedias that gave step-by-step details on how a human would arrive on the surface of the moon. I had latched onto the study of how the universe began, how stars were formed, how life began and evolved on Earth, and the future colonization of other planets as a lifelong interest."

She defied the idea that women were not suited to be astronauts, though few acquaintances shared her belief that she might one day join that elite crew. She wrote, "Then came *Star Trek*, with Lieutenant Uhura, Mr. Spock, and Lieutenant Sulu. Wow! Somewhere, someone else believed that other kinds of people would populate spaceships from Earth. Humans of both genders and all ethnicity would be in space. Here was affirmation!"

C. Jemison
All Hailing Frequencies are Open

Her already active imagination took flight. She saw in *Star Trek* a hopeful view of humanity. As a young girl of color, Mae was entranced to see Lt. Uhura and impressed that she represented intelligence, skill, beauty and that she, too, was a woman of color.

Mae achieved ambitious educational goals. She graduated from Stanford University in 1977 with a bachelor of science in chemical engineering, concurrently earning a bachelor of arts in African and Afro-American studies. She received a doctorate in medicine from Cornell University Medical College, studied at the Los Angeles County – University of Southern California Medical Center, and served between 1983 and 1985 as a medical officer for the Peace Corps in Sierra Leone and Liberia in West Africa.

She applied for and was accepted as a mission specialist and underwent astronaut training with the National Aeronautics and Space Administration (NASA). On 12 September 1992, Dr. Mae C. Jemison soared from Kennedy Space Center, Florida. She rose into the firmament like the bright star she is.

Mae wrote, "The air stirred by the heat of the engines as the space shuttle roared into the sky not only shook the viewing stands six miles away with a chest rattling rumble, but also my future. "I was not only the first African-American woman in space, but the first woman of color in the world to go into space. The trip brought fame and fanfare... But most significantly, my role in the spaceflight provided me a stronger, more visible platform from which to discuss the importance of individuals taking responsibility not only for themselves, but also for how they treat others and this planet."

Mae was assigned to Spacelab J science laboratory aboard NASA's STS-47. She was to conduct prepared experiments, make space walks and launch satellites. Endeavour carried more than forty experiments designed to mirror scientific inquiry that one might find in any serious laboratory on Earth. The results of the experiments were intended to add knowledge to the behavior of crystals, fluids, electronic materials, glass and ceramic,

Courtesy of NASA

Dr. Jemison conducted numerous microgravity materials and life science experiments in Spacelab-Japan, a joint mission between NASA and the National Space Development Agency of Japan. Crewmembers were included as test subjects, as Mae demonstrated here.

metals and alloys and human beings while in the environment of near weightlessness of space. To excite interest and to further scientific inquiry, Spacelab-J experiments in materials processing and life sciences were televised and brought into the living rooms and classrooms on Earth. As Mae had been impressed by Lt. Uhura, she was now in a position to inspire others fortunate enough to see her in real-time from space. At the termination of the flight, the crew landed Endeavour at Kennedy Space Center, Florida, on 20 September 1992. Mission accomplished.

Mae lived her dream; it led to her historic scientific inquiry during 126 orbits of the Earth – three million miles in distance. And, having become an astronaut, she also had the good fortune to meet and become good friends with Nichelle Nichols, the actress who played Lieutenant Uhura.

In 1993, Mae appeared in an episode, "Second Chances," of *Star Trek: The Next Generation.* She noted, "At LeVar Burton's invitation, I became the only Spaceship Enterprise crew member to have actually gone into space. I felt quite honored to be on the set, and in a way become a small part of the *Star Trek* family."

When aloft and beginning each shift with her team, Mae opened each of those shifts with a variation of Lieutenant Uhura's trademark report. She transmitted, "Huntsville, Endeavour. All hailing frequencies are open."

As she gazed from the flight deck windows just prior to the burn that brought Endeavour back from orbit, she saw the Earth, the moon, the stars and she knew unequivocally that she was as much a part of the galaxy as were the planets, the asteroids, or any comets. She asked, "Didn't my body and my mind contain the same atoms and energy as do the stars?"

If asked for advice, Mae recommended, "Don't be limited by others' limited imaginations. And don't limit others due to your limited imagination." She urges us all to ensure that our "hailing frequencies are open."

Florence Klingensmith

Tragedy at the Air Races

As a young girl, Florence Gunderson of Moorhead, Minnesota, was called gutsy, wild, a dare-devil, a live-wire and ready to try anything. Florence, hired to deliver trucks and motorcycles, left high school during her junior year. One acquaintance noted, "Some of us more conservative girls . . . used to look a bit askance when she would race through the streets on her motorcycle."

Florence took a brief fling at wedded life, marrying Charles Klingensmith in 1927; but, the union ended before their second anniversary. On 27 August 1927, two months after her wedding, Minnesotan Charles Lindbergh made a stop in Fargo, North Dakota. Could she have been swept away by the fervor with which the hero was greeted after his remarkable solo flight over the Atlantic? Fargo and Moorhead are sister cities, separated by the Red River of the North, and Florence must have been among the thousands who clustered around the nation's hero.

Eager to learn to fly, she enrolled in classes at Hanson Auto and Electrical School and worked as a mechanic's apprentice at Fargo's airfield, applying her earnings toward flight lessons. In the summer of 1928, her instructor invited her to perform exhibitions and she made her first parachute jumps from his aircraft. Her appetites for speed and excitement were further honed. Literally going door-to-door to persuade Fargo businessmen to sponsor her, Florence raised approximately $3,000 toward the purchase of her own aircraft, a Monocoupe, which she picked up in Moline, Illinois, and promptly named "Miss Fargo."

By June, 1929, she was the first woman pilot to earn her private certificate in North Dakota. She raced her Monocoupe and also attempted to out-loop other women record holders, subsequently setting a record of 1,078 consecutive loops to best a record of 980 then held by Laura Ingalls.

Only four years later, in the Frank Phillips Trophy Race of the 1933 Chicago International Air Races, Florence, daring, pretty, vivacious, and popular, was killed in a crash of NR718Y, the highly modified, two-

Photo Courtesy of the William Heaslip Collection

Having successfully persuaded numerous Fargo, North Dakota businessmen to sponsor her, Florence Gunderson Klingensmith, North Dakota's first licensed woman pilot, purchased a Monocoupe and dubbed it, "Miss Fargo." She won four events at the 1931 National Air Races in Cleveland. Sadly, her flying career was cut short; in 1933, aviation lost a special woman.

seater Gee Bee Model Y Senior Sportster. The tragedy, which occurred the day after her 29th birthday, was reported as a structural failure of the aircraft – a craft built by the Granville Aircraft Corporation in 1930 and purchased by a man from Jackson, Michigan. The Granville Brothers designed the craft for a 240 horsepower engine, but the owner mounted a 450- to 500-horsepower Wright J-6 Whirlwind.

Earlier that day Florence successfully had flown the Gee Bee in the Women's International Free-For-All. Clocked at a speed of 189 miles per hour, she had won a purse of $625. Only Mary Haizlip in the Wasp-powered Wedell-Williams racer had beaten her. Yet, Mary and her husband Jim, both friends of Florence and experienced at air racing, were witness to her fatal crash. They stood next to the Gee Bee designer Zantford Granville on the flight line.

Jim Haizlip later wrote in *The Golden Age of Air Racing*, of the model Y Sportster. He commented on the souped-up engine and enclosed cockpit, but also that there had been no attempt to consider the effects of higher speeds on the rib spacing or rib stitching. He knew that Granville, who had nothing to do with modifications once it was sold, was loath to see it raced.

"Prior to the big race, which was an unlimited free-for-all," Haizlip wrote, "I had stood by while Florence, the only woman entry in the race, was being fitted into the cockpit. . . . Concerned with safety, I couldn't believe it when the ground crew fastened the removable canopy on after the pilot was seated. As I recall, the canopy skirt was fastened at the sides and rear with hook and wire fasteners, like some military airplanes had used for cowlings before the dzus fasteners came along. I could see that the canopy wasn't going to blow off, pinned down as it was; but it was going to require some outside help to get the pilot out after the flight."

Haizlip went on to recall that Florence, who was entered in the race against six male pilots, was keyed-up to be competing with the men. As she banked tightly around a pylon, he and Granville saw a four-by-six-foot chunk of fabric peel away from the inboard top of the right wing. He wrote, "From that instant I mentally and emotionally was flying the airplane. I could feel the buffeting that must have been frightening to her. We watched the airplane leave the airport area in a straight line toward the southeast. . . . With the engine throttled down the airplane would become nose heavy. . . . Undoubtedly the strongest impulse was to get out."

Granville, Haizlip and their two wives watched the airplane continue away from the field about three hundred feet above the trees until a fatal stall augured the Gee Bee into the ground. Haizlip said, "I was more than saddened at what poor Florence must have felt during the last ten or fifteen seconds of that flight. First, the frantic struggle to get the canopy off so that she could jump, then the frenzied efforts to break out that took all of her attention away from flying until the complete stall. Of course, this is all pure conjecture on my part, but reinforced by the discussion with Granville, the unhappy builder whose control of the airplane had passed from his hands when it was purchased . . . I believe the above account is as close as one can get."

In 1998, the Minnesota Aviation Hall of Fame honored Florence Klingensmith by enshrining her among the prestigious ranks of Minnesota's renowned aviators. Florence joined the exceptional individuals who have positively influenced aviation within the state and whose accomplishments reach far beyond its borders. Had she been there, she most certainly would have been pleased with the honor, but in lieu of a gala dinner, she might have preferred to race a motorcycle, a pair of skis, an automobile, or an airplane.

Melba Beard
Aerial Roots

How many of us have searched our family's history only to have been amazed and delighted to find roots reaching into the sky? In this case, the genealogical trip portrayed a parent in an entirely new light. In memory of her mother, Melba Gorby Beard, Arlene Beard Kearney posed in her mother's helmet, scarf, jodhpurs, and goggles alongside her mother's Brunner-Winkle Bird biplane. They were on the set of the Walt Disney movie, *The Rocketeer*, a movie released in 1991 in which the Bird starred. Arlene, who inherited the craft from her mother, was learning to fly.

"I told my mother that I was going to learn to fly her Bird," said Arlene, "but she didn't live to see that happen."

Having been lovingly restored, the Bird biplane was in pristine condition, but Arlene was impressed with more than its beauty. The more time she spent around the antique biplane, the more she discovered how passionately her mother, Melba, loved aviation and, even more importantly, how many loved Melba. As is typical with so many children who know their parents simply as "Mom and Dad," Arlene knew superficially of her mother's earlier exploits in aviation. But she had little concept of the hundreds of aviation enthusiasts who knew of her mother and who spoke of her fondly.

"I feel so lucky to listen to amazing stories about my mother," said Arlene. "I can't help but be proud that she was so admired by those familiar with aviation history."

Melba Gorby, born in 1907, was twenty when Lindbergh crossed the Atlantic Ocean and the aviation craze fired the imaginations of all. She was instructed by the famed Milo Burcham, who later became an engineering test pilot at Lockheed, but not before having captured the title of World Aerobatic Champion. Melba was trained in an International F-17 in 1929 at O'Donnell School of Aviation in Long Beach, California. She had no trouble getting Burcham to teach her to fly, but when she applied for a transport certificate, the examiner told her that he wouldn't give her the flight test.

He said, "Women have no place in aviation."

That examiner met his match. Melba returned the next day, demanding that she be tested. Not surprisingly, she passed and was the 24th U.S. woman to obtain the license.

For four years Melba steeped herself in aviation. A Charter Member of The Ninety-Nines,

the international organization of women pilots, Melba instructed, flew as a charter pilot, competed in air races, and operated a flying school. She served in the Civil Air Patrol and as a Red Cross Nurse's Aide. Married to William Beard in 1933, she gave birth to two children and turned her attention to her family. Her husband, William, after having graduated from Massachusetts Institute of Technology, earned a Ph.D. at Columbia University and accepted a teaching position at California Institute of Technology.

In 1935 at the National Air Races in Cleveland, Ohio, Melba won a purse of $312.50 in a Women's Free for All – an air race in which she piloted her precious Kinner-powered Bird. She also earned the Amelia Earhart Trophy, presented by the donor herself.

Melba never lost her passion for aviation, obtaining a mechanic's license in the 1960s when she elected to restore and preserve vintage aircraft, among them her 1928 Bird. The Brunner-Winkle aircraft

Wearing her mother's helmet, goggles and silk scarf and standing next to her inheritance, her mother's Brunner-Winkle Bird, Arlene Beard Kearney radiated the joy she felt in sharing her mother's passion for flying. The Bird starred in the Walt Disney film, The Rocketeer.

Courtesy of Ann Lewis Cooper

was originally powered by an OX-5, water-cooled, V-8 engine, a World War I surplus engine that was plentiful and relatively inexpensive. With Kinner power came the BK model Bird in 1929, a three-place open cockpit land plane, and in 1931 a CK model with a larger Kinner engine and an enlarged front cockpit to accommodate three passengers.

A pilot for half a century, Melba Beard was named to the OX-5 Aviation Pioneers Hall of Fame in 1971 at the Curtiss Aviation Museum, Hammondsport, New York. Her daughter, Arlene, was fascinated by the impact her mother created as a pioneer among women pilots. She admitted that she'd always thought her father was the well-known and respected parent. It delighted Arlene to learn of her mother's popularity and deserved admiration.

Melba passed away in 1987 at the age of 80. If her beautiful biplane could talk, Arlene would know even more about her mother's dedication to aviation – and the devotion of aviation enthusiasts to her mother.

Melba Beard operated her own flying school and was the 24th U.S. woman to earn a Transport Certificate. She won the Amelia Earhart Trophy (presented by Amelia Earhart) at the 1935 National Air Races, Cleveland, Ohio, and earned her aircraft mechanic license in the 1960s to pursue restoration of vintage craft. Her daughter, Arlene, thought her father, William Beard, to be her more illustrious parent until she started flying her mother's Bird. She relished stories of her mother's fame and popularity. Melba often flew with her husband, William.

Photos on this page Courtesy the William Heaslip Collection and Mid-Week Pictorial, *New York Times* (above).

Captain Lori Cline
Even Today, Firsts Lie Ahead

Numerous records and firsts have headlined the stories of notable aviators in aviation's short, dynamic history – Harriet Quimby, First Woman to Solo Across the English Channel; Anne Lindbergh, First Woman as U.S. Glider Pilot; Jerrie Mock, First Woman to Solo Around the World. Some historic "firsts" have been actively goal-oriented, well-planned for and executed. Others have come unsought – a pleasant surprise and a gratifying compliment to a successful career. Captain Lori Cline, US Airways, has achieved a few of those coveted complimentary "firsts," and Lori asserts that tomorrow's pilots have "firsts" yet to be rewarded.

Lori was honored to be selected as the first woman in her airline to serve as Airbus FAA Designee. In this capacity, she acts as US Airways' extension of the Federal Aviation Authority, having been proven qualified to evaluate pilots and to issue type ratings and other qualifying certificates.

In suggesting that much lies ahead, she noted, "There are still many record opportunities to be scored by tomorrow's women of aviation. As the twenty-fifth woman pilot hired at my air carrier, I was certainly not among the pioneers and held no expectation of being "first" at anything. Yet, I still scored several significant firsts without having sought such goals. Timing and age were helpful catalysts; but, because aviation continues to evolve, there will always be room for a growing list of women's firsts."

As Lori's story will attest, the road to such success is paved with tenacity, persistence, ambition, passion and hard, hard work. She credits members of her family for initiating her career path and having helped her make wise choices. They have propelled her to the top in her field. Her grandfather owned and flew a Cessna 172 and Lori vividly recalls her flights with him, especially one in 1973 at age 13, when she told of wanting to become a pilot. Her dad, Joseph Legat, who had previously logged flight hours, re-enrolled in flight lessons to join Lori so that both of them could pursue their licenses together. In 1978, she was eighteen when she obtained her private certificate.

Opting for a bachelors degree from Indiana State University, Lori took a challenging and difficult double major in aviation administration and professional flight. Amazingly, she completed a four-year bachelor of science in two years while maintaining a 3.58 GPA. "It was a tough two years," she admitted, "filled with summer sessions, heavy course loads and opportunities to fly, fly, fly."

Hired at age 21 in 1981 by a commuter airline, Atlantis Airlines of Florence, South Carolina, Lori was on her way, although it took time for her to upgrade to Captain. "The minimum age was twenty-three for the required air transport pilot (ATP) certificate," she recalled, "I was passed over nine times. Fortunately, the chief pilot and training officer both flew the line for me until my birthday in order to hold open the captain slot. In December 1983, I took to the left seat of the Twin Otter, Atlantis Airlines."

She added, with a smile, "That was a dubious distinction that doesn't exactly elicit passenger comfort and confidence – 'Ladies and Gentlemen, sit back, relax and enjoy your flight. Today your captain is twenty-three years old.'"

The airline's newsletter, Atlantis News, noted, "[Lori's] success is the direct result of her dedication to a goal and the willingness to make the necessary sacrifices to achieve it. Such success should serve as an encouragement to us in achieving our own personal goals."

Piedmont Airlines hired Lori in the early months of the next year. The Captain became a Flight Engineer, Boeing 727, and then moved to First Officer in 1985. Lori regained her Captain's stripes in the F-28 in April of 1987 and, she said, "At age twenty-six, I became the world's youngest Female Jet Airline Captain."

With a diverse background that includes ratings in helicopters, seaplanes, and gliders, Lori has continued to champion aviation as a remarkable career for women. She is past executive countcil member of the International Society of Women Airline Pilots, and she holds

Personal Collection of Lori Cline

Lori Cline, pilot, author, speaker, editor and manager, was in her airline's first all-female A320 flight crew, its first female A320 check airman and the first female to hold a director level management position. Lori predicts firsts yet to come.

memberships in the Whirly-Girls, Wings Club and The Ninety-Nines. In appreciation for the excellent education she received from Indiana State, she has returned to her alma mater to motivate and inspire tomorrow's aerospace achievers. In 1992, representatives of the Department of Aerospace Technology, Julie Hegwood and Vern Knock, wrote to Lori saying, in part, "You were a Hit at ISU! Your combination of experience, personal charm and infectious enthusiasm for aviation was extemely well received by this department. . . . Thank you for giving something back to ISU and to the Department of Aerospace Technology."

In having co-authored two books, *Ladybirds I The Story of American Women in Aviation* and *Ladybirds II, The Continuing Story of American Women in Aviation*, in having designed and erected three museum exhibits featuring female airline pilots and in lecturing extensively, Lori has continued to promote and to encourage countless hundreds of women. For those fortunate to know her, she has led by example. As a member of her airline's first all-female A320 Flight Crew, she was also its first female check airman on the Airbus 320 and the first female to hold a director level management position. Within the entire air carrier industry, Lori was the first female director of flight safety. Hers is an exemplary career.

Limitations were placed upon women in the early air carrier days. "First, society erected barriers dictating what was and wasn't proper for women," she said. "Whether it was sporting pants, driving a car or even voting, piloting an airplane was not perceived as a ladylike thing to do. After successfully hurdling those barriers, women faced another when our government refused to grant military status to the Women Airforce Service Pilots (WASP), preventing women from being candidates for airline jobs when World War II was over. Not until the women's movement of the '60s and '70s, when women moved out of the kitchen in droves, were we successful in changing public opinion about joining the ranks of the gainfully employed, even if it meant setting-up office in the cockpit.

"When you consider the odds against them, it is clear the persistence and determination of aviation's pioneering women propelled them forward to leave a legacy of limitless opportunities and the level playing field currently enjoyed. Today the barriers that dogged our pioneers have vanished, doors are opened wide to entice with new challenges those, male or female, who dare to reach for the sky. The advancements in technology ensure there will always be some new craft to fly, farther and faster than those that went before. As long as there are records to be broken, women have as equal a chance as men to be victorious and to secure a place in future aviation 'firsts.'"

There is a new Airbus, the A380, for example. She said, "It is certain there will be the 'first' woman to pilot it and its 'first' all female flight crew. Even 'firsts' of grand historic proportion have taken more

than one hundred years to achieve as evidenced by Connie Tobias, who became the 'first' female to pilot the exact replica Wright flyer, and Steve Fossett who became the 'first' to fly solo nonstop around the world and 'first' to climb above 50,000 feet in a Perlan Glider!"

Never forgetting her own steps to success, Lori offered advice for those yet to come. She cautioned, "Remember the title, whether sought intentially or bestowed because of time, place and availability, being 'first' often carries with it a price. Once having been named the 'first' in any position, additional scrutiny will accompany the title. Your abilities will be called into question and a higher level of expectation will push you into the spotlight for all to see. Add being a woman to that mix and, for me, 'first' was always accompanied by increased visibility, greater stress, and undue pressure, mostly self induced, in my attempt to ensure that my performance be nothing short of perfection so as to continually make me worthy of carrying the 'first' crown."

As a rarity, a woman in airline management and flight /corporate safety, Lori served US Airways as creator and editor of *Flight Safety* monthly publication. She also was tapped as an air safety investigator, then as manager, flight safety; and as director, flight safety and quality assurance. After five years as director, she resigned, saying, "I wanted to go out on top, like Seinfeld and Michael Jordan, with no accidents under my watch. 'Always leave them wishing you'd stayed' is my motto. I miss being involved in policy making and standard setting. But, my family is paramount and, after my mother died after having been given three weeks to live, that pretty much put things in perspective for me."

Lori joined the air show staff of her husband, George Cline, Airboss. George served in the U.S. Air Force and for 34 years with the FAA as an air traffic controller; he has directed diverse aerial demonstrations and events since 1968. He currently graces the International Council of Air Shows as an ICAS Academy instructor, teaching advanced and ground operations as one of the industry's premier airbosses. In another of her remarkable Firsts, as an airboss staff member, Lori has diversified her talents to reach future aviators through still another venue.

Hers has become a wide web of influence. She recalled the flight she was about to pilot to West Virginia. A man boarded the aircraft with his young daughter who, Lori wrote, "was about eight years old. I was showing her all the bells and whistles, turning everything on for her. Her eyes got about as big as silver dollars. Like any young child, she said to her dad, 'Oh, Daddy. I want to be a pilot when I grow up.'

"He looked at her and said, 'Oh, you could never do this.'"

It was then that Lori Cline saw the disappointed face of a little girl who was not going to find encouragement at home. She has felt compelled to see to it that young women have inspiring role models and that she reach as many as possible to offer support. She has made every effort to be a mentor to those who have their hearts in the sky and need an extra push to follow their dreams. Lori said, "In my own Foreword to *Ladybirds II*, I professed that as the twentieth century drew to a close, women in aviation found themselves at the threshold of a new beginning rather than at the end of an era. There is simply no limit to what a woman can achieve. No truer words could be spoken."

Amy Laboda
Success is No Surprise

No pilot wants to be remembered for having faced an emergency. After all, that is what pilot training is all about – properly handling an aircraft within its specifications, meeting the unexpected and carrying through safely and with a minimum of damage to aircraft, souls on board, or on the ground. Amy Laboda, a remarkable woman, known for her many talents, noted, "An engine failure can happen to anyone."

Yes. But was "anyone" in the skies over the waters off Key West headed to the Cayman Islands as part of the staff for an annual Cayman Caravan? Was "anyone" an experienced flight instructor with an adult passenger in the front seat, her own two daughters and another young adult in the rear? In addition, was "anyone" an anticipated speaker due to lecture Air Traffic Controllers on the then-new technology for ADS - B, Automatic Dependent Surveillance - Broadcast at Cayman Brac and the instructor who had conducted the briefings for other Caravan pilots? Fortunately for all on board, Amy Laboda was in control and, to such a woman, success is not unplanned. Success is one of the goals of her every endeavor.

On Thursday, 14 June 2001 at the Key West, Florida, airport, Amy saw to it that her four passengers were settled in their seats, seatbelts and shoulder harnesses fastened. Her two daughters, Rose and Leah, and a young adult, Kim, were seated first. Amy directed another adult member of the Caravan staff, Lauren, to the right front seat. She had preflighted the craft carefully and briefed the entire crew about the use of life jackets and the aircraft doors. She took the pilot-in-command position of Cessna 210L, N2117S and they were ready to depart.

The engine start, run-up, taxi and takeoff were normal. The sleek 210, its gear retracted, climbed into clear weather and Amy prepared to trim the craft in anticipation of a 330-nautical mile overwater flight across the Caribbean to the destination at Grand Cayman.

But, fate intervened. Following the first power reduction upon reaching approximately 1,500 feet of altitude, a loud bang erupted from the engine and, even though the propeller continued to rotate, the rpm dropped to zero. All aboard were instantly alert and Amy quickly gave directions to the others. There was no hope of the airplane making it back to the Key West airport, so Amy followed her known emergency procedures for ditching a land plane in the water, an element that could have been fatal to all.

She wrote later, "Everyone asks me about the terrible angst of having my kids in the back seat; but, honestly, when that engine let loose I did what I'd always taught others to do. The incident went 'textbook style.' I pushed the nose forward to establish the best glide speed, banked toward land and settled into a controlled and gradual descent. I ran my checklist, barked orders to my passengers as I would have to anyone, and radioed to declare the emergency to Air Traffic Control (ATC)."

The Cessna was only one minute and a half from the water. That isn't a lot of time, but the crucial fact is that it was enough time to get everything done.

"The key was focusing on a perfect seaplane belly landing," Amy continued. "The conditions couldn't have been any better – smooth seas and no wind. I saw to it that the main doors had been opened and advised my crew to brace themselves. I verified wheels up and locked and flared to touch down beautifully on the water. Everyone aboard did what they were supposed to do and got out. No one was hurt and

For two days prior to making an emergency landing in the waters of the Atlantic off Key West, Amy Laboda was charged with teaching others how to ditch an airplane and how to use safety and rescue equipment. That all aboard were unharmed in her craft attests to her excellent response to known procedures she hadn't expected to demonstrate.

we were picked up by boaters nearby."

The Cessna 210 had experienced a fractured crankshaft and one of the main bearings was shattered, its pieces found in the oil sump. Additionally, a bolt for one of the cylinder connecting rods was ruptured near the bolt head, its broken piece embedded in the crankcase near the cylinder opening. It was determined by the National Transportation and Safety Board (NTSB) that, "there was improper installation of the cylinders and failure to assure they were properly torqued."

Irony also came along for the ride. Amy's responsibility for two days prior to her takeoff had been to address overwater pilots, emphasizing the correct procedures for the very emergency she faced and handled perfectly. All Cayman Caravan participants had to be briefed on ditching an airplane, the correct use of safety and rescue equipment and survival techniques. She hadn't intended to give an actual demonstration and took some ribbing from the others for the performance; but, only after they knew positively that the emergency turned out well and that she and her passengers emerged unscathed.

Amy has many claims to fame – from partner, parent, flight instructor, writer, editor, speaker, to successful careerist. And Amy lives the recipes for success with which she empowers and encourages others.

Amy noted, "Everyone wants to know the secret to success, . . . the potent combination of skill and luck and destiny that leads to a life of happiness and fulfillment. It is one of the most 'loaded' words in the English language.

"According to the dictionary, success means to reach the desired result, to thrive and prosper, to flourish, to attain a goal. . . . But, the dictionary gives you a shallow description of a word into which one can delve much more deeply. Success, it says, is 'to do well.' That is a promise, for some, of a comfortable, self-supporting lifestyle. More, it is a feeling of well-being earned from years of hard work and accomplishment; it is about realizing you are living the lifestyle you desired; it is about the quality of the time you have to yourself."

Amy insisted that those were honorable goals; but she challenged her listeners, from her own experiences, to be alert to the many formulae possible. She urged that we all be open and attentive to, "everything you find, not just what you are looking for."

As a young woman, Amy was still attending Fort Myers High School in Florida when she started flight lessons at age 15. She earned her private pilot certificate within two years and went on the following year to upgrade that to a commercial license with an instrument rating while also keeping her sights set on a good education. Amy entered Sarah Lawrence College in Bronxville, New York. This prestigious liberal arts institute has a long tradition of excellence, which further helped to define her.

But, where was she going? What was she going to do with her life? She couldn't have attended a better school. She noted, of her alma mater, "The college fostered creativity by asking its students to write, and write, and write. Every test was an essay exam (yes, even math and biology and chemistry). Every class required a separate individual project with an accompanying dissertation. It was a lot of work."

Following graduation, she took a position as a research assistant. And, in anticipation of traveling with the Peace Corps, she moved to northern California and enrolled in French language lessons. The Peace Corps extended an opportunity for her to teach health education in Africa, but prior to that decision, Amy obtained her flight instructor rating from Dragonfly Aviation at the Sonoma County Airport.

After having returned to the United States, Amy was slightly disoriented – acutely aware that she was no longer a student, not yet a career woman. She applied for and was hired as a flight instructor, with the caveat that she obtain her instrument instructor rating. Within the week she had successfully completed that requirement.

Flight instruction was gratifying and she flew constantly, adding charter piloting in single engine aircraft, ratings in multi-engine craft, and the airline transport pilot (ATP) to her certificates. Amy aimed high, joining the Future Airline Professionals of America and setting airline piloting as her goal.

"And that's where things became complicated," Amy admitted. "I met a magazine editor who suggested that I write an article about flight reviews. I did. He bought it and a beautiful relationship began."

Amy wrote during her mornings and taught flying until nine o'clock at night, six days per week. She met and married her husband, Barry, who held the airline pilot job toward which she was logging time. They moved into a tiny apartment near the outer marker of one of the nation's busiest airports. Amy said, "You could sit in the hot tub at night and watch as one, then another and another heavy popped on their landing lights and lowered their wheels at exactly the same spot – a string of pearls extending out into the night sky. I wanted that."

But, true to her advice of being open and attentive to, "everything you find, not just what you are looking for," Amy refused to close any doors or obscure any possibilities. She exchanged cards with a personnel director for a promising regional airline who spotted her immediately as, "the perfect candidate for the right seat of his airline." She was thrilled.

Then she met a woman who worked for *FLYING*, one of the largest aviation magazines in the world. Her new-found acquaintance mentioned an opening for an associate editor and wondered if Amy would consider such a position. The opportunity was incredible. Invited

For those searching for success, Amy suggests, "Learn to be very careful when you are busy searching so that you pay attention to everything you find -- not just what you are looking for." Hers is the voice of experience.

by the editor-in-chief of *FLYING*, Richard Collins; an interview was arranged.

"That day came," said Amy, "I hopped a Boeing from Dallas to New York, took a bus to Times Square, took an editing test, met some staff and, finally, it was just Mr. Collins and me. He said, real slow, 'You know? You have no real qualifications for this job . . .'

"I inhaled. There I was, dressed to do business, 1,500 miles from home. I had to think, do I want this? . . . I exhaled and answered, 'Well actually, sir, I think that I do. Here's why . . .' and I kept talking until he made it clear that he needed to move on with his day."

Offered the associate editor position, Amy accepted gladly. The move to New York City represented a transfer for Barry, but there was added incentive in that he received the opportunity to fly widebodies on international flights. For Amy, that esteemed position with a highly respected magazine introduced her to many facets of and individuals involved with aviation. It led her to be invited to become a member of the Founding Board of Women in Aviation, International and, not long thereafter, editor-in-chief of *Aviation For Women*, its elegant membership magazine.

She concluded, "So, what then is my formula for success? Hard work? Definitely. A broad-based education? That paid off for me. A willingness to meet and treat everyone and every opportunity, no matter -how small, as if it was an end, not just a means to some larger goal? Yes."

Add to that Amy's ability to live in the now and pay attention to details so as to be cognizant of defining moments of change. She never stopped flying, writing, being open to the exhilaration of learning and the excitement inherent in the various areas in which she excelled. She exuded intelligence, leadership and capability. And, importantly, she personified adaptability, identified change, respected its inspiration and grasped it without regret. Her formula for success, lived throughout her unplanned ditching in the water and all of her life experiences, is a message for us all.

CHAPTER FOUR
CHARACTER & COMPETITION

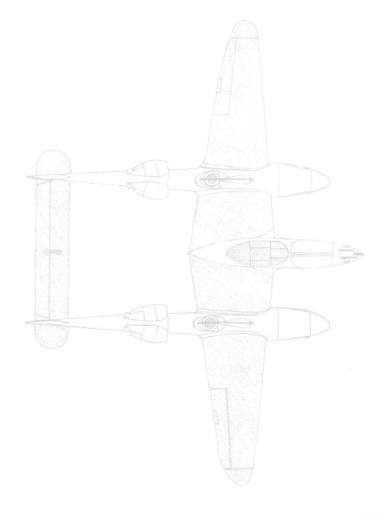

P-38 "LIGHTNING"

Artwork © 2007 Sharon Rajnus

CHARACTER

"In the final analysis, our future depends upon ourselves, our ability, our character, our ideals. If we are to lead mankind through these black years, if we are to be successful in war and peace, we must have clearly in mind what we desire in civilization and what constitutes human progress."

Charles A. Lindbergh, OF FLIGHT AND LIFE

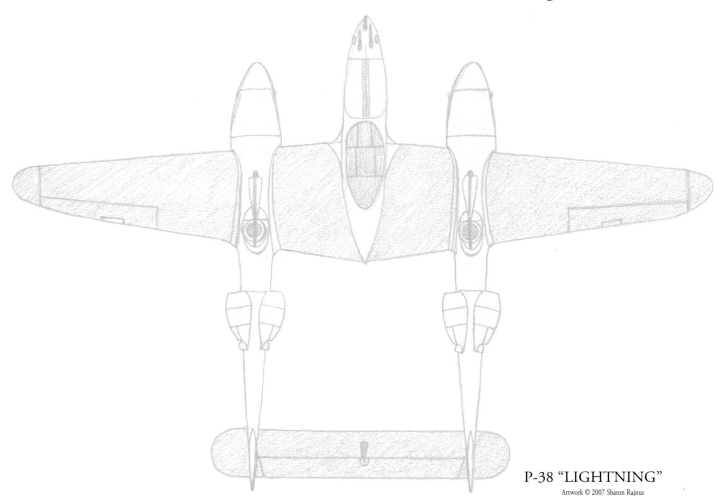

P-38 "LIGHTNING"

Artwork © 2007 Sharon Rajnus

COMPETITION

"To the public I suppose I have often seemed to be the original 'flying fool.' While flying over one hundred and forty different models of aircraft, I have piloted a plane in a plaster cast and a steel corset, too impatient to wait for bones to knit from the last crash. I have frozen my tongue sucking oxygen at sixty below zero, six miles up. I have escaped twice from burning planes. I have clung to a life raft in cold, mountainous seas. I have had most of the bones in my body broken. . . . Maybe it doesn't make sense. I have been told that so often that it has become a kind of background drumbeat to my life. Family and friends have urged me to keep my feet on the ground . . . The only people who haven't tried to change me are flyers. They comprehend."

Ruth Nichols, WINGS FOR LIFE

CHAPTER 4

Dorothy Hester

"Princess Kick-a-Hole-in-the-Sky"

Dorothy learned from two masters: Elrey Jeppesen taught her to fly and Tex Rankin taught her aerobatics. She triumphed as the first woman to successfully complete an outside loop. She said, " – a maneuver that was only three years old at the time."

Artwork © 2007 Sharon Rajnus

When Margaret Burke Hester died in 1919, she left her husband William, an Irish house painter, to care for five lively daughters, the fourth of whom was Dorothy, then nine years old, rambunctious and daring. Seven years later, Dorothy saw a hot-air balloon drift over and dashed after it in vain, calling, "Gimme a ride!"

A neighbor mentioned that she could purchase an airplane ride at a nearby Portland, Oregon airport, and Dorothy initiated a few fundraising schemes. For a small fee, for example, she offered to sleep in her sisters' cold beds to warm them until they returned from dances or she leased her favorite bracelet. By October 1927, Dorothy had accrued the necessary funds and she hopped aboard a streetcar to purchase her first airplane ride. She started running, upon reaching the air field and seeing airplanes buzzing overhead. She admitted, "I was afraid they would all crack up or run out of gas before it was my turn for a ride."

At her flight's end, her enthusiasm was obvious and she said aloud, "If I were a boy, I would certainly learn to fly." An enterprising salesman overheard and immediately moved closer to assure her the Rankin School of Aviation would be glad to teach a girl to fly. A star was about to be born.

John "Tex" Rankin, born in Texas and having similarly been enthralled with flying, had started his own school of aviation in Walla Walla, Washington with a Standard J-1. Seeking the larger potential of flight students in a bigger city, Rankin moved to Portland and, by the time Dorothy Hester was being introduced to flight, his school had hundreds of students.

One of his instructors, Elrey B. Jeppesen, kept a "little black book," of copious notes on landmarks and mileage, which became the foundation for an enormously successful company, now Jeppesen Sanderson, Inc. Tex Rankin called Jepp aside, pointed to Dorothy and said, "That little girl over there has a handful of fifteen minute tickets. Take her up, go around a couple of times and shoot a few landings. Let her get it out of her system. She won't be back."

Jepp later wrote, "I did, and then a few more times and a few hours later, I sent her up for her solo flight. Tex just didn't know how determined that young lady was and how much she loved to fly." Between 1927 and 1928, Tex Rankin and Elrey Jeppesen launched the career that led to Dorothy being touted by adoring fans and newspaper reporters as World Champion Woman Aerobatic Pilot, Sally of Sky Alley, and Queen of the Clouds.

To enroll in Tex Rankin's school, an advance charge of $250 was required for ground school. Dorothy needed more than beds to warm and a bracelet to rent. She discovered that performing a parachute jump would pay $100, but once out of the cockpit, she froze on the wing of the OX5-powered Eaglerock, terrified of letting go. The pilot circled; then he picked up a fire extinguisher and rapped it across her knuckles. Dorothy almost immediately exulted in wafting down through the air under a billowing chute. She sought more jumping opportunities and ultimately pocketed enough money to enroll in Rankin's flight training program. She liked to say, "I bailed out of an airplane in order to bail into one."

Rankin rarely flew with flight students, although he personally gave periodic check rides to test the students' progress and the instructors' techniques and performance. He expected students to request and to schedule such a check with him. After instruction in primary aerobatics, Dorothy challenged Tex to fly with her and to offer criticism of her performance. Rankin biographer Walt Bohrer wrote of this flight, "[W]hen they landed, [Tex] said, 'My stars,' – he always said 'my stars' when something amazed him. 'You fly just like a boy!'"

Dorothy took this as a compliment and soon was trained by Tex as

Courtesy of Oregon Aviation Historical Society

In the 1980s, Dorothy Hester was honored by the Oregon Legislature with a resolution that stated, in part, "for the example she sets [for] all of us in the pursuit of excellence."

he recognized her incredible aptitude for aerobatics. He also understood the marketing bonus that her success would bring to his school.

Tex was flying a WACO-10 at the time and, by 1928, was practicing performing outside loops. It is significant that Jimmy Doolittle, the first pilot in the world to perform this maneuver, accomplished the feat in 1927. This underscores the pioneering times in which both Rankin and Hester were honing their skills and the cutting edge at which this young woman pilot operated.

Tex invited Dorothy to come along as a passenger knowing she could already perform snap and barrel rolls, regular loops and spins. He did not know, however, whether his WACO would stand the weight of two, plus parachutes, in the high negative G environment of an outside loop. As part of their pre-flight briefing, Tex told Dorothy to jump "if the ship broke or a wing came off."

Once airborne and having demonstrated the outside loop, Dorothy asked to try it. Tex reported later that she got half way around and, while upside-down, she got into an inverted spin from which he had to recover. He determined that they had to first practice upside-down spins until she managed safe recoveries. Only then would they turn to mastering the outside loop.

The performance of outside loops took intense commitment, steady concentration and physical strength. With forward pressure on the stick, Dorothy dove in a curving arc for 2,500 feet to achieve 250 miles per hour. By then inverted in relation to the ground, she continued to exert forward pressure to turn skyward, bearing at least 6 Gs and completing as perfectly-shaped a circle as possible. Developing sufficient airspeed to climb at the reverse of the dive was crucial. It was 30 June 1930 that 19-year-old Dorothy Hester made history as the first woman in the world to execute this then-three-year-old maneuver, an outside loop.

Six months of rigorous training for instructor and student alike followed on the heels of her achievement. Before Rankin would permit her to practice solo, he ensured that each step was performed properly. He said, "She went through the most exacting drills of her life – just as exacting as those an accomplished dancer must first master before perfecting the most difficult steps, but far more dangerous."

In 1931, she barnstormed 38 states in a three-month period, flying with Tex in his Great Lakes biplane powered with a 90-horsepower Cirrus engine. The Yakima Indian Tribe dubbed her with an apt nickname, "Princess-Kick-a-Hole-in-the-Sky."

That same year, at the Omaha Air Show, Nebraska, she set a world record for males and females of 56 inverted snap rolls. In addition, she performed 69 consecutive outside loops, 62 of which were credited as perfectly rounded and acceptable to observers for the National Aeronautic Association (NAA). Manufacturers of the Great Lakes aircraft presented Dorothy with her own $3,500 biplane and, for the 1931 Cleveland Air Races, Dorothy was invited to be the first woman to perform as a solo act.

Not all spectators were impressed with women at the controls of aircraft. A disgruntled man at one air show criticized, "Young lady, you ought to be home washing dishes instead of doing this."

Dorothy, generally shy, retorted, "I did them before I left home!"

It was William Shakespeare who wrote, "words are no deeds." In crediting Dorothy with her incredible number of outside loops, it is important to recall that her "deeds" were even more exemplary in light of her equipment. When she was inverted, she not only had to exert demanding pressures on the controls, she simultaneously had to maintain directional control with elevators, ailerons and rudders and she had to keep fuel flowing to the engine via a manual fuel pump, a wobble pump.

Rankin's likening of Dorothy's aerobatic flying to the mastering of dance steps is on target. In the Great Lakes, when inverted, Dorothy was rhythmically pushing and pulling the handle connected to the fuel pump system and forcing gas through the engine driven pump and through flexible fuel lines to the carburetor. For two hours and six minutes in consecutive outside loops while performing ultimate ground-reference to keep herself aware of her place in space, her feet tapped the rudder pedals, her hands moved between the throttle, control stick and wobble pump and her arms exercised fore and aft.

Famed U.S. Navy pilot Al Williams said, "There's a mere slip of a girl doing stunts that chiefs of the [nation's military] units said could not be done a year ago and maneuvers the greatest fliers in the world would not have attempted three years ago – and she is doing it in a light, cheap airplane with a four cylinder engine at only ninety horsepower."

It was no wonder that her exploits remained unchallenged for almost sixty years.

As one of her many honors, Dorothy was installed in the Pathfinder Hall of Fame at the Museum of Flight in Seattle. There her life crosses that of another aerobatic pilot, Joann Osterud, whose familiar and agile Stephens Akro is part of the Museum of Flight's permanent exhibit. In a unique twist, it was Dorothy who invited

Courtesy of Oregon Aviation Historical Society

The first woman pilot contracted to perform aerobatics at the National Air Races, Dorothy was given this new Great Lakes biplane in 1931 by B.F. Goodrich Company, Cirrus Engine Company and the Great Lakes Aircraft Corporation. She posed in Akron, Ohio just prior to the famed air races.

Joann to compete for her outside loop record.

Dorothy believed that her record had stood long enough. She was invited to participate as the Grand Marshall for the North Bend, Oregon, Air Show on 15-16 July 1989 and she made arrangements to be there earlier to watch Joann take her HIgh PERformance BIPlanE – a Hiperbipe – through the grueling, repetitive circles in the sky. Both women were fairly confident that the record was Joann's to achieve, if North Bend's weather permitted.

Joann waited for fog and clouds to dissipate and, when the ceiling rose to 2,200 feet, she took off; however, she was forced to compress her loops to half the normal diameter – 800 feet. A chilly north wind blew, which affected the shape of the loops and the results seemed less stringent in its requirements than had been Dorothy Hester's experience in 1931. Nonetheless, on 13 July 1989, as Dorothy watched from the ground, Joann Osterud performed 208 outside loops in her boxy craft, breaking the records held for both genders.

Dorothy said, "I believed it was well past the time that record was broken. I saw Joann perform in an air show, recognized that she was a smooth flyer. I didn't think she would pull the wings off her aircraft. You can tear any airplane apart if you are tough with it, but her airplane is pretty special."

Dorothy has been honored by inclusion in the OX5 Hall of Fame. She was inducted into the International Aerobatic Club (IAC) Hall of Fame after having been nominated with generous praise by Elrey B. Jeppesen. Much of her memorabilia is exhibited at the Oregon Aviation Historical Society, Jim Wright Field, Cottage Grove, Oregon, and there in 2000, nine years after her death, Dorothy deservedly was installed in the Oregon Aviation Hall of Fame.

She is credited with having said, "You can do most anything to an airplane if you do it smoothly. That's one thing I knew how to do." Princess-Kick-a-Hole-in-the-Sky can rest assured that her place in aviation history is permanent and impressive.

DOROTHY HESTER-STENZEL

Tex Rankin taught eighteen-year-old Dorothy aerobatics in his Great Lakes 2T1 Sport Trainer. Dorothy said, "The Great Lakes was a ground-looping baby. It had hard rubber wheels, no brakes and a small tail, which made it hard to control on the ground." Here we see Dorothy flying inverted, maintaining this attitude for 4 to 5 minutes before "coming up for air".

Fay Gillis Wells

Like a Russian Night Witch

Fay Gillis Wells was an exceptionally accomplished journalist. A knowledgeable, intelligent writer, Fay contributed persuasive prose and rose in the ranks to become a White House correspondent. She spent a decade and a half covering the administrations of Presidents Lyndon Johnson, Richard Nixon, Gerald Ford, and Jimmy Carter.

As a young woman, Fay Gillis received her pilot's certificate in 1929 and was hired by Curtiss Wright in an aircraft sales and demonstration position. When she was in her early twenties – in 1932 – she was given the rare privilege to travel in Russia. While there, she was to make arrangements in Novosibirsk and Irkutsk for fuel depots and maintenance requirements for Wiley Post's celebrated, yet tragically fatal, around-the-world flight the following year. Fay often recounted how she had been invited to accompany Post, an adventure most young pilots would have found impossible to decline. But, Linton Wells had asked Fay to be his bride and Fay followed her heart. She chose marriage, a fortuitous choice that gave her the chance for a long

and fruitful life and the accrual of a multitude of deserved honors. She had much for which to be grateful.

While in Russia in 1932, Fay submitted freelance articles about her experiences, which were published in New York's *Herald Tribune* and a variety of aviation magazines. She also earned an impressive place in history by becoming the first woman to pilot a Russian aircraft, the Polikarpov U-2.

The Polikarpov U-2 (later redesignated the Po-2), more than 40,000 of which were built, was the first trainer for many Russian pilots and later the aircraft of choice for crop dusting. This 99-horsepower, radial-engined biplane – trusty, uncomplicated and forgiving – was nicknamed the Kukuruzni, the Russian word for maize, in reference to those agricultural applications.

Although she could not have known it at the time, by flying the U-2 Fay was linked with Russian women pilots who not long thereafter flew the Polikarpov in combat during World War II. The women,

Courtesy the William Heaslip Collection

In the early 1930s, Fay Gillis became the first woman to pilot a Russian civil aircraft, the Polikarpov U-2. Fay wrote, in her own hand on the back of this rare photograph, "Ivanish Olinivitch, a mechanic in the background, and me. Last minute instructions."

The ubiquitous Polikarpov, which began as the U-2 and later became the Po-2, made a maiden flight in January 1928. Useful and easily maintained, the Polikarpov was manufactured into the 1950s and achieved an impressive total of 40,000 aircraft produced. The Russian women who flew the Polikarpov in World War II flew nearly 1,000 combat missions by 1945.

members of the 588th Night Bomber Regiment, became famous for their nightly bomb runs against Nazi armed forces. Using cunning but dangerous tactics, the women flew their Polikarpov biplanes close to the ground, climbing only at the last minute to close their throttles and make gliding bomb runs. These strategies resulted in disquieting eerie whistling that gave the enemy scant warning of ear-splitting bomb blasts that inevitably followed. Members of German armed forces labeled the women as Nachthexen – Night Witches – as much for the raids, which robbed them of sleep, as for the fact that the pilots and ground crews for the 588th were all women. Nazi ground and air troops resented being surprised, bombed, or downed by women.

As for Fay, her thrilling recollection of having flown their aircraft was greatly enhanced when she met, much later, some Russian women combat pilots. Like those courageous and competent women, Fay was determined and capable, a woman of achievement. In 1929, she authored a letter to the 117 certificated women pilots to invite participation in the organization that became The Ninety-Nines. This organization, now boasting approximately 5,500 members located in 35 nations, has given women pilots a sisterhood of their own. A legend in her own time, Fay stood tall as one of its most outstanding charter members.

In 1973, desirous of creating a living memorial, Fay conceived of the Forest of Friendship in Amelia Earhart's hometown, Atchison, Kansas. Its trees represent each of the fifty United States and thirty-five nations. Memory Lane, an on-going tribute to men and women of achievement in aviation, is a National Recreation Trail – the first to be so designated by the Kansas Department of the Interior.

Just prior to entering the hospital in her final days, she accepted a lifetime achievement award for her contributions in broadcasting. Even up to her death, Fay personified success and transcended self to encourage countless thousands. Fay Gillis Wells' life, well-lived and enjoyed, ended on 2 December 2002. Hers was a life dedicated to her family and to aviation on a global scale.

Dot Swain Lewis

Creating a Legacy in Bronze

Some women are meant to excel. Born to a concert pianist and a judge, niece to a Pulitzer prize-winning musician and sister to a North Carolina State Senator, the young Dorothy Swain Lewis was surrounded by exceptional talent. Dot literally forged her own path to excellence. An accomplished fine art artist, she created lost-wax-process bronze sculptures – her finest legacies.

Having learned to fly in 1941, Dot graduated from Phoebe Omlie's Nashville program and became a flight instructor. She taught flying to U.S. Navy recruits before being hired as a flight instructor for the Women Airforce Service Pilots (WASP) . Seeing her students graduate from trainers into everything the World War II U.S. Army Air Corps had to offer, Dot resigned her position and entered training as a WASP. She flew B-26 Martin Marauders towing targets for B-24 aerial gunnery practice.

Into her nineties, this incredible woman commemorated the WASP in bronze works of art. Her statues grace Sweetwater and Midland, Texas; the National Museum of the United States Air Force, Ohio; the United States Air Force Academy, Colorado; and College Park Aviation Museum, Maryland. Having served with Jacqueline Cochran, it was Dot's pleasure to create a bronze bust of the WASP leader for the Palm Springs, California, Regional Airport renamed in Cochran's honor and, on 31 July 2006, Dot unveiled her latest sculpture at Highground Veterans Memorial Park in Neillsville, Wisconsin.

What remarkable effort resulted in these lasting legacies to the bravery and patriotism of the women with whom she served? As with most artistry, it

Dot Swain Lewis served with Jackie Cochran in the Women Airforce Service Pilots – the WASP. How appropriate that she was selected to create a bronze sculpture of the famed aviatrix to grace the Palm Springs airport named in Cochran's honor.

began with a drawing. For a planned 4.5-foot statue, the drawing was scaled to 1/6th of the original. Step two was to build an armature of heavy copper rod wound with copper wire. Shaped with Styrofoam to keep the form light in weight, the armature was fitted to a sturdy wooden base upon a ¾-inch pipe.

Dot worked outdoors at her home, at 6,000 feet in the San Jacinto Mountains of California. She started with Plaster of Paris, reinforced with hemp, applying the mixture over the skeletal copper wire structure. This demanding effort had to be moved indoors when cold weather adversely affected the plaster.

Simply moving and handling the basic form was a challenge. "But the tedious work," Dot said, "was the trimming to ensure accuracy and form. That was especially challenging in delicate areas such as the arms, hands, fingers and head."

In a lengthy process, a microchrystalline wax was layered over the plaster figure. Dot explained, "The layer of wax was built up to between a quarter of an inch and an inch thick and the details – buckles, goggles, insignia – demanded careful attention. Having started the figure in the month of May, it was the following April before I was ready to deliver my completely wax-covered model to the foundry, Skurja Art Casting in Prescott, Arizona, 350 miles away.

"I wrapped the figure with long strips of cotton sheeting and covered her with bubble wrap and an additional layer of sheeting. I prepared a full-sized drawing of the figure with exact measurements and then loaded the car for the trip."

At the Foundry, Dot spent three days repairing and refining details on the wax figure to prepare it for the creation of the production mold – a hollow sculpture. Once completed the production mold was reusable, allowing Dot to produce additional bronze statues. The figure was divided into sections to be cast into bronze which would later be welded together. Dot admitted, "Each section had to dry thoroughly and this process took days. It was a very important step and I was meticulous, drying each with heat and blowers."

Latex, up to seven coats, was painted onto each piece and reinforced with four-inch squares of netting. As the latex was flexible and fairly thin, several coats of Plaster of Paris were added as support and prevented from adhering by a silicon spray.

In the lost wax process, molten wax is applied to these segments to a 1⁄4- to 1⁄2-inch thickness. When cooled, Dot repaired blemishes. She said, "I corrected and refined the waxes preparatory to the final casting, working for three days with small tools and an alcohol lamp. The wax forms were hollow and the shells had to be filled with a core (of ground fire brick, fine poplar sawdust and water) to maintain shape."

Dot's wax lady and her core were then invested in an additional shell that was heated in a kiln until the wax melted out and all moisture was removed. The form was refilled, this time with molten bronze. Her cooled segments were welded together and, once again, imperfections and defects were filed and smoothed.

Taken outside, the figure was sandblasted, washed and then sprayed with a solution of liver of sulfur and polished with abrasive pads. A blowtorch heated the interior of the figure for ten to fifteen minutes after which Ferric Nitrate was sprayed on the exterior via an air hose. The statue gradually turned brown. Left to cure for a few days, the bronze lady was lacquered, waxed with Trewax and polished. Each of Dot's finished sculptures has required inestimable hours of polishing – during the creation process and in later maintenance.

"But," said Dot, "photos can't do justice to months of planning, the exchange of ideas, sketches created and rejected, the fundraising, and the hard work by members of the WASP Memorial Committee to arrange for erection of each sculpture on its plinth. Each statue has required enormous effort, but each has been a labor of love."

The famed and the talented of the family of Dorothy Swain Lewis bequeathed values to this remarkable woman that she has passed on to those with whom she has come into contact. In turn, with her fine art bronze sculptures, she has left a legacy that celebrates the life she led and the lives of the more than one thousand members of the WASP who performed courageously when their country was in need of their services.

Courtesy of Rose Dorcey

Dot's magnificent sculpture at the Highground Veterans Memorial Park, Wisconsin, honors the service of the 1,074 women who wore the Silver Wings. It is significant that the WASP program was deactivated as of 20 December 1944 without granting veteran status to its members. Virtually all aircraft in the U.S. Air Corps were piloted by these women; they had flown target towing, searchlight and tracking, simulated strafing, smoke laying, engineering test flying, ferrying, and administrative piloting. Had the 1977 Congress failed to award veteran status to the WASP, this sculpture might not have been included in a tribute to veterans – a regrettable omission.

Dot posed by her four and a half-foot tall bronze sculpture at the U.S. Air Force Academy. When asked about her models, Dot insisted that she had one thousand models. She knew them when they were young and found them "capable, brave and beautiful."

Caro Bosca
I Would Have Flown for Free

Courtesy; Dan Patterson, www.flyinghistory.com

Caro Bayley loved to fly and wanted to serve her country during World War II. It was to her good fortune that the Women Airforce Service Pilots were formed. She flew into military history, graduating with Class 43-7. After the war, she flew into aerobatic history.

In the late 1930s, Nazi Germany's assaults of World War II threatened to span the Atlantic Ocean and an isolationist United States was rapidly being drawn into the fray. In Springfield, Ohio, a teenaged Caro Bayley was convincing her father that she wanted to fly and, generously, he treated her to flight lessons.

By 1943, Caro left Springfield to join the trainees in Class 43-W-7 of the Women Airforce Service Pilots, the WASP. Her dad gave her wings and Caro also owed a debt to Jacqueline Cochran and Nancy Harkness Love. In 1941, Cochran recognized the winds of war pressing across both major oceans and she drafted a plan to recruit women as pilot trainees to release male pilots for combat roles. In the fall of 1942, Nancy Love called upon experienced women pilots to ferry aircraft for the U.S. Air Transport Command. The success of her Women's Auxiliary Ferrying Squadron (WAFS) gave a push to the formation of a Women's Flying Training group that became the WASP on 5 August 1943 with the merger of both groups under Cochran's directorship. The women's program was modeled on the training program for male flight applicants to the U.S. Army Air Corps and members of the WASP ferried aircraft and were also successful in target towing, searchlight and tracking missions, simulated strafing, smoke laying, engineering test flying and administrative piloting.

Caro admitted, "Like most loyal Americans during World War II, I wanted to do my part for the war effort. I loved flying and I could scarcely believe my good luck in being able to do something I loved so much for the good of my country. Flying out of Avenger Field, Texas, it was hot, we were tired, and we were sticky half of the time. But, we were having a ball because we had those airplanes. We all loved to fly. I would have volunteered to fly for free."

Having earned her silver wings, Caro followed primary training with an assignment to Mather Field, Sacramento, California to be trained to pilot the B-25 Mitchell bomber.

"I went with twenty other women to Mather," she said, "We got along fine, were well-trained and enjoyed a good experience. From there, ten of us were assigned to Fort Bliss, Biggs Army Air Field in El Paso, Texas. There we were part of a tow target squadron in conjunction with a radar school, although we carried out several assignments and piloted other aircraft in addition to the B-25."

At Biggs, Caro was stationed with her good friend, Kaddy Landry Steele. Kaddy said of the times, "If it wasn't for the war and the fact that they were so short of pilots, we wouldn't have had this chance. They condescended to let us enter the sanctum sanctorum. And they let us know that. They let us in because they needed pilots."

Caro was assigned to radar tracking flights, helping to educate new radar operators at their scopes and her missions in searchlight tracking served to train those operating the lights. She plied El Paso night skies while penetrating light beams sought her craft. Caro also piloted simulation strafing missions and sleeve towing for aerial gunnery practice, bouncing through the turbulence of the mountains, the winds and the hot Texas sun. At Biggs, WASP flew the U.S. Army version of the Curtiss Helldiver, the A25-A, the Douglas Dauntless SBD or A24, the AT-11, and the P-47 Thunderbolt.

The Helldiver suffered, according to some, from a weak airframe structure, inadequate stability, severe buffeting in dives, sluggish ailerons, and strong forces required to handle the stick in flight; yet, the women flew them. The Douglas SBD was nicknamed: Slow But Deadly and the A24, the Banshee; and the women flew them. The P-47 Thunderbolt, powered by an eighteen-cylinder 2,000 horsepower Pratt & Whitney engine, was rugged and heavy. The women flew them and were thrilled for the opportunities. The morning before Caro was due for her first check-out in the P-47, her shoulder suffered an attack of bursitis. She couldn't raise her arm to comb her hair. But, when asked how she was feeling, she answered, "I'm just fine." She wasn't about to give up her chance to control the largest and heaviest single engine fighter in the USAAC arsenal.

Caro also recalled taxiing an A-24 out to Biggs' active runway. She said, "I realized I was about to intercept a long line of B-24s taxiing to the same runway. I tried to decide what to do when the ground controller transmitted to the lead B-24, "Let the A-24 go first. You must be gentlemen.""

Piloting the military version of the Beechcraft Model 18 -- the AT-11 Kansan -- Caro was assigned to participate in training searchlight trackers at Fort Bliss and Biggs Army Air Field, El Paso, Texas. She flew a pattern, enabling searchers on the ground to locate the twin-engine aircraft and to follow it with their lights. All searchlight missions were in the dark of night and required an instrument-rated pilot.

Caro smiled when she admitted, "I didn't wait to hear what the 'gentlemen' had to say to that. I hit the throttle and taxied quickly to the active runway to depart."

General Henry "Hap" Arnold said, at the graduation of the last WASP class on 7 December 1944, "You and more than nine hundred of your sisters have shown that you can fly wingtip to wingtip with your brothers. If ever there was any doubt in anyone's mind that women can become skillful pilots, the WASP have dispelled that doubt. . . . We of the Army Air Forces, are proud of you. We will never forget our debt to you."

These words were seared into the memories of the WASP as it was less than two weeks later – 20 December 1944 – that they were disbanded. Lacking the status of military personnel, they returned to civilian life at their own expense and with no benefits other than pride at having served our country in its time of need.

In the 1970s, when women were accepted into military pilot training and newspapers praised America's "First Women Military Pilots," members of the WASP were insulted. They campaigned for recognition as military veterans and, thirty years late, the 1977 Congress awarded military status to the WASP.

What happened to the many eager, capable and proven woman pilots at the end of World War II? Caro and her sister WASP scattered. Caro moved to Miami, Florida, with a few others, obtained her flight instructor certification and was flight instructing when Jess Bristow, renowned aerobatic pilot, invited her to become a part of his air show. Bristow owned the second of Curtis Pitts' revolutionary small aerobatic airplanes and he introduced Caro to the snappy, short-coupled craft. Caro also met Betty Skelton, who bought that Pitts S-1 from Bristow and flew to Women's National Aerobatic Championship in 1949 and 1950.

Flying Betty's "Little Stinker" cinched the next step in Caro's life. Her father was there for her once again. With Caro performing in the air show business, he ordered the third biplane built by Curtis Pitts. Caro dubbed her Pitts S-1 "Black Magic" and took it to Women's National Aerobatic Championship glory in 1951. One of her memorable acts was to follow Betty Skelton's lead into the low inverted pass toward a thin rope suspended above the ground between two tall poles. Betty was the first woman pilot to clip that rope in an inverted pass and Caro created her own version of the act. Daringly, she dipped low as she skimmed beneath the suspended rope, reaching out toward the grasses as if she was plucking a bouquet. She made a return pass, waving a chunk of grassy sod at her fans. Although she had secreted that chunk of grass in her cockpit prior to takeoff, her fans went wild. They were sure that during her initial pass, she had touched the ground and yanked the grass free.

Just prior to the 1951 Miami Air Show, the beautiful Caro took a Piper PA 12 Super Cruiser to a record-smashing altitude of 30,203 feet – a record held into the mid-1980s. When asked why she liked flying so high, she answered, "You can be alone. No one tries to take your picture at thirty thousand feet."

Before Caro succumbed to pancreatic cancer on 13 September 2007, she had been awarded the Blériot Medal, inducted into the Ohio Aviation Hall of Fame, and had served as president of the WASP. Indicative of her incredible love of life, she arranged for a three-piece band to play music of the Forties at her memorial service. Above all, she instilled in everyone who knew her the same joie de vivre with which she embraced life.

Betty Skelton
"Little Stinker" Did It All

She walked into the spacious new Steven F. Udvar-Hazy Center of the Smithsonian's National Air and Space Museum, her eyes on the ceiling, her footsteps echoing throughout the vast hall. There suspended above her among the world's most famous airplanes hung her own aircraft, "Little Stinker," the second biplane created by Curtis Pitts in 1946 after his prototype crashed and was destroyed.

Betty Skelton had followed the restoration process of her unique airplane at the Silver Hill, Maryland, Paul E. Garber Facility. She knew from the start that the Pitts would be displayed in the Smithsonian's huge addition to its popular museum on the D.C. Mall. But, nothing prepared her for the emotional jolt of actually seeing her beloved aircraft take its revered place in aviation history. Tears stung her eyes and she ached to have the diminutive little red and white jewel lowered to the floor and given a chance to fly again. She would have loved nothing better than to climb into the cockpit and taxi out onto the active runway of Washington Dulles International Airport to take wing. On the other hand, and equally compelling, was the recognition that millions of aviation enthusiasts would see the little plane with which she'd shared such great pleasure. She was filled with joy to recall those hours.

Betty Skelton's adventurous spirit was encouraged from her earliest days. Born to teenaged parents in 1926, Betty, an only child, was taught by Myrt and David Skelton to seek and relish challenge. All three took to the sky with flying lessons when Betty was quite young and, on Old Cory, a small grass field in Pensacola, Florida, she soloed at age twelve.

Collection of the National Aviation Hall of Fame

A lover of tiny, wonderful things, Betty Skelton owned "Little Stinker," one of the smallest airplanes in the world, and snuggled her wee mascot, a Chihuahua she dubbed "Little Tinker," one of the smallest dogs in the world.

To make it legal, she repeated the feat at sixteen. She later added a few years to her age to land a clerical position with Eastern Airlines, using her salary to pay for flight lessons. A determined, assertive woman, Betty quickly amassed the hours and flight experience that qualified her as a certificated flight instructor, a commercial pilot, single-engine and multi-engine rated. When the Civil Air Patrol was founded, she joined and volunteered for any available mission, eventually earning the rank of major.

It was the Jaycees of Tampa, Florida, who inadvertently launched Betty's career into the world of air shows and aerobatic competitions. Little did they realize the heights to which their prodigy would soar. In planning a local air show, someone suggested that Betty perform. She had no aerobatic training and had flown no aerobatics; yet, Betty characteristically grabbed the opportunity and learned to do a loop and a roll. She purchased a 1929 Great Lakes 2T1A biplane and proceeded to thrill crowds, then launched into the world of precision aerobatic competition.

In 1948, she participated in the 16th Annual Miami All American Air Maneuvers at which two significant events took place. Triumphantly, she rolled, spun, looped and tumbled her Great Lakes to the International Feminine Aerobatic Championship. On the tarmac amid the cluster of airplanes perched like so many seabirds on the sand, she first glimpsed Curtis Pitts' Special biplane, the tiny single-seat taildragger with a 15-foot wingspan equal to the length of its fuselage and a weight of only 564 pounds, then owned by Jess

Betty took possession of her tiny biplane in 1948 and won Feminine Aerobatic Champion for the second and third times in 1949 and 1950. Her outstanding performances in the Pitts Special revolutionized aerobatic flying and rocketed the Pitts biplane to prominence and popularity.

Bristow and flown by Phil Quigley.

As the first of what would evolve into phenomenal Pitts Specials to compete in precision aerobatics and to participate in the world's air shows, this short-coupled, nimble craft drew curious crowds. Each rib and spar had been built and fitted by Curtis Pitts himself; the fabric stretched tightly over the forms was stitched meticulously by Pitts' wife, Ellie Mae. Betty, who barely tipped the scales at 100 pounds, was captivated; she had always loved small things. Her pet dog, "Little Tinker," was a tiny Chihuahua. This Pitts Special seemed to be designed just for her.

She asked Bristow for permission to climb into the cockpit, a request that was denied. The refusal only further piqued her interest and she pressed for its purchase, coaxing Bristow to relent a scant few weeks prior to the Cleveland National Air Races in September 1948.

On her introductory flight in her new airplane, she departed Gainesville, Florida, and flew to Tampa, slow-rolling her way home. However, not appreciating how rapidly she needed to apply braking to maintain directional control on landing and in front of a crowd gathered to welcome her home, Betty and the craft whirled into a groundloop. The aircraft named itself as an embarrassed Betty muttered, "You Little Stinker!"

It was an inauspicious introduction to an outstanding relationship – a determined, capable and petite young woman and a tiny new aerobatic airplane that captured the imagination of the aviation world and became the airplane of choice for thousands. Investing hours of aerial practice into mastering the Pitts, Betty entertained the air show fans at Cleveland, Ohio, and returned Little Stinker to Florida to train arduously and precisely for the 17th Annual Miami All American Air Maneuvers and a repeat of her Feminine Championship title. A perfectionist, she often flew three and four times daily in strenuous preparation. If a particular maneuver eluded her in any way, she repeated that maneuver for an hour or more, seeking straight lines, exacting turns, split-second timing and faultless execution. Betty's performances contributed to dramatic changes in aerobatic precision and she was largely responsible for rocketing the Pitts Special to prominence and popularity. She followed her 1948 championship win with the International Feminine Aerobatic Championships in 1949 and 1950.

All of her flights carried with them the dangers inherent in pitting a small, lightweight craft against the forces of nature, the challenges of distance flights from one air show to another and the stressful gyrations of aerobatics. In pressing to meet her schedules, Betty faced hazardous weather many times. In one cross-country flight from Tampa to Oshkosh, Wisconsin, she became hopelessly trapped by towering cumulus storm clouds over Tennessee. Betty dove for an off-airport landing, side-slipped into a farm field and purposefully groundlooped to a rapid stop. As a violent thunderstorm pelted her with wind, hail, and rain, she jumped out to roll the Pitts into a ditch and grabbed one wing tip. Luckily, a young farm boy dashed out of the farmhouse to hang on to the opposite wing. Though drenched, the pair managed to keep the craft from being dashed to pieces.

Airborne to participate in a show across the Allegheny Mountains from her departure in Washington, D.C., Betty climbed to maintain adequate ground clearance and to stay above billowing and threatening clouds. She felt desperate; she was at 12,000 feet with no visual contact with the ground and Little Stinker had no radio and no instruments. A DC-3 airliner passed and Betty frantically rocked her airplane's wings. The DC-3 pilot circled back in assistance, let her tuck her biplane into formation, lowered the gear and flaps and led her to a safe landing in Pittsburgh, Pennsylvania.

She recalled one attempt to penetrate fog in North Carolina by following railroad tracks, the pilots' "iron compass." It occurred to her that military pilots often used the same guide and maintained the center line of the tracks; she pulled to the right. Within moments, a

Holding the trophy that accentuated her diminutive size, Betty Skelton claimed the feminine championship for her second win in 1949. An annual award in her name, first issued in 1988, is given to the woman pilot with the highest score at the United States National Aerobatic Competition.

Collection of the National Aviation Hall of Fame

P-51 Mustang came blistering over the center of the tracks from the opposite direction. She avoided a head-on collision by not more than ten feet.

Occasionally, inclement weather wasn't the culprit. Betty performed in Kentucky and, carelessly distracted from replacing her aircraft gas cap by a young fan asking for an autograph, she rolled inverted on the takeoff. When less than thirty feet above the ground, she was blinded by a face-full of gas. She instantly rolled upright and coaxed the craft to the ground. That wasn't the last time her well-honed aerobatic reflexes saved her life. Having pressured her good friend, the famed Steve Wittman, to let her attempt the dangerous inverted ribbon cut, he insisted that he be the one to coach her. She planned to take off, make a high straight inverted pass above the ribbon, not attempting to cut it, then return with a second pass or a third to finally be low enough to snap the ribbon.

She recalled, "Suddenly, I was horrified that I was too low to cut the ribbon; I was going well beneath it! Then, less than two seconds later and without any warning, the engine stopped dead."

Betty used a margin of extra airspeed to half-outside-snap-roll Little Stinker to an upright position a mere instant before the wheels touched the ground. She rolled to a stop just short of a drainage ditch. Steve Wittman checked the fuel injection system, gave her a bit of time to settle down, then handed Betty her helmet and goggles with the directive, "Go fly your airplane." Betty's hands shook; but she took to the sky and, not long after, became the first woman to accomplish the inverted ribbon cut in U.S. air shows.

A woman of achievement in several disciplines, Betty Skelton climbed to 29,050 feet in a Piper Super Cub in 1951 to set a new World Lightplane Altitude Record. She and her husband Don Frankman were awarded the Silver Award for co-writing and producing the Best Industrial Film of 1965, *CHALLENGE*, at the International Film Festival. Having retired from aviation in the 1950s, she went on to become a top woman executive with one of the world's largest advertising companies, Campbell-Ewald, and was named Top Career Woman of Detroit in 1964.

Fascinated with automobiles, Betty established speed records at the Chrysler Proving Grounds in Michigan, Daytona Beach in Florida, and the Bonneville Salt Flats, Utah, where she became the first woman to drive a jet-powered car faster than 300 miles per hour. Another of Betty's most exciting firsts came in 1959, when, with the assistance of *Look Magazine*, she was given the opportunity to become the first woman to take NASA tests, the same physical and psychological tests given to the seven newly-selected, original astronauts. She was given the nickname "7 and 1/2." No human had yet been in space and Betty was pleased to undergo the tests. "But it didn't take me long," she admitted, "to learn that it might take a gal a lifetime to penetrate NASA's 'space wall.'"

Betty Skelton was the first woman to receive the race driver's AAA license, to drive "jump boats" at Cypress Gardens, Florida, and to be enshrined in both the International Aerobatics Hall of Fame and the International NASCAR Motor Sports Hall of Fame. She was named to the Tampa Sports Hall of Fame, the Florida Women's Hall of Fame, the Tampa Bay Walk of Fame, the Women in Aviation, International Pioneer Hall of Fame and, in 2005, honored with induction into the National Aviation Hall of Fame in Dayton, Ohio.

When you visit the Smithsonian's Udvar-Hazy Center, look high to see a resplendently restored "Little Stinker." When Betty flew this unique craft, it was the only Pitts Special in existence. Let the diminutive, red and white "Little Stinker" remind you of this very special lady who flew it to its esteemed place in aerobatic and aviation history.

At the controls of her 1929 model Great Lakes 2T1A biplane, Betty was the first woman to perform the ribbon cut while in inverted flight. She occasionally added humor to her act. Fully intending to cut the ribbon suspended between the two poles, she initially aimed straight for one of the pole holders, who, in on the act, dropped the pole and dashed to safety. Another picked up the pole and Betty concluded her act with a ribbon cut.

Collection of the National Aviation Hall of Fame

Mary Haizlip
Darling of the Air Races

Two stars shined in aviation's Golden Era – Mary and Jim Haizlip – who quickly claimed leading roles among the most colorful and admired air racing couples. At the 1932 National Air Races, in Cleveland, Ohio, an intense 22-year-old Mary Haizlip competed in the Shell Speed Dash, thanks to her husband Jim's intervention. When Jim was invited to fly Jimmie Wedell and Harry William's new, fast and relatively unstable Wedell-Williams #92 in that year's Bendix Trophy Race, Jim requested that, were he to win his race, Mary could compete in #92 against other women pilots. Harry Williams didn't care much for women pilots and he was careful about choosing pilots for his racers. He only reluctantly agreed.

Jim Haizlip did win the Bendix and Williams honored his agreement. In a fifteen-minute solo flight, Mary familiarized herself with #92. Although many pilots shrug and say, "Once you've flown one airplane, you can fly them all," this racer was fueled with 100-octane gas, its first usage in an aircraft. Some believed it suicidal – that the airplane would explode in flight.

From the first international air race in Rheims, France in 1909, male pilots knew well the challenges and thrills of close, demanding air racing. It was twenty years later before Cliff Henderson, Elizabeth L. McQueen, and Lou Greve joined in the belief that women pilots were imperative to aviation's progress. They recruited female pilots from the seventy U.S. women who were licensed to fly at that time and Greve, industrialist and president of the National Air Races, sponsored the Cleveland Pneumatic Tool Race/Aerol Trophy Race for women pilots that became the Women's Air Derby. Invitations were distributed and women pilots had unparalleled opportunity to prove their mettle; some of them achieved overnight fame and others were injured in accidents. One tragically lost her life.

Nineteen year old Mary Haizlip was representative of the group; she exuded stamina and vitality. Born Mary Hays in Washington, D.C., in 1910, she had begun flight lessons prior to traveling to Oklahoma City to visit her father, a mining engineer. There Mary pursued additional training at the Graham School of Flying in Norman. Impetuously, she married her flight instructor, Jim Haizlip, only two weeks after having met him.

Mary joined nineteen other women pilots to race from Santa Monica, California to Cleveland, Ohio, their race timed to coincide with the popular 1929 National Air Races. It was a wonderful opportunity for women to show that airplanes had no interest whatsoever in the gender of the pilot and each woman was determined to succeed.

In one mishap, Mary was forced to replace her craft and she arrived a day late in Santa Monica in an American Eagle 129. She had to land twice to unclog fuel lines and, as her craft carried only two hours usable fuel, had to make frequent refueling stops, often coasting to the ground on the fumes.

Her challenges were shared. Some whispered of sabotage as not everyone agreed with the importance of women's contributions to aviation. Bobbi Trout, Pancho Barnes, Claire Fahy, Ruth Nichols, and Margaret Perry had difficulties that took them out of the competition. Louise Thaden, eventual winner of the heavy aircraft division of the Derby, was almost overcome with carbon monoxide poisoning from exhaust fumes. Despite the fact that the Travel Airs were open cockpit aircraft, her experience alerted Travel Air's Walter Beech to the need to provide fresh air to all pilots in Travel Air aircraft. Tragically, Alaska's Marvel Crosson crashed to her death in Arizona's barren Gila River Valley in a Travel Air. Carbon monoxide fumes were blamed.

Although headlines demanded, "Air racing for

Mary entered her first air race at Terre Haute, Indiana in 1929, sponsored by the National Exchange Club. She entered the 1929 All Women's Air Derby in an American Eagle and finished in a respectable seventh place among heavier aircraft. By 1932, Mary flew the craft in which her husband Jimmy had won the Bendix Trophy and set a new speed record for women.

women should be discouraged as a far too hazardous adventure," the gutsy participants flew on. Collectively they agreed to honor Marvel's memory by staying in the race. Mary and the others flew approximately 2,400 statute miles in eight days, fully aware that this was a crucial test for women.

Having come in seventh in the heavy division, Mary waited only a matter of weeks before she became the only woman to participate in the 1929 National Air Tour. In a long-nosed, "anteater" version American Eagle, Mary departed Dearborn, Michigan on 5 October 1929 and flew an impressive 5,017 miles in a round-robin throughout the eastern United States as a demonstration of aviation's capabilities and reliability.

One year later, she was flying in the closed-course pylon races at the 1930 National Air Races, Chicago, Illinois. Piloting an Inland Sport, Mary came in first in a Women's Open race for a prize of $500. In the McCormick Trophy Women's Free-For-All, she flew 50 miles in a bright red Warner- powered Cessna GC-2 to a second-place finish, winning $750. In her third event, $300 was awarded her third place finish.

The men's and women's purses differed: Jim Haislip earned $4,450 for two firsts and one second place. Mary, for her first-, second- and third-place finishes earned $1,550. The comparative winnings told a story of their own.

In June, 1931, Mary flew a Buhl Bull Pup to a World Altitude Record and, by September, she was competing in the 1931 Cleveland National Air Races, again flying from Santa Monica to Cleveland in the Transcontinental Handicap Air Derby. She piloted a Lambert-powered Monocoupe to second-place and the handsome reward of $1,800. In closed-course racing, she raced seven times, jumping from a La Blond-powered Davis (1st place), to a Menasco Gee Bee D for two races (two 2nd places), to a Wright R 750 Travel Air (2nd place), to a Wasp Jr. Laird racer (2nd place) and to a Ranger- powered Laird (2nd place). In Event 33, Greve's Aerol Trophy Race, she took 2nd place in a Wasp-powered Laird and the monetary prize was an impressive $2,250. With her total of $4,850, she was the second highest money winner – male or female!

In the Golden Age of Air Racing, her proud husband, Jim, wrote, "At Cleveland in 1931, Zantford [one of the Granville Brothers, designers of the Gee Bee aircraft] came to us hurriedly and asked if Mary would fly one of their airplanes . . . [The Menasco-powered Gee Bee Model D Sportster.] We were across the field from the starting line and the race was due to start in less than ten minutes. One of the boys taxied the Gee Bee across while we went by car. I showed Mary the ignition switch and the throttle and reminded her that after the race there was plenty of fuel to fly a little familiarization before landing which it turned out she didn't need. She placed in the race ahead of the other identical Gee Bee and turned the airplane back to the Granvilles in perfect condition. That year she had competed in eight different race events for women in six different airplanes including one of her own that she flew in the coast-to-coast derby. In all the contests she entered she placed either first or second to the delight and admiration of the other airplane owners." By 1932, Mary was obviously a force to be reckoned with on the annual air racing circuit.

Making a name for herself among air racing fans in Cleveland, Ohio, in 1932, Mary Haizlip flew the Model 44 Wedell-Williams #92 to a world speed record for women of 255 miles per hour. Her record remained unbroken for seven years.

Now, in Cleveland for the 1932 National Air Races, Mary was quickly introduced to the Wedell-Williams #92. She climbed into the cockpit and, after her short indoctrination, raced in the Aerol Trophy Race Free-For-All against Gladys O'Donnell in Howard's Ike, Betty Lund in a WACO Taperwing, and Florence Klingensmith in Livingston's Coupe. When the race was called at the end of four laps because of an imminent storm, Mary was awarded $1,250 for a second-place finish behind O'Donnell. Harry Williams was delighted and Mary entered #92 in the Women's Shell Speed Dash for a speed record over a 3 kilometer straightaway course. With all eyes on her, Mary enjoyed her shining moment. First to finish, she set a speed record of 255 miles per hour, forty-five miles per hour faster than the previous record – a speed record that stood for seven years!

Two years later, during the 1934 Dayton Air Meet, Frances Harrell Marsalis crashed to her death as she rounded a pylon and Mary and Jim were eye-witnesses to Florence Klingensmith's death in her Gee Bee. Air racing has never been for the faint-hearted.

Mary admitted, "Racing planes didn't necessarily require courage. But, it did demand a certain amount of foolhardiness and a total disregard of one's skin."

That was the gutsy attitude of this strong, capable, daring, and athletic woman. Mary Haizlip put her life on the line and disdained any fears that would keep her from savoring the sweet joys of success.

Laura Ingalls

Solo Over the Andes

In 1934, Laura Ingalls, solo in the open cockpit of her Lockheed Air Express, coaxed her craft to 18,000 feet through the Uspallata Pass, now a major transportation route between Chile and Argentina in the lofty Andes Mountains. Additional artwork for Ingalls on pages 2 - 3.

Artwork © 2007 Sharon Rajnus

A dome of rare air surrounded Roosevelt Field, Long Island, New York in the early days of aviation, focusing upon the greats of aviation. The achievements were legion and daring men and women leapt from the runway into the inviting new frontier. There, Brooklyn-born Laura Ingalls soloed on 23 December 1928 and went on to receive her private pilot certificate after having first tried and rejected nursing, secretarial work, and performing on the stage as a Spanish dancer. Nothing captivated the young Laura as did flying and, although she told her parents she was selling real estate, she was an avid flight student at Roosevelt Field Flying School.

Laura traveled to Lambert Field, St. Louis, Missouri, and, in September 1929, received her limited commercial certificate and on 12 April 1930 she upgraded that to transport. Laura became the first woman to obtain that advanced certificate at Lambert Field and 15 April in the United States.

The following month, in a de Havilland Gipsy Moth, Laura shattered a women's record of 47 consecutive loops by performing an astounding 344 in one hour and three minutes. Soon thereafter, offered a dollar for every loop she could perform above her 344 by aviation enthusiasts in Muscogee, Oklahoma, she bettered her challenge by 636 loops and earned 980 dollars.

From loops to rolls, Laura returned to Lambert Field where she rolled her Moth for three hours and 39 minutes to perform 714 barrel rolls and break both the men's record of 417 rolls and Bettie Lund's women's record of 67. She flew her Moth that same year to set a record east-to-west coast flight of 30 hours, 27 minutes.

Later, she wrote, "I shall always love the Moth – for the Moth taught me to fly. Five times that tiny ship carried me across the Rockies; five times we fluttered small but determined over the enormous western miles against big bullying head winds. Our cruising speed only 85 mph in still air and, when held back by a velocity of 30 or 40 mph, it gave a ground speed of but 45! . . . Not only at low speed does the wind take greater toll in drift, but the interminable approach to watched-for landmarks dissolves certainty into doubt. We doubt our time; we doubt our speed . . ."

"Still the mountains rise blue in the far distance – still ahead an even higher range which must be cleared, although the little Gipsy engine is straining every cylinder and unable to climb higher. It seems almost unfair. The immensity of Earth, the immensity of Wind – against one small speck – which continues, nearly at a standstill, to remain aloft and inch indomitably toward the West."

Laura yearned to be the first woman to solo across the Atlantic Ocean and searched for an aircraft that matched her determination. She located a Lockheed Air Express, NR-937-Y that was completed in May 1931 and belonged to the Atlantic Exhibition Company. Powered by a cowled Pratt & Whitney Wasp engine and flown from a single-seat, open cockpit located behind the cabin, Laura prepared to fly it over the Atlantic Ocean to an historical first when leaking fuel tanks grounded her. Her dream failed.

"Another stark defeat," she wrote. "Why do things always seem to mean life or death to me; why must I want things with such blind desire that nothing else exists but that one thing - and denied it, I am plunged in darkness and despair? Is it because Rhapsody waits at the other end, for those who go down to the depths? No matter - I would give much to take disappointments in a humdrum way - lightly, casually; instead of knowing every nerve taut and quivering in anguish."

By 1932, Amelia Earhart and her red Lockheed Vega soloed the Atlantic and captured the honor and the adoration of the world. Rising competitively to the challenge of Earhart's success, Laura purchased the Air Express, refitted the cabin windows and set a record for a round-trip transcontinental flight between New York and Los Angeles; she flew thirty hours into westerly winds and lopped five hours off that time with tail winds on the reverse course.

She christened her Lockheed, "Auto-da-fè" – "Act of Faith," a name with important implications for her next feat. Laura prepped for an ambitious long-distance flight and she departed Jackson Heights, New York on 28 February 1934. Having stopped in Miami, she then took off on a remarkable eight-week flight that would have daunted the best of pilots. Laura's route took her to Havana, Cuba; Mérida, Yucatan, Mexico; Managua, Nicaragua; Cristobal, Canal Zone; Talara and Lima, Peru; Arica, Antofogasta and, on 13 March, into Santiago, Chile.

From Santiago, Laura lifted into the hills. She became the third woman in the world, the first from the United States, to cross the Andes Mountains. She coaxed a normally-aspirated, open cockpit, single-engine aircraft over the lofty range, choosing a pass that carried her between peaks that reached 20,000 feet above sea level and higher. Inherent in mountain flying are the unpredictable winds, turbulence, updrafts and downdrafts that can toss an aircraft about like a small cork bobbing on an ocean. She couldn't have made it above the tallest peaks had she wanted to. Even the pass was dauntingly high for her aircraft. Nonetheless, Laura pressed on to Mendoza, Argentina. She not only faced the challenges of controlling her plane, she is fortunate that she wasn't bleeding from the nose, gasping for air, having her eyesight blur or fatally losing consciousness.

On she flew – from Mendoza to Buenos Aires and then north to Rio de Janeiro. Having left the Andes behind, Laura still relied heavily upon her determination. Between Rio, Paramaribo, and Port au Spain, Trinidad, torrential rain forced her to descend as she attempted to cross the mouth of the Amazon River and pursue the coastal jungle. Down to a scant 15 feet above the waves, she weathered the storm on instruments alone. She curved north along the West Indies, landed once again in Cuba and arrived in Miami, Florida, on 23 April 1934.

The flight from Miami to New York was a joyous hop for Laura. Flying into her native state, she wrote, "Enveloped in the dark speed of high altitude, we rush on - we are abreast, we dominate New York. New York! The dream city of them all. A legendary city, set upon the sea, in unbelievable magnificence, reaching fabled towers into the dawn. Looked upon at night, from the vast dome of sky, incredible! . . . In a swift leap, I am above the field - shoot past - and swing back to circle down by gradual degrees."

In her historic flight, Laura logged 16,897 miles with her only companions the ocean mists, billowing clouds, the wind and the rain. In addition to having completed the longest flight by a woman, Laura received the Harmon Trophy as the Outstanding Woman Pilot of 1934. Her flight records included first woman to fly from North to South America and the first pilot to complete a solo flight around South America in a landplane.

In 1935, Laura purchased a Lockheed Orion and renamed her new craft with the same name. Between Floyd Bennett Field, New York, and Union Air Terminal, Burbank, California, she completed the first non-stop east to west transcontinental flight by a woman. In September, competing with Amelia Earhart's women's record of 17 hours, 7 minutes, Laura bested her rival and flew nonstop from Los Angeles to New York in 13 hours, 34 minutes.

During the 1930s, Laura Ingalls held more U.S. transcontinental air records than another other woman. She said, "There's no thought of danger. It's a game. You watch for landmarks, measure your time, smile, go on. Every real flier becomes one with the elements and just hates to land."

Laura became involved in the anti-war, America First movement in 1939 and was first grounded and then jailed. She spent a year in the West Virginia Women's Reformatory for violation of the Foreign Agents Registration Act of 1938 for not registering as a German agent.

Renowned artist Charles Hubbell wrote of her, "In 1934 she was the world's outstanding woman flyer and by 1942 she lost all she had gained in life . . ."

After World War II, Laura Ingalls lived quietly in California. Having pushed her envelope wide, she died at the age of 66 in Burbank on 10 January 1967.

Laura Ingalls credited her mother Martha with the ability to hurdle difficulties and achieve the reputedly impossible. Posed by her de Havilland Gipsy Moth in which she set aerobatic and speed records and crossed the Rocky Mountains five times, Laura profited by her mother's good example.

Bonny Warner
Goals are Meant to be Achieved

In the poignant scene in *South Pacific* in which "Bloody Mary" introduces her daughter to a U.S. Navy Lieutenant, she sings, "Happy Talk." She coaxes, "You got to have a dream, If you don't have a dream, how you gonna have a dream come true?"

Twenty years later, in 1976, Bonny Warner, a fourteen-year-old high school freshman, acted on such wise counsel. She turned dreams into goals and goals into outstanding achievements.

Having heard explorer Dr. John Goddard speak at her high school assembly, Bonny was motivated further. Goddard's philosophy challenged: "To dare is to do; to fear is to fail." He had personally listed more than 100 ultra-challenging goals – exploring the world's rivers, climbing its highest mountains, driving a dog-sled in the snow of the High Sierras – to help him to live his life to the fullest. As he spoke to Bonny Warner's schoolmates, he urged that they compile a list and he added, "If you really know what you want out of life, it's amazing how many opportunities will come to enable you to carry them out."

Bonny created that list. After having written, "Go to a top college," she added, "become an Olympian, work for ABC-TV, obtain a private pilot license, and build a log cabin."

Bonny already enjoyed field hockey in school and she opted to excel. Indicative of her drive, she queried the Field Hockey Association as to the requirements for becoming an Olympic field hockey player and, with a response of "experience at the college level," her next goal was obvious. Bonny was accepted at Stanford University, where those who matriculate with sports scholarships are required to be athletes and scholars. So much for the first item on her list. Few colleges can top Stanford and the Palo Alto location was relatively easily accessible to her home and family.

Holding tightly to her schedule, Bonny missed one school quarter to attend the Olympic Winter Games of 1980 in Lake Placid, New York, as one of 50 Olympic torchbearers, an honor she earned through an essay contest. While at Lake Placid, she participated in a beginner's luge camp and was encouraged to pursue the sport competitively. Having won $5,000 in a random drawing at a nationwide clothing store, she applied those winnings to a trip to Konigsee, an idyllic spot overlooking the deepest lake in the Bavarian Alps and home to a world-class training center for luge.

Luge is a single athlete competition that requires the racer to lie supine, feet first, and to careen down an icy "half-pipe," a narrow chute with banked curves and narrow straights. A luge racer experiences a run of up to 80 miles per hour as the sled and the body are wrenched around fourteen to twenty curves during a sizzling 40 to 60 seconds.

Bonny arrived in Konigsee filled with determination, but she lacked the ability to speak German. She wanted to be taught to slide and she made her desire to try a run apparent. The Germans, who assumed she was a top slider in the United States, directed her to the top of the icy course.

A lesser woman might have balked. Not a determined Bonny Warner. H.G. Frautschy wrote, "She made it through two turns before crashing, sliding, bouncing, and ricocheting off the rock-hard ice walls of the track."

Bonny refused to give up. She careened down the chute repeatedly, hanging on the sling and gradually getting the feel of steering, which was accomplished by pushing on the runners and using shoulder pressure and precise body movement. Bonny was bruised and sore, but she doggedly returned to the top of the chute to try again and again. She earned the respect of the Germans, who continued to offer advice and guidance. She made the U.S. National team the following year.

Bonny competed on the U.S. Women's Luge Team at the Sarajevo Olympic Winter Games in 1984. She competed at the Calgary Olympic Winter Games in 1988 and placed sixth – the highest any U.S. citizen, man or woman, had achieved in the sport at that time.

Between these obviously challenging and rewarding experiences, Bonny graduated from Stanford with a degree in broadcast journalism and worked as a reporter for KGO-TV, an affiliate of ABC in the San Francisco Bay area. Check off another item on her list.

With a sizeable education grant from the U.S. Olympic Committee, Bonny took

Courtesy of Bonny Warner Simi

Taking to this two-person bobsled after having been women's luge national champion for five years, Bonny demonstrated her Olympic style. Her brakeman crouched behind her out of the wind. Bonny was on the bobsled national team between 1999 and 2002.

Simi

Bonny, who also pilots the Airbus 320, transitioned to Brazil's Embraer 190 of JetBlue Airways. Having set goals as a teenager, she completed and surpassed all that initially motivated her and has continued to establish new, challenging directions for her life. She is a beacon for those who seek fresh perspectives.

to the air. She not only became a private pilot, she continued to amass certificates and ratings. She went to the top – an airline transport rating (ATP) – and, having been hired by United Airlines, from first officer on the Boeing 737 and 777 to captain on the Boeing 727.

Bonny placed 10th at the 1991 World Cup just after finishing initial airline piloting training at United. She was national champion five times and a U.S. National Luge Team member every year from 1981 through 1992. With more international top-five finishes than another other U.S. slider, she was the first U.S. gold medal winner in World Cup competition and ranked third in World Cup standings in 1987, higher than any other U.S. luge competitor.

She went on to be an Olympic contender in two-place bobsled and Olympic commentator for CBS in 1994 and 1998. In 1996, Bonny married Tony Simi and, two years later, they welcomed their daughter Kaitlin. She later transitioned to the Airbus 320 and Embraer 190 with JetBlue Airways. Hers were action-packed years.

Can anyone fully appreciate the tenacity and the effort that lies in reaching Olympic and World Class status without having accomplished it oneself? From the toning and strengthening of the body – Bonny did sprints, weights, and plyometrics (explosive jumps) – to hours of exercise and speed training – she devised a device designed to increase speed and strength for the running start in bobsledding, a sport she took up to get back into shape after her pregnancy. Two years later she was ranked 3rd in the world. It is with awe to recognize Bonny Warner Simi's incredible accomplishments.

Bonny's goal-setting continued. Perhaps one crowning achievement of this inspiring athlete has been to inspire and help others to achieve. One writer wrote, on an aol.com members blog, "In 1988, after attending the Calgary Winter Olympic Games our sons (Brian and David) had developed an interest in the sport of luge. They were selected from a program called 'Luge Challenge.' Bonny Warner

(1984, 1988, and 1992 Luge Olympian) inspired kids to participate in Olympic sports. As a result, Brian and David participated in the U.S. Luge Association Program for three years."

Bonny co-chaired, with Brian Boitano of Men's Figure Skating, the U.S. Olympic Spirit Award Selection Committee for the 2002 Olympics. She had taken a leave of absence from airline piloting for the grueling preparation for Olympic participation when the terrorist activities of September 11, 2001, caused her to return to work.

She said, "It occurred to me that because I'm the . . . mother of a three-year-old, perhaps the American public would realize that, if I'm out flying when I didn't have to be, then maybe I could send a message that it is really safe to fly."

When involved with Women in Aviation, International, at the 2003 Conference held close to Dayton, Ohio, Bonny practiced her ability to network. She said, as reported in the *Cincinnati Enquirer*, "I shared a cab [to the hotel] with a United mechanic who specializes in avionics . . . and who thinks she may be furloughed. The next day, I sat next to a woman who is in an avionics firm and put her in touch with the mechanic. That's how it works."

Bonny has blended all of her talents – journalism, athletics, adventure, media broadcast, parenting and piloting – into a vital message for youth. A speaker, a writer, and a publisher, she actively searches for ways in which she can inspire and motivate others, especially the young. She recalled Dr. Goddard, who, at seventy-five, was still setting and realizing new targets. In turn, she challenges us to take a fresh perspective, to respond to our curiosity, to stretch our capabilities and to fully live life. She would say, to those who are open and willing to accept challenges, the same thing she would say to her daughter: "You can do whatever you dream. You can amaze yourself with your accomplishments."

Ruth Maestre
With ATC, Bringing Them Home

As a student, Ruth Maestre pursued a degree in forestry from Purdue University and worked for the Bell Pizza House to finance her education. Bell Pizza's owner was an airport traffic controller (ATC) at the Lafayette, Indiana, Airport and he and his wife suggested that an ATC career might prove lucrative to Ruth. While contemplating the difference in salary between prepping pizza dough to controlling aircraft, Ruth was persuaded to submit an application to the Federal Aviation Authority. She figured that she had nothing to lose, filled out the paperwork and, thanks to an aptitude in mathematics, passed a test that generally weeded out at least half of each class. She said, "I took the test in Indianapolis the fall of 1983 and was offered the job in the early part of 1984. I knew nothing about planes, flying or controlling a variety of aircraft, but I don't give up easily. Being just a bit stubborn is a good quality for a controller. I went to Oklahoma City for the training and I didn't pass by a lot, but I passed. It was a question of stick-to-itiveness."

When nearly a quarter of the century has been spent in one career field, does not one consciously reach for balance, an equal distribution of the easy times with the hard? Ruth has faced the vagaries of her job. She has contrasted glorious sunny days – bright cheerful aviators, the rhythm of arriving and departing aircraft: properly spaced, properly flown and easily handled – with greyer days, snafus, confusions, and spirits dampened by a wide variety of circumstance. One such event was a catalyst for her emotions; one particular work day brought a search for understanding, best attained by reaching out to share.

Ruth wrote, "I currently serve the flying public from the Air Traffic Control tower at Cleveland Hopkins International Airport. Is my job stressful? You bet. Is it fun? Oh, yeah. There are times when I think they don't pay me enough for all that is required and other times that I can't believe I'm being paid for the pleasure that is mine. But, my view from the tower is one most people will never see. On one Monday

evening, my view was one that I wish that none of my co-workers all over the United States have to see."

Ruth recalled that particular evening, remembering the sultry breeze that swept over the airport from Lake Erie, the long shadows that were cast by the setting sun as day became twilight. "I was working the local position as the controller whose task it is to clear pilots for takeoffs and landings," she said. "We had just experienced the end of an 'arrival bank,' a typical occurrence that refers to a relatively short time period in which several airplanes arrive for sequencing to land. Typically, for an hour or so, landing air traffic is heavy. The tempo slows for thirty to forty-five minutes and then a series of departures rev up to leave.

"In the brief respite, from the birds'-eye position high above Concourse B, I was scanning 'my' airport, which is how every controller who operates the local position feels, and I noticed some unusual activity on the tarmac. A Boeing 737 was parked at its gate, but fire trucks and police cars attended it."

Below her red lights swept in circular motion, alternately reflecting from the silver fuselage of the jet and deepening in color to stripe the darkness of the macadam. A bus pulled up.

"Generally," Ruth continued, "if there is any type of medical emergency, organs being flown in or out, major sports teams arriving or departing or the like, we in ATC know about it. But, this time, no one had alerted us at all. Yet, all of the Cleveland Airport's emergency vehicles were there. Even more intriguingly, the firemen, policemen, TSA Airport Security personnel and ramp workers were lining up as if to greet a dignitary who would disembark from the jet.

"Then I saw a hearse back toward the aircraft. I quickly realized that, indeed, a very special dignitary was onboard that aircraft. One of our own had come home. Not the way anyone wanted, but in a manner the soldier had known was possible from the day of enlistment, the day

Courtesy of Ruth Maestre

From Mesa, Arizona to Menominee, Michigan, the Air Race Classic, 20-23 June 2006, took Ruth (left) and Denise Waters across Texas to Louisiana, Oklahoma, Kansas, Minnesota and to the terminus. The duo, formidable racing opponents, flew Denise's Grumman Tiger. They placed second as Team #1.

From her unique view of an airport tarmac, this scene is not as rare as this air traffic controller would like. Ruth said, "I want those serving and their families to know that we grieve with them and, while God is watching your loved ones, so are the air traffic controllers. We want to bring everyone safely home."

Artwork © 2007 Sharon Rajnus

the soldier chose to represent our country and protect the freedom we, so ungratefully sometimes, enjoy."

Ruth had read in the local newspapers about the loss of a Cleveland boy, a young man who sacrificed his life fighting for our country. She alerted the rest of the ATC crew and each one was silent, watching the event unfold. As the hearse backed up, they saw a group of people leave the bus. She said, "They were holding one another. I didn't need binoculars to know that they were crying. I choked up and had to turn away from the window to regain some composure."

As other aircraft were taxiing toward their gates, the tower and ground controllers maneuvered planes carefully. They tried to ensure that their instructions resulted in providing as quiet an atmosphere as is possible at an airport. Ruth said, "I am sure that, if you were aboard any of those aircraft, you didn't mind the extra minute or two that it took for arrival at your gate. Thank you."

And for the people aboard the Boeing 737, she added, "I wondered if the passengers on that flight knew what a precious cargo had lain below them."

When the luggage ramp conveyed the casket from the cargo hold, six meticulously uniformed military men, the honor escorts, marched to the end of the ramp; they stood at attention, ready to welcome their fallen comrade. The door to the hearse was opened and, after having carefully draped the casket with the flag of the United States, the six lifted their precious burden and carried it to the hearse. All the witnesses on the ramp stiffened to rigid and respectful attention.

Ruth said, "It was all I could do not to cry. The other operators in the tower were silent. It seemed, for a precious moment, the entire airport fell into silence. Then, as life slowly crept toward normalcy, doors were shut, people climbed back onto the bus, everyone drove away and the airport became, again, an airport.

"I had just witnessed a family grieving, a country's loss and the

price of freedom. My view from the tower lasted only a few minutes, but it will last forever in my heart. I am thankful that, in a very small way, I was able to pay respects to one of our own.

"I am thankful, too, for our freedoms, those for which that young man paid with his life. Northeast Ohio has taken very hard hits in the war against terror. It has shed its share of heroes' blood and this same scene played out for me again. It has brought home to me the need to extend my thanks to those serving and to their families who support them. Please know that we grieve with you and, while God is watching over your loved ones, so are the air traffic controllers.

"My job has never been about the money. It is about bringing everyone home safely. It has been my honor and privilege to serve."

Ruth Maestre has felt personally the despair that grips family members who have lost a loved one. Her husband, Jon, a talented avionics expert, was taken from her in a tragic aircraft accident. They were youthful, full of life and love, and filled with the expectations of a wonderful future ahead.

As with the family members of the fallen soldier, Ruth was forced to call upon her own remarkable reserves of strength. She continued, as a dedicated ATC controller, to assist pilots; she took on some important volunteer roles in the organization Women in Aviation, International, giving of herself for others. Often teaming with Denise Waters, she participated successfully in several air racing events, winning and placing in many, including successfully completing the London to Sydney Air Race in 2001; and she dove into the hard work of building her own aircraft – a kit-built Lancair IV. Ruth is especially devoted to her three nieces and two nephews, sharing with them the joys of aviation and introducing them, step-by-step, to the creation of an airplane in which she can look forward to flying with them. She will make every effort, with those – her special passengers – to bring them safely home.

Denise Waters
Race the World, Ride the Sun

In Charles Van Doren's *A History of Knowledge: Past, Present, and Future*, the author defines Renaissance Man. He identifies him as an Aristotelian ideal of the educated person, "critical" in virtually all branches of knowledge, an individual blessed with broad intellectual interests and accomplished in the arts and the sciences. There may be many, but one aviatrix, Denise Waters, stands tall in qualifying for the enviable title of Aviation's Renaissance Woman, a model for Van Doren's ideal.

Making one of life's serious and life-altering decisions, Denise chose early retirement from her position with NYNEX in Manhattan to pursue other goals. Although she continued in a consultant role for the communications industry, that is just one of her hats. She also oversees the company specializing in construction and business management that she founded with her partner, Martin Pine. In addition, she and Martin are active in marine education and safety consulting, yacht deliveries, and offshore sailing.

Denise Waters and Ruth Maestre joined the London to Sydney Centenary Air Race in 2001. The 12,000 mile flight with more than 24 stops took the duo from Ohio to the race departure site in England. There they joined 37 other teams from Australia, Canada, Hong Kong, the Netherlands, New Zealand, Portugal, Switzerland, the United Kingdom, and the United States. Two women pilots perished prior to reaching the race start, six aircraft later withdrew, and Denise and Ruth joined 31 planes to complete the competition. From Australia, Denise pressed on and crossed the Pacific to an eventual terminus in Ohio. She joined the relatively rare elite of around-the-world pilots.

On the cultural side, Denise is a musician, having received her bachelors degree in music education from Ithaca College, New York, and a masters in music performance from Florida State University. An athlete, she participates in marathons, shorter races, and mini-triathlon events, competitive in running, biking, and swimming. That list can be lengthened with Nordic skiing, hiking, horseback riding, sailing, and, of course, flying.

Within her realm of aviation, she is equally diverse, talented and tireless. Having learned to fly in 1987 at one of the busiest general aviation fields in the United States, Teterboro Airport, New Jersey, Denise added a commercial certificate and her instrument and multi-engine ratings in Vero Beach, Florida, and her seaplane in Naples, Maine. Denise responded to the lure of homebuilding and within one year of having received her license, she was shopping for a kitplane to build. She anticipated sharing this project with her parents, Dick and Jane (E.J.) Waters, and found that the building process led to a deeper, wider, and more expansive knowledge base for greater understanding of the physics and mechanics of flight.

Denise said, "I had progressed in my flight training and was frustrated with the high costs and the inconveniences of renting airplanes. I wanted my own plane and, more importantly, I wanted to know how everything worked – a thorough understanding of what is happening behind the instrument panel and in front of the firewall. My father, a pilot and mechanic, and my mother, a student pilot, were in aviation before I was born. They left it behind when faced with the financial demands of family. I thought it would be fun working with them and returning them to their earlier passion."

In choosing a building project, Denise was careful and meticulous about the purchase. She developed and analyzed a series of questions before signing on the dotted line: Financially, can I afford this? Is this airplane safe? Technically, could I do this? Do I have a large enough work area? Do I have the necessary tools and equipment? Do I (and my family) have the stamina to complete this if it takes forever? Will the airplane's functions answer my needs? What about the company support? Is the firm reputable? Am I ready and willing to accept realities that go with an experimental aircraft? What will I do if I have to stop prior to completion? What will I do if the company stops before I do?

Delivery trucks followed shortly after the decision was made. The project was based in Dick's upstate New York workshop. Although it involved an added challenge of commuting over 500 miles to work on the project, Denise was grateful to have her father as mentor. "My parents couldn't have been more supportive with their time, space,

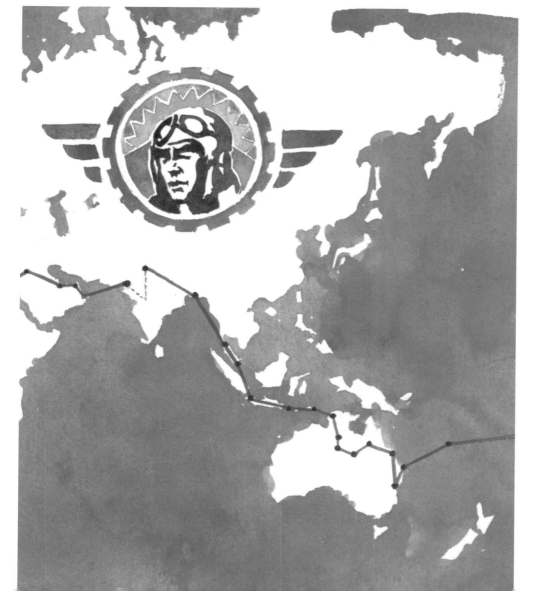

and encouragement. I feel fortunate in our relationship and am pleased they found their own pleasure in my endeavor."

Sadly, Dick Waters didn't live to see the completion of their joint adventure; but he had insisted, "When she bought her Express kit at Oshkosh in 1988, I think a lot of people felt that 'Daddy was buying Denise an airplane.' They couldn't have been further from the truth. She is paying for this. She is doing the work of building.'"

Denise's choice, the Express kitplane, one of the fastest, conventionally-configured true four-place aircraft, marked a new period in homebuilts, leading the way for both experimental and production composites seen on flight lines today. While Denise progressed on her project, the company, still in its infancy, stumbled; an accident blamed on an engine failure claimed the prototype resulting in a non-fatal crash. To make matters infinitely worse, a few years later, during an economic recession and market saturation, the second prototype crashed killing all aboard. Rumors flew and the verdict was pilot error.

Later, Denise wrote, "The tragedy left me with very mixed emotions. I had flown with that pilot; he was a staunch advocate of the Express. He is also the first that I have personally known in the flying community to no longer be with us. But, his accident is a lesson to us all, many times over, about the overconfidence that can envelope one when his or her feet are free of the earth for so many hours."

Denise dealt with more than human loss; she also witnessed the bankruptcy of the company and its aftermath – the cycle of multiple company restarts and upheaval for 290 builders who had depended upon a supply of parts, construction details, and mutual support. She wrote then, "This is not a pleasant situation for anyone – kitbuilders, the manufacturer, employees, suppliers and creditors. The grand hopes of finishing within a few years are now in a holding pattern. What now seems the impossible may just take a little longer, but it will be worth it. The Express was not meant to lie in pieces collecting dust; it was meant to fly and taste the wind."

To keep her piloting skills sharp while building an airplane for her future, Denise purchased a 1979 Grumman Tiger. She wrote, "Martin delivered a boat to Bermuda. I'd been scheduled to go, but a paying customer came along and I was bumped. I chose to fly over fall foliage in the Adirondacks, Vermont, and New Hampshire. Martin spent ten days on the open ocean with gale force winds and rain. I spent the sunny autumn days in the air, touring artisan studios on the land, relaxing and getting some much needed exercise on their quiet roads. You can't convince me that flying isn't more fun than sailing!"

While embroiled in aircraft building and obtaining licenses and ratings, Denise paralleled with work in general aviation maintenance, starting on her Tiger; engine overhaul, complete instrument and avionics upgrade, new upholstery, and exterior paint. She learned from and worked with professionals to gain experience. She wrote, "I helped to disassemble the airplane for inspection. It was great being there because, if they found anything, they could show me, give me options and get the answer on the spot – all great experiences that prepared me for work on my Express."

Acknowledging that there was far more to learn about structures, systems and mechanics, Denise continued work on general aviation aircraft accumulating the required field hours and enhancing her apprentice work by attending evening courses in airframe, powerplant, and avionics, near her home in New York City at the College of Aeronautics. She completed her FAA mechanic certificate with airframe and powerplant ratings. She also was awarded maintenance training scholarships from Simuflite through Women in Aviation, International, and Pratt & Whitney via the Association for Women in Aviation Maintenance (AWAM).

Flying for Denise took on an entirely different dimension when she found an all-consuming passion for air racing. She has honed her skills and become a formidable opponent in a variety of racing venues: Air Race Classic, U.S. Air Race; Great Southern Air Race, Great Hawaiian Air Race, Around New Zealand Air Race, and the Bicentennial Women's Air Derby. She has multiple wins, has placed numerous times

Few push their capabilities further than Denise: Pilot, Mechanic, Aircraft Homebuilder and Air Racer. Having attained her latest challenging achievement, she set sights on her next.

and enjoys the challenges, education, and camaraderie. Through the American Yankee Association she met another Grumman Tiger owner, Ruth Maestre, air traffic controller, air racer, aircraft homebuilder. Ruth and Denise, whose individual skills complement each other to make a winning team, have shared many a cockpit together on their racing wings.

Both women carried racing fever to a new high when they entered the London, England to Sydney, Australia Centenary Air Race, March and April 2001. En route to the start, they held in Goose Bay, Canada's minus temperatures with their recently purchased Piper PA 30B Twin Comanche. Upon weather forecast improvement, they chose to fly 3,000 miles on a northerly heading via Greenland, Iceland and Scotland.

The 28-day race began in Biggin Hill, London. Denise and Ruth, with the support of friends, family and strangers from around the world, raced *Niner-Eight Yankee*, with thirty-eight teams, representing nine nations, to exotic places most never have the opportunity to see: Cannes, Corfu, Crete, Cairo, Luxor, Bahrain, Dubai, Muscat, Karachi, Delhi, Calcutta, Yangon, Phuket, and Singapore. Leaving Jakarta before sunrise on the 22nd race day, for Bali, Kupang and the Timor Sea crossing, they made Darwin as lightning flashed to the east and the south. Denise shouted, "We did it! Australia!"

Ruth wrote, in their race log, "This is our fifth continent. . . . The race isn't finished yet, but it feels like we've really done it! We made a good decision to stay in Jakarta. One of the other teams fought thunderstorms from Bali and experienced aircraft damage."

The duo crossed Australia to the terminus in Sydney – one of thirty-one teams to successfully complete the 12,000-mile race. As work beckoned, Ruth returned to air traffic control via a commercial flight from Australia.

Denise worked on *Niner-Eight Yankee* in preparation for the Pacific crossing. She was joined by Dee Bond Wakelin, a New Zealander and London-to-Sydney Air Race administration member. Denise and Dee flew the Australian coast north, then east to cross the vast ocean. With stops that included Noumea, Fiji, Samoa, Christmas Island, and Hawaii, the pair arrived in Oakland, California, just days prior to the Air Race Classic 2001.

Denise didn't simply cross the United States to Ohio, she *raced* to Ohio, becoming one of the few women pilots to have circumnavigated the world. She quickly was tapped to lecture on her experiences and to offer encouragement and expertise to others. In appreciation for what aviation has given to her, this exemplary woman has established scholarships to involve youth in aviation. She is a writer, a speaker, a mentor to young men and women interested in mechanics, competition piloting, aircraft construction, and the myriad of subjects in which she is well-versed. She is amazingly accomplished; a Renaissance Woman.

CHAPTER FIVE

CURIOSITY
& CONQUEST

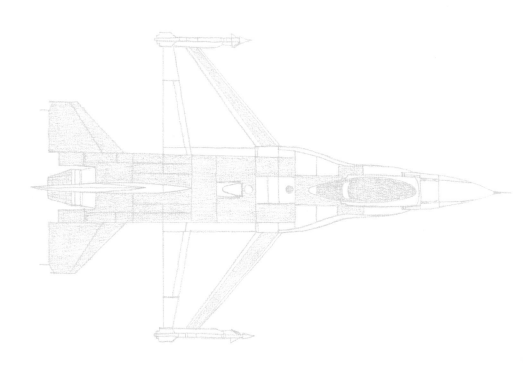

F-16 FIGHTER

Artwork © 2007 Sharon Rajnus

CURIOSITY

"Daredevils . . . need to live close to the edge to feel fully alive . . . For me, it's just a case of my curiosity leading with its chin: things fascinate me whether they are dangerous or not. I don't need to fly because flying doesn't frighten me; I need to fly even though it frightens me, because there are things you can learn about the world only from 5,000 feet above it just as there are things you can learn about the ocean only when you become part of its intricate fathoms."

Diane Ackerman, ON EXTENDED WINGS

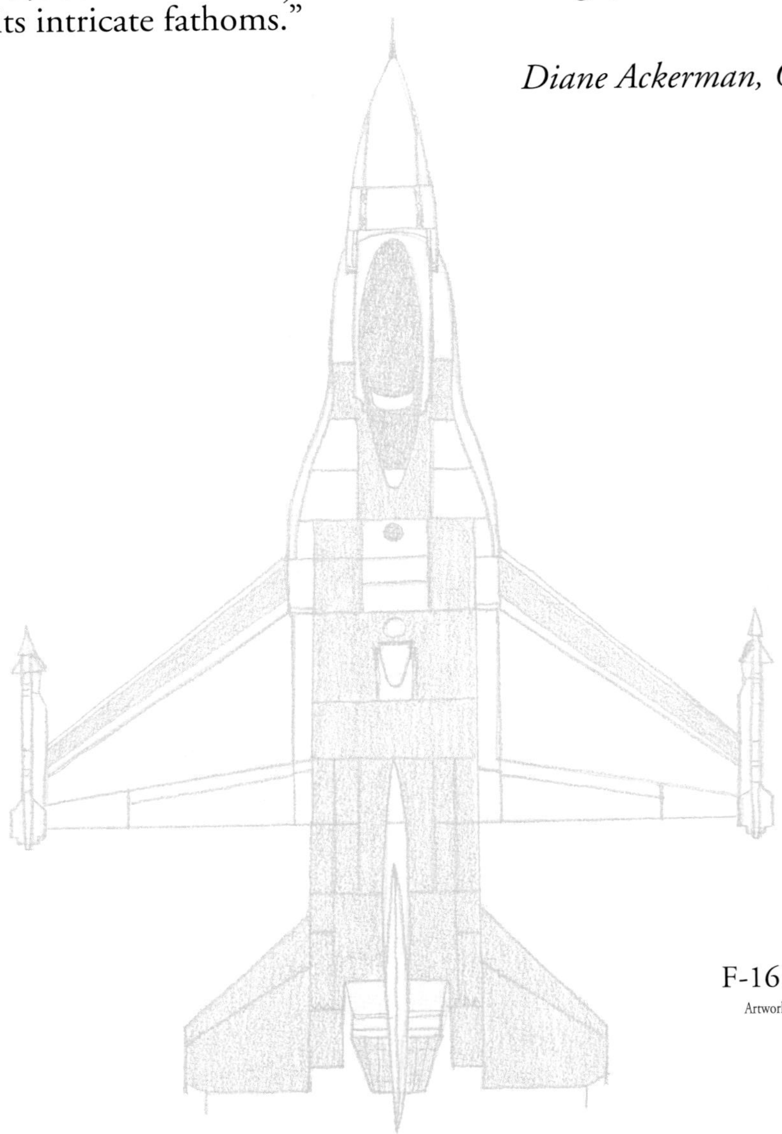

F-16 FIGHTER

Artwork © 2007 Sharon Rajnus

CONQUEST

"I . . . take off into the night. Ahead of me lies a land that is unknown to the rest of the world and only vaguely known to the African – a strange mixture of grasslands, scrub, desert sand like long waves of the southern ocean. Forest, still water, and age-old mountains, stark and grim like the mountains of the moon. Salt lakes and rivers that have no water. Swamps. Badlands. Land without life. Land teeming with life – all of the dusty past, all of the future. The air takes me into its realm. Night envelops me entirely, leaving me out of touch with the earth, leaving me within this small moving world of my own, living in space with the stars."

Beryl Markham, WEST WITH THE NIGHT

CHAPTER 5

Connie Bowlin

"Once you've flown one, ..."

Every pilot is introduced to emergency procedures before pocketing a certificate; but, pilots training in or transitioning to rare and valuable World War II warbirds take those procedures very seriously. Most learn essential steps through long practice at repetition. When an emergency occurs, time is precious. Having committed the checklist to memory can mean the difference between life and death.

Connie Bowlin, a captain with Delta Airlines and an experienced pilot with more than 20,000 flight hours in more than 70 types of aircraft, flew as part of the 1998 warbird exhibition during AirVenture, the world's largest air show at the Experimental Aircraft Association (EAA) Convention. She was flying the P-51D *Old Crow*, a warbird owned by pilot and performance engineer Jack Roush and painted with the insignia and colors of the craft piloted during World War II by Clarence E. "Bud" Anderson, a triple ace and the leading ace of the 363rd Fighter Squadron, 357th Fighter Group – the Yoxford Boys of the Eighth Air Force. Skies were clear, the sparkling blue of Lake Winnebago was teased with widely separated whitecaps and the heavy iron encircling the field held the attention and awe of thousands of aviation enthusiasts below.

Bud Anderson, still an active pilot who often flew this P-51, was on those grounds and anticipating flying *Old Crow* later in this show. He was part of an incredible crowd of 650,000 aviation fans, 10,000 airplanes from every state and many other countries, 2,500 air show aircraft, and 800 commercial exhibitors, which converge at Wittman

Field in Oshkosh, Wisconsin, annually.

This colorful mosaic was Connie's to enjoy from above until, suddenly, when she selected gear down to bring the Mustang in for a landing, a red landing gear warning light on her panel gleamed defiantly – gear unsafe!

Fortunately, Connie's husband, Ed Bowlin, was airborne in a similar P-51 and flying her wing. Ed pulled slightly to the side and dropped below her for a visual check of *Old Crow*. He confirmed the Mustang had a left gear extended and a right gear that refused to extend. It was a dangerous situation.

In the P-51D Mustang, the landing gear (or, as it was titled by North American Aviation early in the 1940s, the "alighting gear") is controlled via mechanical linkage and hydraulics. As Connie well knew, a failure of the hydraulics will affect gear operation and that "no provision is made in the airplane for a pilot-actuated hydraulic hand pump."

With no manual pump, Connie was challenged to bring this broken bird back to the busiest airport in the world during the incredible week of EAA's convention. Further, she was to land as judiciously as possible to preclude further damage her craft, endanger anyone on the ground and, of course, to walk safely away from the inevitable incident.

Connie flew into clear airspace away from Wittman Field and went through every possible procedure that would shake loose the stubborn right wheel. She reaffirmed that the gear handle was down and yawed

the Mustang to loosen it. She knew, further, to pull the fairing door emergency handle and again try to force the gear down by yawing the airplane. She also ran through the checklist for the emergency she faced.

Connie was busy. She said, much later, "It never occurred to me that I might get hurt. That's hard to believe, I'm sure, but it's true. I truly didn't believe I might get hurt."

Those words are spoken by a woman who started her aviation career in 1970 as a flight attendant, who applied for and was hired as an airline pilot in 1978, and who has worked hard to achieve her enviable position as one of the most accomplished woman pilots in the world. In meeting, falling in love with and marrying Ed Bowlin, Connie married her best friend. Ed encouraged her every step of the way. He provided her with his Cessna 182 in which to initially learn to fly. He shared with Connie an airplane sales business that meant the purchase, flying and delivery of a wide variety of airplanes – each one contributing to her experience and confidence. Now he maintained his position on her wing. Having Ed alongside was a major factor in the successful outcome to the emergency.

A wingman is trained in formation flying, in assessing any problem that can be visually apparent, and in staying with the troubled craft. Ed radioed Connie of her disparate situation. Even a belly landing would have been preferable. The manual noted, "better no gear than one extended and one retracted."

Connie said, "I flew around for an hour, analyzing the problem, reducing the fuel quantity and checking every conceivable method of getting the gear extended. It was nice to have all the support from Ed and from people on the ground who were on the radio with me. Their knowledge and assistance were invaluable. Two guys parked their black jeep at the spot north of the cable that stretches across the runway so I would have a reference point for my touchdown. They were helping me avoid having my gear door snag that cable.

"As I committed to landing, there were two videos taken of the event. One was filmed from the Wittman Field Control Tower and the other by members of the official EAA photography staff. I took them by surprise. They were pretty excited. I, on the other hand, was busy – just doing what I needed to do. Ed buzzed the right side of the runway as I touched down. He followed me all the way."

Corwin H. "Corky" Meyer, renowned test pilot, was directed to test and evaluate the P-51 for naval operations in 1944. He wrote, in his biography, "My task was to check the stall characteristics to see if [the P-51D] had met the standards acceptable for carrier requirements. It had not. The Mustang still had severe wing dropping with little aileron control for recovery. What was worse was how easily the P-51D went into secondary accelerated stalls in the clean and landing configurations when trying to recover from the initial stall."

Landing configuration requires flying just above stall. Connie's predicament was serious. *Old Crow's* left gear was out and down. The

Hers has been an exemplary career. From a scholarship as "Miss Winston-Salem" to becoming a flight attendant for Delta Air Lines, Connie Bowlin moved into the cockpit and became a Delta Captain. She has thousands of flight hours in more than 70 types of aircraft, counting the World War II warbirds as her favorites. Demonstrating living history, she preserves America's Aviation Legacies and, through the EAA Young Eagles Program, encourages youngsters toward aviation careers. She and her husband Ed Bowlin pilot the P-51 Mustangs, "Old Crow" and "Glamorous Glen III," for appreciative and nostalgic air show audiences.

touchdown and rollout would be crucial and the right wing had to be held off the ground as long as possible.

Once committed, her landing was smooth and straight. The aircraft held steady for a time; then, inevitably, the right wing dropped and smacked the ground. Connie and *Old Crow* swept off into the grass in a cloud of dust.

"Ed buzzed past just above me one more time after the airplane stopped. I jumped out as quickly as possible to wave to him and show him that I was all right. Someone wanted to report him for 'hotdogging,' but he wasn't hotdogging; he was doing exactly what a wingman knows to do – check on the downed pilot."

There was damage. That was unavoidable. Connie joked, "A runway light flew off as I struck it with the wing while leaving the runway. Later, when the airplane was in the hangar, Ed kidded me saying, 'You could have missed that light and you wouldn't have dented the wing.' I knew he was kidding, but someone nearby heard him and thought he was being a real jerk. I knew better.

"Jack Roush, who built the engine, wanted to know if the Mustang was running well before the incident. That was good of him – to give me the benefit of the doubt right away. My answer was, 'Yes, Jack. It ran great right up until the prop hit the concrete.' Unfortunately, with the damage to the gear door and gear mechanism, we'll never know exactly what caused the malfunction."

But, Connie is also a horsewoman. She knows the wisdom of climbing right back onto a horse that has just thrown you. She flew another P-51 in the air show the next day and *Old Crow* was completely repaired and airborne again within a month.

Not that Connie lacked an airplane to fly. Retired from flying as a Captain for Delta in the Boeing 767 and 757, Connie holds type ratings for the Boeing B-17 Flying Fortress, Douglas DC-3 / C-47 Skytrain, Douglas DC-9/MD88, and Cessna Citation. She is also authorized to fly, in addition to the Mustang: the Republic P-47 Thunderbolt, Curtiss P-40, Chance-Vought F-4U Corsair, Douglas AD-1 Skyraider, North American T-28 Trojan, Lockheed T-33 Shooting Star, DC-B26, and Jet Provost. When she said, "It was nice to be very comfortable in the Mustang," hers was the voice of experience.

Feeling privileged to be entrusted with equipment that brings so many memories to the heroes and heroines of this country, Connie never ceases to be honored and humbled in meeting World War II veterans who gather around the aircraft with deep and obvious emotion.

She said, "I think of the young people who worked on and flew these planes; the pilots, gunners, armorers and mechanics; those who were youngsters barely out of their teens when they went to war. They make flying the warbirds so special. They are the ones for whom I am grateful and in awe. I realize that there will be a day when we can no longer fly these aging aircraft and I feel very privileged to have a small part in keeping memories alive.

"In addition to the veterans, this living history reaches vast numbers of people who otherwise would have no opportunity to see the planes that figured so heavily in assuring the freedoms we enjoy today. Of course, the fact that Ed and I get to fly together makes it just that much more fun, too."

Connie's wisdom connects with us all as she urges anyone who has a passion to nurture that joy. She suggests that no matter what it is that people do, they should see that it is a lot of fun.

Retiring from the cockpit of the Delta Air Lines 757/767 simply gave Connie Bowlin more time to pilot rare and aging warbirds. Connie, one of the few women entrusted with the controls of the B-17, owes a debt of gratitude to the members of the WASP who flew B-17s during WWII. Connie was honored as an "Eagle" at the annual Gathering of Eagles and is an inspiration to all who know her.

Teddy Kenyon
God Willing, Weather Permitting

A daring 18-year-old in 1923, Cecil MacGlashan, called Teddy by all who knew her, sped by on her brother's new motorcycle and horrified her mother with, in her mother's words, "...behavior inappropriate for a young lady." Enrolled in a Boston Finishing School, Teddy met a senior engineering student and pilot, Ted Kenyon, and by the time Teddy married Ted Kenyon three years later, her mother was resigned to her daughter's vigorous pursuits. Teddy barnstormed with Ted, selling tickets for his airplane rides from a 1,300-foot cinder strip in Boston – a humble airfield known today as Logan International Airport. Eager to fly, she soloed after only four hours of instruction and received her pilot certificate with only ten flying hours of experience.

Although her husband urged her to avoid inclement weather and to avoid aerobatic stunts, Teddy subscribed to only the first of those admonitions. Their private airplane was named "GWWP, God Willing, Weather Permitting," a note commonly added to flight plans. But, in 1933, clearly capable of having her aircraft maneuver through all three axes, Teddy was awarded the title of "Miss America of the Air" at an American Legion Meet in Boston, winning a silver trophy and $300 in twenty-dollar gold pieces. At Roosevelt Field on Long Island at the National Air Pageant, she borrowed a WACO biplane and successfully flew an aerobatic maneuver that she'd never before performed. She captured the Women's Championship, a second silver trophy and $5,000, sharing $1,000 with the owner of the WACO and purchasing a WACO of her own.

The Ninety-Nines was founded in 1929 and Teddy was an original charter member of this organization of licensed women pilots. Teddy was chosen by The Ninety-Nines to receive the Kimball Cup as New England's outstanding woman pilot for 1935.

In the spring of 1942, when male test pilots were at a premium, Teddy and two other women were hired by Grumman Aircraft as production test pilots. With minor preparation, the trio went to the flight line, climbed aboard newly-manufactured Grumman F6F Hellcats and took off – literally and figuratively. But her mettle was tested one year and 500 flight hours later. Teddy was at 6,000 feet when her Hellcat's left aileron jammed. She was urged to bail out over Long Island Sound, ditching the craft; but, she responded, "I wouldn't hurt this aircraft for anything." Returning to the field without any ability to bank, she relied on rudders to skid the fighter in a wide arc and into position for a smooth landing.

Teddy Kenyon, extraordinary test-, fixed wing- and rotary wing-pilot, died at age 80 in 1985. Her passion for flight remained throughout her long life – and inspires still.

Courtesy William Heaslip Collection

Before Teddy Kenyon became a test pilot of F6F Hellcats during World War II for Grumman Aircraft, Long Island, New York, she borrowed this WACO biplane and won the trophy and $5,000. She was competing in the National Air Pageant of 1933. Her winnings made possible a generous gift to the WACO owner and the chance to purchase an airplane of her own.

Jean Batten

Success at Any Cost

From the moment of her birth in 1909 in Rotorua, New Zealand, Jean Batten was influenced, molded, guided, and encouraged by her mother, Ellen Blackmore Batten, a possessive and headstrong woman. Were Ellen's hopes and dreams stifled in cultural mores of the turn of the twentieth century? Jean was the beneficiary of her mother's love and attention, but few recognized the extent to which this love equated to domination.

On the positive side, under Ellen's control Jean blossomed into a renowned aviatrix. Jean sincerely believed she was destined to represent New Zealand and the British Empire in aerial exploits and that much was owed her by others. She developed a staunch faith in her own capabilities and, although Ellen attempted to stifle Jean's relationships with men, Jean learned to become a skillful manipulator of those who befriended her.

Jean was a woman of her time, inspired by the remarkable achievements of men and women of the air. She longed for similar adulation and she became both ruthless and accomplished.

Inspired by Amy Johnson's solo flight of a Gipsy Moth from England to Australia in 1930, Jean dedicated herself into learning to fly and to besting Johnson's record. She and Ellen left New Zealand for England under the guise of pursuing music lessons while relying upon financial support from Jean's father, Fred Batten, from whom her mother was estranged. When Fred discovered the deceit, he brought an end to Jean's allowance. Jean turned her wiles on others and found several who staked her to airplanes, to training, to support, and to sponsorships of long-distance flights.

Between 1933 and 1934, Jean made three attempts to solo a Gipsy Moth from England to Australia. On her third try, she set a women's record in May 1934 of 14 days, 22 hours and 30 minutes. She achieved her dream – cutting over four days off Amy Johnson's time. Instantly, headlines declared her achievement and Jean became the newest darling of the air.

Within a year, she made aviation history again. By flying from Australia to England, she became the first woman to solo both directions. She demonstrated an uncanny ability to navigate – faultlessly planning her route and meticulously flying her plan. Her achievements are legion, considering her navaids consisted of a turn indicator, a magnetic compass and a watch and that near-disasters plagued her. Undaunted, she faced snapped connecting rods, engine failures, wrecked airplanes, bent and broken propellers, fuel leakage, sand- and windstorms, driving rains, turbulence, accidents, incidents and long, solitary open-cockpit hours.

Jean celebrated her 26th birthday by taking delivery of a Percival Gull 6 – a low-wing monoplane with electric starter, fuel pumps, a metal propeller, brakes and flaps. She was overjoyed to move up to luxury of the Gull – its closed cockpit alone represented protection from relentless battering of wind, sun and rain. It was twice as fast as the Moth and, when extra fuel tanks were added, could fly twice the range.

So many long distance, endurance and altitude records had been set by 1935 that Jean felt pressured to find a goal not yet attained. With the capable Gull, she challenged herself to be the first woman to solo across the South Atlantic: destination, Brazil.

Ready to depart from England on 10 November 1935, she admitted feeling "the thrill of anticipation and exhilaration that glowed in my heart before every big flight."

Then she was handed a written directive from French authorities that forbid her to cross the Sahara to Dakar without a radio. Jean took

Jean accepted delivery of her Percival Gull in 1935 on her 26th birthday. With long-range tanks, it was capable of carrying her from Africa to South America, if nothing went wrong. Her major fuel leak after reaching Rio de Janeiro meant the difference between life and death.

Artwork © 2007 Sharon Rajnus

the letter to the ladies room, tore it into bits and flushed it away. She was ready to fly and nothing was going to stop her.

Jean flew to the southeastern corner of England in preparation for what she hoped would be a record-breaking solo flight. From England to Dakar in West Africa and from there to make the 1,900-mile crossing to Natal, Brazil. At dawn on 11 November, she flew to Casablanca, spent the night, and flew on to the Sahara Desert. The Dakar airfield was temporarily closed and she had to operate out of a neglected military field that added unnecessary miles to her overwater flight. Concerned that her Gull was over gross weight with 147 gallons of fuel, she lightened the load by leaving behind a signal pistol, revolver, rockets, cartridges, torch, toolkit, spare engine parts, and emergency water drums. She was carrying neither a life raft nor a lifejacket, believing them only of temporary assistance in a survival situation.

With only two or three hours of sleep, Jean received her weather forecast and took off for approximately 1,300 miles of open ocean. Concentrating on time and her magnetic direction, she flew close enough to the ocean waves to use them to monitor her drift. It was mandatory that she be accurate within five degrees as she had measured her fuel requirement carefully and her supply was limited. She had been briefed that she was headed for a permanent low pressure depression near the equator, but she wasn't told that other pilots referred to it as, "the Black Hole." It was almost her undoing.

Her biographer, Ian Mackersey, wrote, "When she was approximately 200 miles north of the Equator, she flew into the South Atlantic convergence zone, the familiar black wall of rain that rose threateningly from sea level to a much higher altitude than she was capable of reaching. She plunged into it with determination, but it was so torrential she had to drop to within 50 feet of the water to maintain visual contact with the sea."

Having dived low to see the water, she suddenly recognized the danger of being forced into the sea. Jean climbed into the rain-blackened clouds and, for a seemingly endless time, flew blind, tossing in the volatile turbulence and forcing herself to concentrate solely on her heading of 242-degrees.

"Then the terror began," Mackersey continued. "To her horror, the compass needle slowly swung around the dial. . . . In ghastly motion,

Designed by Britain's Edgar Percival, his sleek Gull was fitted with a Gipsy six-cylinder engine, a starter motor, brakes, flaps and could cruise at 150 miles per hour. Jean's Gull 6 was relatively rare – only 19 were built. In it she became the first woman to solo the Atlantic from England to Brazil and in the fastest time.

it swung through 180 degrees. In the blackness of rain pounding relentlessly on her windscreen, she could find no point with which to orient herself . . . no glimpse of sea, sky, or sun. She fixed on the turn indicator, trying to hold course."

Jean later wrote, "I knew I couldn't accurately steer another thousand miles to Natal on that alone. . . . Perspiration was now trickling down into my eyes . . . every muscle in my body was tensed."

Although she heard later about the erratic magnetic phenomenon from French mail pilots, she knew nothing of it prior to her flight. "Semi-paralyzed with fear and near desperation," Mackersey wrote, "she broke out of the storm into brilliant sunlight after what had seemed an eternity. The compass needle, though agonizingly slow, again steadied."

Having been airborne for more than seven hours, Jean was completely exhausted. She was approximately 1,100 miles from her African departure and still 800 miles from her Brazilian landing. She admitted, "I spent the next few minutes trying to ascertain accurately the amount of drift and calculated it at eight degrees to starboard. I altered course eight degrees to port to compensate for it. . . . I began to feel very lonely . . . empty blue sea everywhere . . . a vast blue waste."

She had not imagined that such loneliness existed. Her relief was obvious when, after 13 hours and 2,000 miles of ocean, she finally made landfall within half a mile of her planned destination site.

In 1935 this International News Photo was published with the following information: London, England . . . Miss Jean Batten, young New Zealand woman flyer, shown with the plane [de Havilland Gipsy Moth] in which she left Lympne Airdrome here for Morocco today, November 11. Miss Batten will then await favorable weather at Morocco, for the start of her planned solo, South Atlantic flight. If successful she will be the first woman to have accomplished the feat. Natal, Brazil, will be Miss Batten's objective.

But, Jean's ordeal was not over. She announced that she would spend the night in Natal and fly 1,400 miles to Rio de Janeiro the next day. She took off, but she didn't arrive. Brazilian Air Force pilots equipped with WACO biplanes searched for her and discovered that she and the Gull had endured a forced landing on a beach 175 miles north of Rio. A loose connection in her fuel line drained her last gas tank dry. The timing was crucial – had the fuel line disconnected over the Atlantic, she might never have been seen again.

Intriguingly, the record for crossing the Atlantic from England to Natal had been held by Amy Johnson's husband, Jim Mollison. Jean was able to beat his record by almost a day. Her reception in Brazil was every bit as thunderous and generous in praise as had been her adoring crowds in Australia and in England.

Much was accorded Jean in her glory years. In addition to receiving the Order of the Southern Cross, an honor previously limited solely to British Empire members of royal birth, the Harmon Trophy was presented three times to Jean by the United States. Jean also received the Challenge Trophy from the U.S.-based Women's International Association of Aeronautics (WIAA). This organization was founded by Mrs. Elizabeth Lippincott McQueen, an exceedingly wealthy woman who, though thwarted in her own attempt to become a pilot, became a sponsor and benefactor of other women involved in aviation. Beth McQueen, instrumental in helping to organize the 1929 "Powder Puff Derby," joined the long list of those who lavished honor on Jean Batten, an aviatrix who personified courage, persistence and great accomplishment.

Aida de Acosta

She was First to Fly

As the nineteenth century turned into the twentieth, discoveries, inventions and experiments in powered flight abounded. Kites, balloons, dirigibles, and flimsy hand-wrought winged machines consumed the passions of creative minds. Engineering drawings probed the secrets of flight and the architects of adventure explored their fantasies. The opportunity to fly hovered but one discovery away.

Alberto Santos-Dumont was part of this feverish curiosity. Enamored with balloons and airships, this Brazilian-born French engineer proved more inventive than most. It began, oddly enough, with his becoming aware of an Arctic adventure that caught his attention and inspired him – Andrée's Polar Expedition of 1896. In hopes of reaching the North Pole and fascinated with long balloon voyages, Professor S. A. Andrée and two crewmen departed Sweden in a quest for fame and discovery via exploits in a hydrogen balloon. Their departure was publicized in periodicals and news items and Santos-Dumont became interested in the choice of strong, but light Chinese pongee silk for the bag and in Andrée's planned use of directional drag ropes that dangled beneath the balloon and directed its course. That the Andrée party disappeared mysteriously only intensified the publicity and further excited the imagination of this clever man. Santos-Dumont determined to become adept in the design and art of flying lighter-than-air ships.

He sought the engineer of the Andrée balloon to place an order. While waiting for a balloon to be built to his specifications, Santos-Dumont practiced making balloon ascents and landings and, by 1898, he was ready to solo his own design – his "Number 1".

Santos-Dumont continued designing, building and flying and, in 1901, he was heralded for having powered a balloon with an internal combustion engine. His activities excited a wide following and, after he flew his "Number 6" over Paris, circling the Eiffel Tower and returning to his departure point at Parc Saint Cloud, his fans were ecstatic. For this feat he earned the Deutsch Prize of 50,000 francs. After giving generously to his workmen, he offered a sizeable amount of the award to the poor of Paris. This further endeared him to the public and, in his native Brazil, he became honored as the Father of Aviation.

But, it was Santos-Dumont's "Number 9", the "Baladeuse" that captured the attention of Aida de Acosta, a privileged teenaged Cuban/American who was visiting Paris with her mother. The young Latino evidently demonstrated such keen interest in his airship that he gave her instruction in the control and handling of his aerial machine.

Santos-Dumont, who had never allowed another to fly his dirigibles, gave Aida de Acosta three lessons and then allowed her to solo the airship between Neuilly and Bagatelle in June 1903. To assist in the navigation, Santos-Dumont pedaled his bicycle within gesturing distance below her route of flight.

It is generally true that those at a pivotal point in history do not think of it in those terms – they are simply living life and pursuing their interests and their dreams. That they achieve notoriety, media attention, fame, or, in particular instances, establish a first, is generally an accident of time, place, effort, and fate. It may be, however, in this plucky young woman's case, that she actually did say to Santos-Dumont, as she is attributed on the early aviators website: "I want to fly alone. I want to be the first woman to pilot an aeroplane."

And fly she did! Aida became the first woman to solo a powered aircraft, coached by her mentor below. His "Number 9," which rose with a gasbag capacity of 220 cubic meters and was powered by a three horsepower motor, was created to demonstrate the feasibility of urban travel. Now, Aida took the controls and handled "Baladeuse" toward a large gathering of sports enthusiasts enjoying a polo match. She not only landed in the field, she took off once again and returned. The crowd went wild and, when her parents heard of her amazing achievement, they insisted that the voices of the press be silenced.

It wasn't until 1933 when Helen S. Waterhouse, the aviation editor of the *Akron Beacon Journal*, disclosed the little known truth of this momentous flight. Believing that a young woman should be named in periodicals only when she marries or when she dies, Aida de Acosta's parents pressured Santos-Dumont to withhold their daughter's identity and, according to *Women in Transportation*, "The negative publicity and parental outrage caused Santos-Dumont to conceal the identity of the pilot, describing her only as 'the heroine, a young and very pretty Cuban, prominent in New York Society,' in his book *Dans L'Air*."

It was also in the 1930s that the mystery of Andrée's Polar Expedition of 1896 was solved. A study from the University of Kansas reported that a Norwegian vessel reached White Island. The men aboard were hunting for seals and walrus and also carried a scientific expedition to study the glaciers and seas of the Arctic Ocean. White Island was normally inaccessible as it was generally blanketed in thick ice fog and surrounded by thick polar pack ice. Purely by happenstance, they came upon a boatswain's hook engraved with "Andrée's Polar Expedition, 1896." They pursued the initial artifact and, though the task was arduous and grim, discovered human remains of the ill-fated balloon voyage and saw to it that they were returned to Sweden. The Norwegian Expedition found valuable relics of the Swedish Andrée Expedition at about the same time as Helen Waterhouse discovered the truth about the first woman to solo Santos-Dumont's powered aerial machine.

Major Nicole Malachowski

A Team Player

Thunderbirds live in legends and myths, symbolizing power, agility, strength and nobility. Thought to be a mighty god by some Native Americans, the Thunderbird is also believed to be a giant supernatural bird inhabiting the highest summits. At Nellis Air Force Base, Las Vegas, Nevada, hangared beneath dramatic, rugged, red mountains, these legendary creatures have taken a human form. There the Thunderbirds, members of the United States Air Force Flight Demonstration Team, are one with the sleek F-16 Fighting Falcons that give them wing. Like their legendary counterparts, they also represent power, agility, strength and nobility.

When you pass through the doorway of those hangars, part-work space and part-museum, the walls bear colorful images resplendent in red, white and blue that celebrate the teamwork essential to a successful unit. A plaque states, "In these halls you will find mirrored an honest pride, an almost unbelievable attention to detail, and a spirit of achievement that touches and inspires everything that is done here."

Since November 2005, when she was selected, and March 2006, when she first performed as a pilot and team member, Major Nicole Malachowski has been unique in attaining a place in the Thunderbirds' lofty aerie. She is the first woman pilot selected to fly with the elite squadron. She is the first woman to fly as a pilot with any major U.S. military demonstration team. She is a legend in her own time.

As a high school student, Nicole, who calls Las Vegas home, enrolled in flight lessons and during her leisure hours, she rode her bicycle to the North Las Vegas Airport to hang out with pilot friends. She credits the Nevada Civil Air Patrol with having made flying a reality for her and she credits her parents for their supportive role. With the remarkable Air Force team based in Las Vegas and operating in and out of Nellis AFB, she couldn't have helped but be inspired by those whose ranks she now has joined.

A 1996 graduate of the United States Air Force Academy, with a bachelor's degree in management, Nicole was trained in gliders at the Academy. She went on to become an instructor pilot, a role in which

Photos: Department of the Air Force, USAF Thunderbirds

she served for three years. Following undergraduate pilot training at Columbus AFB, Mississippi, she trained in the F-15E at Seymour Johnson AFB, North Carolina and was assigned to F-15Es of the 494th Fighter Squadron, RAF Lakenheath, England. During her training, she flew the T-37, T-38, AT-38, F-15E and now flies the F-16C/D, No. 3, Right Wing. As a Thunderbird, Nicole personifies precision, professionalism, pride, and patriotism.

Acting on a suggestion that she apply to become a Thunderbird from her husband, Major Paul Malachowski, an F-15E weapons systems officer, a "Whizzo," she sought her coveted assignment. To submit an application, she had to have logged a minimum of 1,000 flight hours in fighter or trainer jets, include letters of recommendation, a biography and a detailed explanation of her motivation to fly with the elite crew. Selected to be interviewed and flight tested at Nellis, she made history.

"The Air Force has so many great opportunities out there," she said, "and all you have to do is apply. It never hurts to try!"

Interviews and recommendations must have indicated beyond a doubt that Nicole had exemplary flying skills. Of almost equal importance, she understands and practices the skills of being a team player. Being "a good stick" is paramount, but close, fast, tight formation flying demands the utmost in mutual dependency and trust. Nicole doesn't simply exhibit the values and character traits necessary to be an aerial team player, she lives them.

"I never thought I could be a Thunderbird," she once said. But, a Thunderbird she is! Until November 2007, she will be a vital member of this Air Combat Command unit composed of eight pilots (six are demonstration pilots), four support officers, four civilians, and approximately 120 enlisted personnel who represent the Active USAF, the Air National Guard and the Air Force Reserve. Officers accept two-year assignments and enlisted personnel serve for between three and four. Replacements annually alter the mix of experience levels as reassignments affect almost one third of all personnel.

Flown smoothly and artistically, formation flying is compelling; a powerful aerial ballet; the pride of the pilot at the controls inspires the countless air show fans who stand in awe below. As the presentation of the best of the U.S. Air Force, it is intended to motivate, inspire, retain and recruit for the modern U.S. Air Force. Two solo pilots, including, for 2007-2008, the Thunderbirds' second woman pilot, Major Samantha Weeks, demonstrate precision maneuvering to showcase the capabilities of the Lockheed Martin multirole fighter. The objectives of the entire team are: to instill confidence in the competence of the nation's air forces, to inspire esprit de corps among those who wear the Air Force blue, to enrich Air Force community relations, and to be representatives of freedom and of good will around the globe.

Since its activation in 1953, the Thunderbirds represent the professionalism of those who fly, maintain and support their aircraft, their service and their country. In 2005, then-Captain Nicole Malachowski was the first woman pilot selected for this highly specialized unit. Women represented the Thunderbirds in a wide variety of roles; Nicole was the first pilot.

Nicole noted, "What better way could there be to share the Air Force story?"

During the 2007 schedule, the Thunderbirds represented over 500,000 men and women of their service in commemorating the 60th Anniversary of the United States Air Force. They flew in 70 air shows in 22 states and nine countries. For the first time in Thunderbird history, the team performed in Ireland. Their performances overseas mark the first European tour since September 11, 2001.

Knowing what it is to serve, having piloted F-15Es during Operation Iraqi Freedom, Nicole continued her service to our nation in the role of ambassador of the U.S. Air Force. Clad in the crisp uniform, earning the trust of her teammates, flying in incredibly close proximity to one another at breathtaking speed and demonstrating the excellence of one of the finest fighting forces in the world must have been the penultimate experience and responsibility this young woman had yet undertaken. In her historic role, she embraced the qualities of her team's namesake as she mounted her wings of red, white and blue. Few role models have such a platform on which to perform and such an opportunity to instill pride in countless millions of fans. May she – and they – keep their eyes on the sky.

Having gained high-performance fighter experience as an instructor and flight commander in F-15E Strike Eagle aircraft, Nicole flew during Operation Iraqi Freedom Watch. She recalled an unforgettable moment in January 2005 in which she led a two-ship of F-15Es over Baghdad as part of Armed Support for the Iraqi's first election. She said, "Baghdad is a bustling city and we flew at an altitude that made it obvious we were patrolling to make their first vote as safe for all Iraqis as possible. The streets were so empty that my heart sank. I longed to see the people feel confident enough to go to election booths. I was hopeful that Iraqis would get their opportunities to exercise what we in the United States take for granted – our vote. I saw one man walking alone in the middle of the street and called him the 'Pied Piper of Sadr City.' Soon, people emerged from buildings to follow him and then there were hundreds of people following along in an organized, orderly line that stretched far behind him. I was so proud of our Americans, so proud of the Iraqis."

494TH FIGHTER SQ

Mimi Tompkins

Aftermath!

In one agonizing, horrific, and thunderous clap, life changed decisively for then-First Officer Madeline "Mimi" Tompkins. It was her turn at the controls; the weather allowed for visual flight rules; no threatening meteorological conditions had been reported and the takeoff and climb had been unexceptional. Yet, having just hand-flown the Boeing 737 from Hilo, Hawaii to 24,000 feet toward a destination of Honolulu, Oahu – a flight she'd made innumerable times – the unimaginable became reality. In lieu of her expected twenty-eight minute, normal, and uneventful flight, a fuselage crack had widened and, with a ferocious whoosh, 18 feet of the fuselage's upper crown skin – from the cabin entrance door to just forward of the wings – tore away. Aloha Airlines Flight 243 suffered explosive decompression!

Mimi, as the second to be flying right seat for Aloha Airlines that fateful day, had begun her trip routinely. Prior to her boarding, at 11 a.m. of 28 April 1988, the captain, Robert Schornsteimer, and another first officer had started at five a.m. and completed three of the airline's planned six round-trip inter-island flights. For Aloha's crewmembers, island-hopping was familiar and pleasurable. Accustomed to the happy babble of tourists enjoying aerial glimpses of the beautiful volcanic islands, they were especially conscientious about their passengers' comfort. They reveled in sharing their home, their special island paradise, with travelers.

Flight 243 was crewed by two pilots and three flight attendants; a FAA air traffic controller occupied the jump seat and 89 passengers were aboard. When the horrendous blast occurred, Mimi felt her head snap backwards and she saw debris, including pieces of gray insulation, floating in the cockpit. The professionalism of the two pilots immediately kicked in, Captain Schornsteimer took the controls, all

Hired by Aloha Airlines in 1979, Mimi Tompkins made history as Aloha's first woman pilot. Her career path has taken her to the left seat as a captain and has given her opportunities to help others by becoming a spokesperson and educator for Critical Stress Management.

three in the cockpit donned oxygen masks and the captain opened the flow of oxygen to the passengers.

The noise was deafening and the pilots gestured with hand signals to communicate with one another. As the captain initiated a rapid descent, Mimi turned to the radios. She tuned the transponder to 7700 – the emergency code – and she attempted to transmit their intentions to divert to their nearest alternative, Maui's airport located east of the town of Kahului.

Flight 243 departed Hilo at 1:25 p.m. The horror began at 1:43 p.m. and, acting quickly, Mimi declared the emergency. Although the captain admitted later that he'd glanced over his shoulder and noticed the cockpit door missing and blue sky in lieu of the ceiling of the first class cabin, the immediacy of the situation demanded complete concentration on a safe descent and a landing as soon as practicable.

In the cockpit, as the captain handled the controls, Mimi transmitted to the Air Route Traffic Control Center (ARTCC), but the noise level precluded hearing any response. She couldn't be sure of having reached controllers' ears; yet, she continued to transmit and ultimately switched frequencies to the Kahului Tower. At 1:48, Mimi had established two-way communication with a tower operator on Maui. She again declared the emergency and the Maui Air Traffic Control facility took over the handling of the flight. Five minutes later, she radioed, "We cannot communicate with the flight attendants. We'll need assistance for the passengers when we land."

Two minutes later, one gear-down light failed to illuminate upon extension of the gear and Mimi advised, "We won't have a nose gear. We'll need all the equipment you've got."

Shortly thereafter, their difficulties were compounded again. In maneuvering for the approach, a yaw indicated the failure of the left engine. Fortunately, both pilots were thoroughly familiar with the airport, located on an edge of a land bridge between Haleakala and the West Maui Mountain Range. Captain Schornsteimer established a descent for landing, touching down at 1:58 – a thirty-three minute ordeal that has been called a "miracle." With a total of 95 aboard, it was miraculous that only eight were seriously injured, 57 suffered minor injuries and 29 were spared.

It wasn't until they were on the ground that Mimi and Captain Schornsteimer learned of the tragic loss of one of the flight attendants; C.B. Lansing was swept from the aircraft with the explosion. Her body was never recovered. They also learned that a second flight attendant sustained serious injuries – a concussion and head lacerations – and of heroic bravery on the part of the third, who crawled along the aisle to assist terrified and wounded passengers.

Right before their eyes was unspeakable confusion; the portion of the ceiling ripped from the fuselage, wires dangled, seats were askew and debris was widely scattered. People were bleeding, moaning and crying. Although Mimi and others hurried to help administer to the injured, she felt woefully lacking in nursing skills. And, too soon, her angst was complicated by pressure from news reporters who competed for attention.

In the days and weeks that followed, incredible stress affected all who were involved. For the flight crew, Mimi admitted, "We are trained for emergencies. We simply did our job."

Yes, she and the crewmembers acted quickly and well. But, some emergencies demand more than others and some factors are beyond the training an airline pilot receives. In the aftermath of those terrible moments, Mimi was faced with repetitive and countless inquiries from the Federal Aviation Administration (FAA), National Transportation Safety Board (NTSB), insurance companies, and attorneys, and besieged with hearings and media interviews. She was granted little time to come to grips with the terror she had experienced.

Mimi returned to work and soon upgraded to captain; yet, she suffered sleeplessness, sudden nightmares, and recurring dreams. In 1989, when flight 811, a United Airlines 747 en route from Honolulu, experienced an explosive decompression that was fatal to nine passengers, the damaged aircraft returned to and was parked on the Oahu airport within her view. Intrusive memories, so common to post-traumatic stress disorder (PTSD), plagued her.

Through intervention from the FAA's Dr. Pachel, Dr. Audie Davis,

Mimi was at the controls of Flight 243 in 1988 when the Aloha Airlines Boeing 737 experienced explosive decompression. Working feverishly, the two-person cockpit crew recovered at Kahului Airport on Maui in what has been termed, "a miracle landing."

and Dr. Don Hudson, she received vital guidance and help. She not only conquered the inevitable stress that follows such a tragedy, but in turn, she has devoted time and comfort to help countless others whose lives have also been shocked with sudden and frightening realities. She has strengthened her courage and deepened her compassion.

Mimi has written, "Hijackings, passenger medical emergencies, system malfunctions; as professional pilots, our jobs place us in a high-risk category. We must perform routine duties with a constant awareness that routine could turn to crisis in a split second. What is often forgotten is that stress reactions as a result of trauma are normal. Post-traumatic stress disorder (PTSD) is a more serious psychiatric diagnosis. . . . While the professional crewmember has honed risk awareness and instant appropriate responses to a razor-sharp edge, he/she often has not been as effective in learning how to handle the medical and psychological aftermath of a critical incident."

The Executive Board of the Air Line Pilots Association (ALPA) established a critical incident response program (CIRP) to educate members about critical incident stress management and to help prevent the onset of post traumatic stress. Mimi wrote, "All of the crewmembers and one of the flight attendant accident investigators for the Aloha 243 accident developed PTSD within two years of this event. Crewmembers have a tendency to feel that asking for support is a sign of weakness. Unfortunately, ignoring the side effects of stress can have almost irreversible effects. And proper treatment is essential to ensure complete recovery. Regardless of the degree of critical incident stress or PTSD, early intervention can greatly reduce the time and expense of the treatment. . . . By providing an avenue for people to talk about a particularly stressful event soon after the event occurs, they are better able to process the event."

Mimi served on a task force to investigate critical incident response and accepted the responsibility of researching existing programs to evaluate them for use with pilots. "We all had different skills," she said. "People would listen to what I had to say because of the accident, but the program would never have gotten off the ground without the hard work of the capable people I served with on the project team."

Firefighters, paramedics, EMTs and police officers have undergone and benefited from aspects of this program. It was time for aircraft crewmembers to follow suit. Mimi was involved in forming the task force and continued to serve after ALPA adopted the program. The first class was taught in 1994 and, to offer assistance after a crash fatal to all aboard occurred in October 1994, she was part of the group called upon to debrief accident investigators who worked at the crash site.

"It was pretty frightening," Mimi said. "We'd been through the training and we'd all been certified, but suddenly we were faced with a real-life crisis. We avoided the use of the term 'counselor' and labeled our effort as education. Now, as educators, we were going to have to prove ourselves."

When critical incident response was elevated to an official committee status, Mimi accepted the role of chairperson and served from 1996 to 2002. She will tell you that she gained more than she has given, but those she has helped might differ. Many who have suffered from PTSD, and who have not received intervention, have left their careers for other jobs. She knows personally the effects trauma can inflict upon behavior, emotions, and one's physiological and spiritual well-being and she has been tireless in educating others. Having helped to create a model for critical incident stress management, she and others have intervened to mitigate the affects of stress and to enable flight crewmembers and their families to get back to normal after having undergone crises.

First Officer Mimi Tompkins performs the walk-around ground inspection on her first day with Aloha. Relatively few women pilots had been hired by any U.S. airlines prior to Mimi's becoming a crewmember in 1979 and her first day on the job drew media attention. Little did she know the extent of such attention until the fateful 1988 incident.

Courtesy of Mimi Tompkins

Through ALPA, all airlines profit from the expertise Mimi obtained and has been willing to share. Captain Mimi Tompkins ably continues to handle the controls of Aloha Airlines' Boeing 737s. She exudes experience and confidence. Perhaps, best of all, she has the satisfaction felt by the educator who has, through sharing experience, knowledge, and expertise, helped countless others avoid being paralyzed by stress.

E. Lillian Todd

A Mother of Invention

Radio Club of America

Who could have predicted that New York City's E. Lillian Todd could have wrought such wonders? Not only did she design and build a flyable model dirigible, but she is the first woman in the world to design and build a heavier-than-air machine. Her ingenuity extended to powered flight and beyond.

Her biplane glider was exhibited in 1906 at a show in New York's Madison Square Garden. It was to be carried down an incline at the run until its fans revolved, which activated two propellers. To land the craft, she created a valve exercised by the pilot that reduced the air reaching the fans which, in turn, slowed the propellers and allowed a settling of the craft onto pneumatic wheels.

Miss Lillian improved upon her designs, involving the Wittemann brothers, who had opened the first U.S. airplane manufacturing plant on their family estate on Staten Island, New York. The Wittemanns built their first powered craft in 1906 and she benefited from their experience.

Miss Lillian proposed testing her "aeroplane" on a Staten Island street; but, her request was denied by the Commissioner of the Borough of Richmond of New York City. He wrote, on 20 September 1909, "I took up . . . the matter of your proposed aeroplane test on Southfield Boulevard and we are advised that such an application should be denied as the charter does not in its present form contemplate any such use of the public street . . ."

Undaunted, Miss Lillian pressed for flight testing on Long Island. Her biplane, with curved, bird-like upper wings, proved its airworthiness by being flown on 7 November 1910 by Didier Masson, a French pilot. The next day the *New York Herald* noted: "After years of effort, Miss E. Lillian Todd realized her ambition when she had the pleasure of seeing a biplane, the work of her hands and brain, fly across the Garden City aviation field. . . . [Masson] ran the machine across the ground, then went to the air for twenty feet and made a turn at the far end, returning to the starting place, where he was enthusiastically received by Miss Todd and the crowd."

Undoubtedly the crowd included teenaged boys Miss Lillian encouraged in their interest in model airplanes: Frank King, W. E. D. Stokes, Jr., George Eltz, and Frederick Seymour. In 1907, Miss Lillian had mentored these young men and formed the Junior Aero Club of the United States. Her biplane and hot air balloon models were exhibited at their Junior Aero Club Exhibition in 1909 and, for club activities, Miss Lillian urged the design, building and testing of their own aircraft models. She led by example, building model airplanes, a steamship, an electrically operated doll, which was credited with having raised $435 for the purchase of gramophones for World War I aviators, and an electric powered hot air balloon inspired by those created by the famed balloonist, Thomas Scott Baldwin.

Exploring additional interests, the boys delved into the idea of sending messages without wires and branched eagerly into experiments with wireless telegraphy. They named Miss Lillian as the Honorary President of their new pursuit, which became the Junior Wireless Club, which formed the historical beginnings of the Radio Club of America, Inc. The inventive Miss E. Lillian Todd can be credited with more than historical firsts in aviation; she can be highly respected for having played a major role in the creation of RCA.

E. Lillian Todd was a creative inventor. She encouraged yougsters to form the Junior Aero Club. Its members' dual interests in aircraft and wireless telegraphy has resulted in the Radio Club of America – RCA.

The National Aeronautic Association (NAA) grew out of the 1905 Aero Club of America (ACA) that, with the merger with eight others, became the Fédération Aéronautique Internationale. Miss E. Lillian Todd– the first female aircraft designer – showed her biplane model at the Junior Aero Club Exhibition in 1909 and followed that with her own powered aircraft.

Connie Tobias
Harriet is Whispering, "Go, Connie!"

The night was festive. In the vast gallery of the National Museum of the United States Air Force, Dayton, Ohio, celebrants gathered to honor the 101st Anniversary of Powered Flight and to remember the momentous contributions of Dayton's own Wright Brothers. It was 17 December 2004 and the legacies of Wilbur and Orville surrounded the guests. From the huge B-52 Stratofortress and the sleek F-22 Raptor to the pilotless Global Hawk, these fruits of the Wrights' labors emphasized the debt owed to the brilliance and tenacity of the famed brothers. There to repeat the admonition that Dayton's heritage should be widely celebrated and long revered was the featured speaker, Dayton native Connie Tobias.

Connie, an Airbus 330/300 pilot, demonstrates the same qualities of those fellow Daytonians. A Summa Cum Laude graduate of Ohio University with a bachelors degree in aviation and an academic masters degree in engineering, Connie has spent her post-college years with her head and her heart in the sky. Connie was one of the earliest women hired by Piedmont and currently flies for US Airways. She can list over 21,000 flight hours and sixty-plus aircraft that she has flown. But, Connie can also claim having piloted several fascinating aircraft that make her accomplishments unique.

Having logged four hours of flight in a Blériot, which gave her experience with wing warping techniques, Connie went on to fly airplanes that replicated test flights made only by the Wrights themselves. She successfully piloted exact replicas, built by the Wright Brothers Aeroplane Company: the 1902 and 1902 modified Wright Gliders, the 1903 Wright Flyer, and has trained to fly the 1905 Wright Flyer III.

How would a modern pilot obtain flight experience in a 1909 Blériot? Because of her airline piloting and her likeness to the pioneer pilot, Harriet Quimby, Connie was invited by members of the Collings Foundation to perform as Quimby. Connie recognized opportunity knocking and accepted immediately.

The stated purpose of the Collings Foundation is to support

Connie Tobias' sights are set on piloting a Blériot across the English Channel in commemoration of Harriet Quimby's 1912 aviation first. She was impressed with Harriet's obvious mastery of, "a machine that modern aviators struggle to get aloft." Connie has the tenacity and the talent to recreate history.

Courtesy of Connie Tobias

transportation-related events and to present living history in an effort to encourage Americans to better understand their heritage. As the Foundation owns a 1909 Blériot XI, they searched for a woman pilot to reenact the role of Harriet Quimby. Connie was a natural. In Harriet, Connie met her alter-ego. Like her, Connie is a tall, slender, beautiful brunette and, like her, Connie has the same daring and determination necessary to stretch her wings and achieve great things.

Connie said, "We were both born into modest, hard-working families; we were competitive and goal-oriented and we, of course, shared our passion for flight."

Harriet Quimby is remembered as the first U.S. woman to achieve a piloting license, #37, issued in 1911 by the Aero Club of America and the Fédération Aéronautique Internationale. She learned to fly in New York in a Moisant monoplane, built on the lines of the Blériot monoplanes designed in France. In 1912, Harriet borrowed a single-seat Blériot XI and made history as the first woman to pilot an aircraft across the English Channel. She took off from England on 16 April 1912 into the soft advection fog of early morning and landed 59 minutes later on the sandy beach near Hardelot, France. Harriet should have been regaled with the royal treatment given to such aerial explorers as Anne Lindbergh, Amelia Earhart, Jean Batten, Amy Johnson, and the others about whom publicity hounds thronged. However, the RMS Titanic struck an iceberg just before midnight on 14 April 1912 and sank almost three hours later, taking with it approximately 1,500 persons. It was excruciating news and it dominated the attention of the media.

Over the ensuing years, Harriet's flying outfit has probably received as much, if not more, attention than the woman. She was avant-garde; she designed a striking purple satin flying suit that tucked into tall shiny boots; she covered her head with an attractive and protective hood. Connie, too, looks striking in the outfit that matches Harriet's, complete to goggles and gloves.

Having learned a great deal about the woman, it was up to Connie

Only five pilots, in addition to Orville and Wilbur, have succeeded in flying a 1903 Wright Flyer. Connie Tobias has over 21,000 flight hours. As the only woman among the five, she pilots a rare group of replica aircraft: the 1902 Wright Glider, 1903 Wright Flyer, and a 1909 Blériot.

to familiarize herself with the aeroplane. She said, "I traveled to Stow, Massachusetts, to fly with the Collings Foundation. The Blériot was something else! For a start, there were no ailerons, no brakes, no instruments other than the rpm and oil pressure gauges, no turn and bank, no airspeed. After all we're taught today about the dangers of skidding an airplane, the best way to turn the Blériot was by flat, skidding turns. With the lifting tail surface, there is a tuck tendency to this plane in the air. And, drag? It took full power constantly to overcome the drag. The rudder was small and there wasn't sufficient response. I became a human trim tab.

"Actually, only one attitude struck me as safe – straight and level. It was increasingly impressive that Harriet had safely crossed the Channel in this plane. Her mastery of a machine that modern aviators struggle to get aloft secures her status as a true and fearless aviation pioneer. She must have been truly exceptional!"

Connie appeared as Harriet at an Aviation Heritage Festival at Daniel Webster College, Nashua, New Hampshire. Resplendent in her purple flying suit, Connie drove a 1905 Cadillac to the Collings' 1909 Blériot and participated fully in the flying tribute to aviation's past. Her goals: education and inspiration.

Connie has taken that inspiration into a highly successful effort to assist young people who have, like she, their heads and hearts in the sky. Connie's education was gained at Ohio University's Fritz J. and Dolores H. Russ College of Engineering and Technology. Through her alma mater, she has established the Harriet Quimby Scholarship Fund. The scholarship is awarded to a female or male student at Ohio University who exemplifies Harriet's attitude and drive.

Connie demonstrated those qualities when she spoke at the 101st Anniversary celebration of the Wright Brothers' first powered flight. After her compelling description of her training and execution of those unique and challenging flights, Connie was presented with the National Aeronautic Association's Commendation Award.

Connie said, in part, "I flew a lot of antique aircraft, especially taildraggers, to regain the touch and the feel of hands-on control. I took up hang gliding in preparation for the Wright Glider.

"I earned wisdom! Despite all the preparation, my first 1902 Wright Glider flight ended with an unceremonious smack onto the ground. During my second glide, I simply could not hold onto the craft during the landing. My body sailed through the air and I sheepishly belly-flopped onto the sand. Interestingly, I read that same evening that Wilbur Wright had the same hilarious mishap one hundred years prior to mine. We both solved the dilemma by moving back more deeply into the hip cradle.

"Then, on the third and final try, the wind was higher and more brisk. It took courage to ask the team to launch me. But, once launched, I whispered aloud, 'I've got it!' I hovered like a bird; it was rhythm, precision, and timing."

Other than Wilbur and Orville Wright, only five pilots in the world have successfully flown controlled, sustained flight in a 1903 Wright Flyer. Connie made history as the first and only woman to succeed. She has set a goal to recreate Harriet's Channel crossing.

This high-flying pilot who has crossed the Atlantic Ocean over 1,000 times has her heart set on piloting a fragile, wood, wire and fabric Blériot across the English Channel. Our eyes will be on her bit of sky.

Joann Osterud

Inverted

Once Dorothy Hester Stenzel had invited Joann Osterud to tackle her long-standing record in outside loops, Joann trained hard to ready herself for the bodily punishment of inverted flight. Joann's doctor said she would "look like hamburger when she got done," but she trained anyway. She not only ended the long reign of Dorothy's record; but, accompanied by music played over her in-cockpit tape recorder that rhythmically kept the beat, she looped on to better the male record of 180.

Prior to the record setting flight in July, 1989, Joann had been preparing her airplane and her own body for weeks. Her airplane, a small, boxy Sorrell Hiperbipe, a negative stagger biplane that she named *Supernova*, was equipped with an electric transfer pump to keep the fuel flowing while inverted. Special straps were added to hold her feet on the rudder pedals and to reduce excessive flopping of her head. To accustom her body to the rigors of hanging from her seat and shoulder harnesses for an extended time, Joann had a contraption built that would condition her to negative Gs and strenuous outside maneuvering. The equipment allowed her to hang upside down for long periods of time.

Joann's was not simply a record-setting flight; it benefited charity. United Way of Southwestern Oregon received the results of pledges, which obligated the donors to pay United Way according to the numbers of outside loops completed. In addition, the youngster who collected the most pledges was rewarded with a flight with Joann.

"It was the highlight of 1989 to set the world record at North Bend, Oregon, Airshow," said Joann. "I did 208 outside loops in two hours, four minutes and thirty-eight seconds. That's 1.6774 loops per minute. It was a double thrill for me to know that Dorothy Hester Stenzel was in the audience. I've always admired her and, knowing she was there rooting for me, well, it kind of eased the pain of taking away her fifty-eight-year-old record. In the process, we raised considerable sums for United Way, so it was more than a silly stunt, although some people still question my intelligence."

This from a Reed College graduate, with post-graduate work in science and public policy taken at Massachusetts Institute of Technology. However, having already been introduced to flight while in college, Joann would be the first to admit that much of her time at MIT was spent gazing out of the windows at the billowing clouds that invited her into the sky. She opted for a career in aviation and holds the distinction of being the first woman hired as a pilot by Alaska Airlines. Hers has been a long and successful career.

It is fact that preparation, experience, practice and talent

Joann Osterud, air show star, was hired as the first woman pilot by Alaska Airlines in April 1975. Four years later, at the Abbotsford Air Show, she soared to aerobatic fame piloting the Stephens Akro.

contributed to Joann's successful record, but it is lesser known that, having accustomed herself to flying upside down, she sought further records in inverted flight. In 1990, she eyed the records for endurance and distance. Again, she aimed to best a record held 58 years.

During the Depression, Milo Burcham sought an endurance record to focus attention on aviation jobs. He purchased a Boeing 100 from Pratt & Whitney that had been used as a flying test-bed for engines. His mechanic suggested that he invert the engine itself and Burcham, who later became a world aerobatic champion and a Lockheed production test pilot, set his inverted flight record in 1933 by completing a flight from Long Beach to San Diego and back in four hours, five minutes and 22 seconds.

In 1990, when Joann was preparing, a French pilot, Jean-Jacques Lancereau, set a world record flying inverted for 300 miles. She challenged his record, too.

Joann plotted a course from Vancouver International Airport, British Columbia, over the sparsely populated, but geologically dramatic Fraser River to Vanderhoof. She was accompanied by another renowned air show star, Bud Granley, flying chase. Less than half-way into the flight, Joann noticed a drop in oil pressure. Initially she attributed it to a gauge malfunction; but, aware of the mountainous terrain and long miles ahead, she landed at Lillooet. It was a fortuitous decision; her aircraft had only one cup of oil remaining. Her record attempt was thwarted.

By the next year, and in a Gordon Price Ultimate 10-300S biplane, Joann prepared again. She called it "taking care of unfinished business."

Again escorted by Bud Granley and by additional chase planes necessary to obtain media coverage and record verification, Joann departed Vancouver on 24 July 1991, rolled the Ultimate inverted and proceeded upside-down to Vanderhoof. There she was scheduled to perform during the three day Vanderhoof Air Show. Again she raised money for a good cause, this time the Vanderhoof Air Cadets, Squadron #899. The Cadets sold time estimates of Joann's trip and set aside the proceeds in support of their many programs for youngsters between the ages of 12 and 18.

Joann set world records for endurance and distance by flying inverted for four hours, 38 minutes and 10 seconds over a 658-mile course. Her flight, sanctioned by the Fédération Aéronautique Internationale, the world's air sports league, through the Canadian Sport Airplane Association, was a spectacular success. That she went on to perform in the air show during the rest of the weekend attests to her tenacity and her commitment.

She wrote, "Now, I have flown upside-down longer and farther than anyone else on record. I also know why the previous record stood for fifty-eight years! If I had known all the time (and money!) that would be involved, I'd never have started. But, once begun and once

The Ultimate 10 – 300S, designed by Gordon Price, was meant to offer competition pilots a wing with an improved roll rate over the Pitts. It took on a life of its own and Joann took her Ultimate – the original "Bluehawk" – to record-breaking achievements in inverted distance and endurance. Its inherent strength proved to make a difference between life and death.

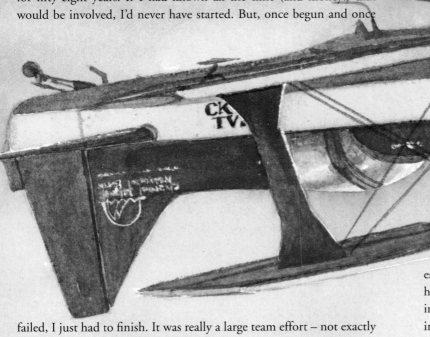

failed, I just had to finish. It was really a large team effort – not exactly something you just go do on a Sunday afternoon. I'm in the Guinness Book three times. I just hope no one tries to break my record any time soon so that I'll have to do it again."

It comes as no surprise that air show stars consistently look for new and difficult challenges with which to interest fans. Yet, for all of her advanced preparation and more than a quarter century of aviation experience, Joann endured an agonizing accident on 11 April 1997 – exactly 22 years from the date of her hire by Alaska Airlines. She is fortunate to have survived.

At Yuma International Airport, Arizona, Joann was performing aerobatics to Elvis Presley's "Hearts are Burning," Johnny Cash's "Ring of Fire," and four other fire-related songs. As sunset painted the Arizona desert lavender, she performed her impressive inverted flaming ribbon cut by diving and making two passes in inverted flight through a huge flaming ring. For the third pass – her ribbon cut – her target was a ribbon held on poles across the runway beyond the ring; a strand of fire burned along the ground and fireworks were attached to the tops of the poles. On that fateful pass, seeking to slice the ribbon with her propeller blades, she impacted the ground.

Joann later recalled the turn-around, rolling inverted and establishing her sight picture for the run-in. The next few seconds, however, were a total blank. She did recall hearing the sound of the impact and her visual picture resumed with the sparks created by the inverted slide. An FAA inspector reported that the "Ring of Fire" routine required the pilot to fly directly into the setting sun, then turn around for the inverted passes. The light conditions undoubtedly played a crucial role in the accident; the fact that Joann had purposefully chosen the non-active runway, this one a strip of black asphalt with no centerline or runway markings also figured in the crash.

Joann said, "I lost peripheral vision. My biplane and I slid about one thousand feet, totaling the Ultimate. When the music ended, I remember hearing what sounded like funeral dirge being played over the loud speakers. Renowned air show announcer Danny Clisham was at the microphone, reassuring stunned and silent onlookers.

"I crawled out of the wreckage and headed for the announcer's stand. My ego and my pocketbook were sorely damaged, but I was very lucky to be alive."

Joann's appearance must have elicited a huge collective sigh of relief from her fans. Later, a blogger on the Internet noted, "She showed a lot of class when she rushed up to apologize to the crowd for frightening them."

Joann retired from her successful career as an airline pilot, leaving United Airlines in 2007. The blogger is right. Throughout her long and distinguished career, Joann has shown a lot of class.

Mildred Hemmons Carter

Tuskegee's Own

A young Mildred Hemmons Carter waited throughout World War II for the return of her husband, Herbert Eugene "Gene" Carter, a pilot and maintenance officer in the original 99th Fighter Squadron of the Tuskegee Airmen. Gene and Mildred met as students at Tuskegee Institute and discovered they had more in common than their college educations. Both learned to fly at Tuskegee as part of the Civilian Pilot Training Program (CPTP) launched in 1939 at colleges and universities throughout the nation. It was customary to accept one woman per training class of ten men into the program and, as that special woman at Tuskegee, Mildred was a stand-out. She was highly respected for her determination and her capability.

Only sixteen when she matriculated as a freshman, Mildred had been offered the opportunity to pursue a work/study program and was hired by the coordinator of the Pilot Training Program. This personal introduction was all the inspiration she needed and she sought the chance to fly Piper Cubs with Tuskegee's best. Although she was too young – the minimum age was 18 – Mildred waited another year and her application was accepted. In 1941, the same year that she graduated, she earned her private pilot certificate on February 1st and secured a place in history; she will always be remembered as the first black woman to receive a pilot certificate in the state of Alabama.

In learning to fly under the tutelage of C. Alfred "Chief" Anderson, the man who has been called "The Father of Black Aviation," Mildred and the others had the good fortune of taking lessons with a master. As a young man in 1927, Chief Anderson had saved enough money to pay for flying lessons, but found the way barred.

It was virtually impossible to find someone willing to give flying lessons to a black man. Chief borrowed money from friends to purchase a small aircraft and then searched for someone willing to give him lessons. Fortunately, he discovered a German who, after having served his own country in World War I, migrated to the United States and started an airfield in Pennsylvania known as the Flying Dutchman. In 1929, Chief Anderson became a certificated private pilot and within three years was the first black pilot in the U.S. to obtain the Transport license.

When the United States entered World War II, Gene and the other male pilots began to train for combat roles. Mildred was as qualified as the others; but she was left behind. At that time, U.S. women were not included in military pilot training.

Patriotism engulfed the United States as the citizenry was caught up in the war effort. Qualified men were drafted into military service, including several male graduates of Tuskegee who were licensed pilots, but were drafted into enlisted ranks before the start of the Tuskegee experiment. Mildred was as excluded as they, but more cutting and unforgettable was the abrupt and cold rejection she received in response to her application to become a member of the Women Airforce Service Pilots. She volunteered to fly for her country and was summarily dismissed because of her skin color. She was not the only woman of color to have an application denied, but she would have performed to the best

Mildred, the first black woman to become a Private Pilot in Alabama, was honored to meet the nation's First Lady, Eleanor Roosevelt, when she visited Tuskegee. In the background was Daniel "Chappie" James, the first black four star general in the United States Air Force.

of her ability. It was crushing to know that her service was refused.

Chief Anderson, who also knew what it meant to face discrimination, was a perfect person to encourage Mildred as a flyer. He knew there was a joy in being in control of an airplane and having earned the coveted wings. Mildred profited from her training and gained confidence and self-esteem simply knowing that she was a licensed pilot. During her student days at Tuskegee, she was one of the few to be introduced to and to speak with the nation's First Lady, Eleanor Roosevelt. Mrs. Franklin Roosevelt visited Moton Field and even accepted a ride in a Piper Cub with Chief Anderson as part of her demonstration of support for the Tuskegee Experiment. For her part as a special woman of the Tuskegee Airmen, Mildred has subsequently been feted by other U.S. presidents and their first ladies.

Mildred credited Chief Anderson for the opportunities to continue to fly despite her rejection by the WASP. She said, "He would call and ask, 'Mil, do you want to fly today?' I always said yes. I wasn't logging flight time; I was just having fun." The Carters had returned to live in Tuskegee in 1965 and these flights continued until Chief Anderson was in his eighties. He passed away in 1996.

Women had to campaign for their opportunities to fly for the Women's Auxiliary Flying Service and the Women Airforce Service Pilots. They served without military recognition until 1979. Black men had to fight to prove themselves capable of flying and, thanks to the success of the Tuskegee Experience, they were instrumental in seeing integration occur throughout the United States Air Force. As Bessie Coleman, Willa Brown, Janet Bragg, Dr. Mae Jemison, Mildred Carter, and so many others discovered, black women had the roughest road to hoe. They are all owed hearty kudos. We are enriched by their efforts, their determination and their accomplishments.

Although refused by the WASP, Mildred did participate in WWII as the star of her husband Gene's aircraft. Painted on the fuselage of each of his three P-40s was, "MIKE." Gene gave her the nickname "because she was a tomboy and because she was a pilot who graduated from the same program as I".

Mildred pinned on Gene's Lieutenant's insignia. In one entry in his daily diary, he wrote, "6-Mar-44: We lost Mike III yesterday. I guess I win. Three out of three and I am still here to talk of it. Jerry flak shot a whole section of the engine out. Was able to make a dead stick landing on the beach with the wheels down, so a new engine will fix her up again. But, by then, I hope to have named a P-47 'Big Mike'".

Courtesy H. Eugene Carter Collection

Louise Thaden & Blanche Noyes

A Classic Upset

Louise Thaden and Blanche Noyes were not the first women to compete in the famed Bendix Transcontinental Speed Dash, but they made history in their initial attempt. When introduced in 1931, the Bendix was open to men and women. No women competed. In 1933, Amelia Earhart and Ruth Nichols each raced; both failed to finish. In 1935, Amelia finished in 5th place and Jackie Cochran raced, but fell short. Triumphantly, Louise and Blanche were the first women to take the Bendix Trophy in 1936. Importantly, they were not alone; Laura Ingalls finished in second place and Amelia Earhart came in fifth. It was a memorable year.

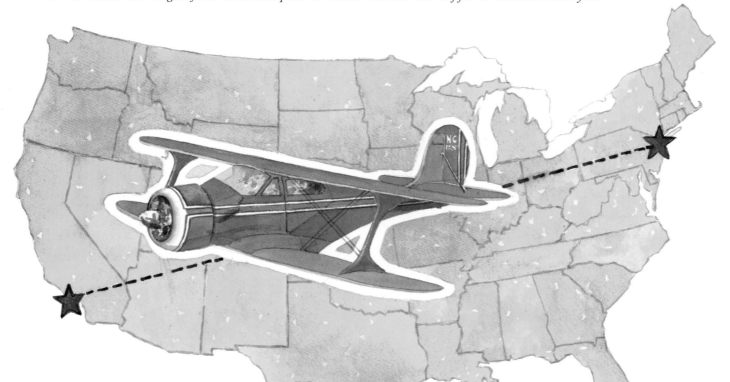

1936 BENDIX TRANSCONTINENTAL

Courtesy William Heaslip Collection

Louise and Blanche piloted a stock Beech C17R Staggerwing powered by a Wright Whirlwind nine cylinder radial engine. It was one of two Bendix airplanes. The airplane that won the race was constructed as #77. Because that particular Staggerwing was sold prior to the race, it was construction #81 that was flown around the country in celebration of the Bendix triumph.

A dealer interested in distributing Travel Air aircraft in San Francisco, California, approached designer Walter Beech in 1927 in Wichita, Kansas. Upon negotiating a deal, he received more than an opportunity to market Beech's biplanes, he gained a marketing assistant. Young Louise McPhetridge was intrigued by aviation in 1927; she was brimming with enthusiasm and eager to be part of the fledgling industry. The dealer, D. C. Warren, agreed to teach Louise the business of aviation and, while they were about it, to fly. It was a young woman's dream come true. On 2 April 1927 she flew to California with her new employer in a Travel Air Model B. Hers was a date with destiny.

By 1929, Travel Air was the world's largest producer of mono- and bi-plane commercial aircraft and Louise helped in their sale by setting record after record. After having received her pilot's license in 1928, she took a Travel Air to an altitude record of 20,260 feet. She set a women's endurance record by remaining aloft in for 22 hours and 3 minutes and, in August 1929, won her division, the DW Class limited to aircraft powered by engines rated up to 800 cubic inch displacement, of the Women's Air Derby. To further warm up for her entry into the 1936 Bendix Transcontinental Speed Dash, on 29 May that year she set a speed record for women of 197.958 mph in the C17R Beechcraft popularly known as the Staggerwing.

The stage was set. Louise invited Blanche Wilcox Noyes to join her as navigator for a cross country race in the Staggerwing. Blanche, raised in Ohio, had hoped for a stage career. She changed her career path abruptly when she fell in love with an airmail pilot, Dewey Noyes. As Dewey wanted his bride to share his passion in flying, he purchased her first airplane for her and taught her to fly in only four hours of dual instruction. When she earned her pilot's license in Cleveland in July, 1929, Blanche became Ohio's first certificated woman pilot.

Committed to showing off the Staggerwing to its best advantage, Louise and Blanche climbed aboard the 420-horsepower C17R Beechcraft to leave Floyd Bennett Field, New York, early on 4 September 1936. Averaging an impressive 166 miles per hour, they landed in Los Angeles 14 hours and 55 minutes later. Having contended with adverse weather and radio problems, the two were pleased to simply complete the race. Little did they realize immediately that they had made history. For the first time for women, they took first place in the classic Bendix Transcontinental Speed Dash, the most famous cross-country air race in the United States.

All of the contestants were competing for $15,000 in prize money. In addition to a monetary award to those who finished second, third, fourth, and fifth, prize money was to be divided between the first-place finisher – which was assumed to be a male pilot – and the first-place finisher among the women. Louise Thaden and Blanche Noyes received both first-place prizes – $7,000 as the "man's prize" plus $2,500 for the "feminine pilot making the fastest time." Louise set a new women's east-west transcontinental speed record, beating the previously set time of 18 hours, 23 minutes. To enhance the ironic situation, Laura Ingalls brought her Pratt & Whitney-powered Lockheed to a touchdown in second place in a time of 15 hours, 39 minutes and a prize of $2,500; and Amelia Earhart, also in a Pratt & Whitney-powered Lockheed, landed in 16 hours, 34 minutes for a fifth place finish and $500. As the "outstanding woman pilot in the United States in 1936," Louise Thaden was awarded the Harmon Trophy, awarded by the Ligue Internationale des Aviateurs.

Ambassador Clare Boothe Luce once said, "Because I am a woman, I must make unusual efforts to succeed. If I fail, . . . they will say, 'Women don't have what it takes.'" Clearly, Louise and Blanche, Laura and Amelia dispelled whatever doubts race officials entertained about women pilots prior to the 1936 Bendix. In 1937, Jacqueline Cochran finished third overall in the Bendix and, in 1938, piloted a Seversky fighter plane to a first place victory in 8 hours 10 minutes. Women in all areas of achievement owe debts of gratitude for such stalwart leaders and outstanding role models.

Kathy La Sauce
Leading in Air Force Blue

In 1990, Fred Reed, a columnist for Universal Press Syndicate, wrote in the *New York City Tribune* about military women. He stated, in part, "There seem to be only two positions on women in combat: firmly for and firmly against. . . . My own views, for what they're worth, are as follows. First, no group, whether a racial or gender group, should enjoy special privilege. Men do not enjoy the privilege of deciding whether they want to go to war. Neither should women. . . . Second, the dispute rests on hot air because of the lack of historical experience. I am against the idea in part because, having read a lot of military history starting with the Sumerians of the third millennium B.C., I have encountered no example of a body of women in combat. The presumption is that they either won't or they can't do it."

Sumer was a flourishing Mesopotamian country in today's Southern Iraq; however, Sumerian women were under total domination without recourse or protection under the law; they had no luxury of choosing how they would like to live, much less whether to go to war. Sumer declined four thousand years ago and was later absorbed by Babylonia and Assyria.

Let us take a giant leap forward to the modern era. Forty-eight years before he wrote his article, members of the Women Airforce Service Pilots (WASP) were flying virtually every airplane in the U.S. Army Air Corps' arsenal and serving their country with distinction. Also participating in World War II were three regiments of Russian women who flew as fighter and bomber pilots. They engaged in night combat missions so successfully they were nicknamed the Night Witches for their harassment of Nazi soldiers. Fred Reed missed these accomplishments.

And in 1972 , one particular woman was making her career choice to join the U.S. Air Force. Reed should have met the likes of Kathy La Sauce!

Kathy entered the United States Air Force

Kathy La Sauce, with nine other candidates, earned jet pilot wings from the U.S. Air Force as they completed Undergraduate Pilot Training at Williams Air Force Base, Arizona.

Courtesy Lt. Col. Kathy La Sauce, USAF Retired

during the Vietnam conflict and was among the first women in USAF history to serve as an aircraft maintenance officer. After a year of extensive training on all aircraft systems, she was assigned to Travis AFB, California, and, in 1974, was transferred to Andersen Air Base, Guam. As a maintenance officer, she supervised flightline maintenance, launch and recovery of C-141, C-5 and WC-130 aircraft and was responsible for over 120 maintenance personnel.

Even Kathy couldn't have foreseen the major opportunities that lay ahead. The Air Force, Navy and Army decided to open all service academies to women and, in 1976, the Air Force initiated a test program to train women as pilots in the same curriculum as the men. Kathy was among the first ten women officers selected to be trained as U.S. Air Force pilots. Assigned to Williams Air Force Base, Arizona, she was the first of the women to fly the prop-driven T-41 trainer; the first to fly the T-37 jet trainer and, on 1 November 1976, the first to fly the Northrop T-38 Talon, a supersonic tandem-seat jet – the first woman undergraduate pilot trainee in the history of the U.S. Air Force to fly a jet aircraft.

Kathy would be quick to insist that her nine compatriots Mary H. Donahue, Connie J. Engel, Susan D. Rogers, Victoria K. Crawford, Mary H. Livingston, Carol Ann Scherer, Christine E. Scott, Sandra M. Schott, and Kathleen A. Rambo-Cosand were close behind. Each was a proud officer and, on 2 September 1977, they were the first women to graduate from USAF Undergraduate Pilot Training (UPT) and to earn pilot wings.

Kathy went on to accumulate over 3,000 flight hours in the C-141 Starlifter. Indicative of her talents, she was upgraded to instructor pilot and subsequently to wing flight examiner/instructor pilot, placing her in a very select group. She completed Air Command and Staff College, Armed Forces Staff College and was

Courtesy Lt. Col. Kathy La Sauce, USAF Retired

In 1974, cockpits of the U.S. Navy were opened to women. In 1975, the U.S. Army trained women helicopter pilots and, in 1976, women were given the opportunity to fly for the U.S. Air Force.

Kathy took to the skies in this T-37 Jet Trainer – affectionately known as "Tweetie-Bird" or "Tweet." In 1993, combat roles were opened to women and Kathy played a role in making that possible.

Presidential support aircrew personnel. She went on to become deputy commander for Air Transportation, 89th Airlift Wing and Commander, 93rd Aerial Port Squadron at Andrews Air Force Base.

There she supervised 150 persons and the arrivals and departures of notables. Kathy was on scene for England's Prime Minister Margaret Thatcher, President Mitterand of France, Russia's Raisa Gorbachev, and First Lady Barbara Bush, to name a few. Kathy recalled a memorable moment, ". . . the day that President Ronald Reagan took his last flight in Air Force One. It was my extreme pleasure that, as he boarded the airplane, he gave me his last salute and a wink."

When Lt. Colonel Kathy La Sauce retired, she was the senior ranking woman pilot in the U.S. Military. Despite having set a sterling example, it was after Kathy retired, having spent 20 years in her career field, that women were admitted to flight training with no restrictions on flying first-line aircraft. Kathy and the other nine members of her Air Force class are due admiration and appreciation for having helped lift the ban on combat flying that finally occurred in 1993.

Fred Reed, try to meet outstanding women of achievement in the U.S. military service like this exemplary woman. Perhaps the men of Sumer should have reconsidered the value of women in their society. War for the ancient Sumerians might have gone differently had they given women a chance to serve.

promoted three years below-the-zone to major. She earned her master's degree in aeronautical science from Embry-Riddle Aeronautical University.

The 89th Military Airlift Wing (MAW) stationed at Andrews Air Force Base, Maryland, is the unit responsible for providing air transportation for the U.S. President, the Vice President, Cabinet members, members of Congress, senior Defense Department officials and foreign heads of state. Kathy was the first woman pilot selected to fly with this elite wing. She flew the VC-135 aircraft, a specialized variant of the Boeing 707, and scheduled flight operations for 225

To react positively in challenging situations – COURAGE
To hold a belief, act accordingly and morally – CONVICTION
To impart, discuss and exchange ideas – COMMUNICATION
With awareness, to put another above self – COMPASSION
To be qualified and to exhibit capability – COMPETENCE
To follow a course of action to which bound – COMMITMENT
Ethical strength and moral attributes – CHARACTER
To test ability and skills, to contest – COMPETITION
To seek education and gain knowledge – CURIOSITY
To embark on a quest for victory – CONQUEST

THE POWER OF PERSISTENCE

It is reassuring to know of the existence of women like these *Stars of the Sky*. They truly are the stuff of legends and their qualities should inspire. Their opportunities were seized eagerly and it is stimulating to witness the positive attitude and will to succeed that is demonstrated by each and every one. Like so many other outstanding women of accomplishment, each of the Stars has faced and overcome obstacles with remarkable stick-to-itiveness. Her success reflects the power of persistence.

In analyzing paths taken to rewarding and remunerative careers, from the accidental as in Air Traffic Controller Ruth Maestre's encouragement from her boss in a fast-food restaurant to those determined in early childhood as in Astronaut Dr. Mae Jemison's study of the solar system that drew her to science, the options vary widely. At this writing, almost five thousand job opportunities are listed as available on the website: www.avjobs.com. The website www.careersinaviation.org lists opportunities in fields such as: aircraft design, systems engineering, test

piloting, search and rescue, human factors, air traffic control, jet mechanics, electrical engineering, computer systems, airport management, space exploration, and customer service in the aviation/aerospace industry.

Women in Aviation, International, via its website: www.wai.org, provides a variety of avenues for career opportunities, vocational guidance and networking possibilities. The site states, in part, "During the last two decades, the number of women involved in the aviation industry has steadily increased and women can be found in nearly every aviation occupation today. However, the numbers are small by comparison. Women pilots, for example, represent only six percent of the total pilot population.

"At the first Annual International Women in Aviation Conference in 1990, participants recognized the need for more women in the industry and for a support group to serve as mentors, advisors and interested colleagues. Following a number of successful conferences, Women in Aviation, International (WAI), was established as a professional, non-profit organization in 1994 to address those needs."

Women in Aviation, International, has taken huge strides to promote and assist women in all facets of the aviation and aerospace industries. As a vital and important organization, it has gained wide recognition and made a series of valuable partnerships, all of which extend its sphere of influence.

This throws wide the doors of opportunity to those with the interest, the drive and the tenacity to pursue their dreams and to exert the power of persistence. The essential message of the preceding stories is one of encouragement for you, the reader, to aspire to fulfill your hopes and your dreams and to make worthwhile and satisfying choices. Emulate these heroines who competed with the elements of nature, faced the unknown

and surpassed even their own awareness of their capabilities. Not one has taken "no" for an answer. If she had talent, she went on to hone it; if she gained education, she applied and enhanced it; if she was the beneficiary of some good fortune that might be termed "luck," she applied herself and put it to use. Above all, when she was introduced to some element of aviation, she persisted in dedicating herself to success. There were no shortcuts; each woman chose her own destiny and made it happen.

There are lessons to be learned from such women – lessons in reaching beyond one's boundaries and in calling upon inner strength when goals are worthy. There are lessons in starting anew when necessary. Their values can encourage you to assess your values; their choices can inspire you to make wise choices. Their "can do" attitudes are contagious and their joys are irrepressible

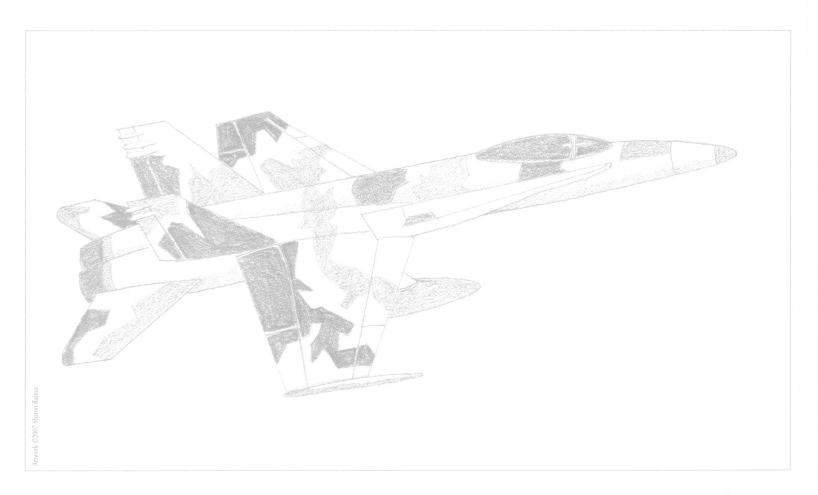

Artwork ©2007 Sharon Rajnus

The F-18 Hornet is an all-weather attack/fighter operating either from carriers or land bases. It is superb as a fighter escort, suppression of enemy air defenses, reconnaissance, all air control and support, and day and night missions. It has a digital control-by-wire flight system providing exceptional handling qualities. This system provides excellent maneuverability and allows the pilot to concentrate on the weapons system as evasive action is taken. The fractal camouflage paint shown is used to reduce a visible signature to deceive and confuse the enemy.

Bibliography

Stars Of The Sky, Legends All

Books:

Bohrer, Walt. *BLACK CATS AND OUTSIDE LOOPS, Tex Rankin: Aerobatic Ace*, Plere Publishers, Oregon City, OR, 1989.

Bragg, Janet Harmon. *SOARING ABOVE SETBACKS, The Autobiography of Janet Harmon Bragg*, Smithsonian Institution Press, Washington and London, 1996.

Cooper, Ann. *HOW HIGH SHE FLIES, Dorothy Swain Lewis*, Aviatrix Publishing, Chicago, IL, 1998.

Cooper, Ann. *RISING ABOVE IT, Edna Gardner Whyte*, Orion Books, Crown Publishers, New York, 1991.

Cooper, Charlie and Cooper, Ann. *Tuskegee's Heroes, featuring the Aviation Art of Roy E. La Grone*, Motorbooks International, Osceola, Wisconsin, 1996.

Dillard, Annie. *THE WRITING LIFE*, Harper & Row Publishers, New York, New York, 1989.

Dwiggins, Don. *HOLLYWOOD PILOT, The Biography of Paul Mantz*, Doubleday & Co., New York, 1967.

Earhart, Amelia. *FOR THE FUN OF IT*, Reprint, Academy Chicago Publishers, 1977. Originally Published by Harcourt Brace, New York, 1932.

Haskins, Jim. *AFRICAN-AMERICAN ENTREPRENEURS*, John Wiley and Sons, New York, NY, 1998.

Hodgson, Marion Stegemen. *WINNING MY WINGS*, Naval Institute Press, Annapolis, Maryland, 1996.

Holden, Henry and Griffith Cline, Captain Lori. *LADYBIRDS II, The Continuing Story of American Women in Aviation*, Black Hawk Publishing Company, Mt. Freedom, New Jersey, 1993.

Jackson, Donald Dale and the Editors. *THE AERONAUTS*, Time-Life Books, Alexandria, VA, 1981.

Jemison, Dr. Mae. *FIND WHERE THE WIND GOES, Moments from my Life*, Scholastic Press, New York, NY, 2001.

Jessen, Gene Nora. *THE POWDER PUFF DERBY OF 1929*, Sourcebooks, Inc., Naperville, IL 2002.

Ladd, Michelle. *PRINCESS KICK-A-HOLE-IN-THE-SKY, "Golden Age Aerobatic Ace."* Essay for Professor Schmitz, America Between the Wars, December 11, 1987.

Lindbergh, Anne Morrow. *THE UNICORN and Other Poems*, 1935-1955. Pantheon Books, Inc., New York. 1956.

Long, Elgen M., and Marie K. *AMELIA EARHART, The Mystery Solved*, Simon and Schuster, New York, NY, 1999.

Mackersey, Ian. *JEAN BATTEN, The Garbo of the Skies*, McDonald & Company, Ltd, London, England, 1990.

Maurer, Richard. *THE WRIGHT SISTER, Katharine Wright and Her Famous Brothers*, Roaring Brook Press, Brookfield, CT, 2003.

McCallister. Bruce. *WINGS OVER DENALI*, Roundup Press, Boulder, CO, 2004.

McDaniel, William H. *BEECHCRAFT, FIFTY YEARS OF EXCELLENCE*, McCormick-Armstrong Co., Inc., Wichita, Kansas. 1982.

Mead, Margaret. *BLACKBERRY WINTER*, William Morrow & Company, Inc., New York, 1972.

Meyer, Corwin H. *FLIGHT JOURNAL, A TEST PILOT'S TALES OF DODGING DISASTERS – JUST IN TIME*, Specialty Press, North Branch, Minnesota, 2006.

Mitchell, Charles R. and House, Kirk W. *FLYING HIGH, PIONEER WOMEN IN AMERICAN AVIATION*, Arcadia Publishing, Charleston, SC, 2002.

Mock, Jerrie Fredritz. *THREE-EIGHT CHARLIE*, J.B. Lippincott Company, Philadelphia / New York, 1970.

Oakes, Claudia M. *UNITED STATES WOMEN IN AVIATION THROUGH WORLD WAR I*, Smithsonian Studies in Air and Space, Number 2, Smithsonian Institution Press, Washington, DC, 1978.

Phillips, Ed. *TRAVEL AIR, WINGS OVER THE PRAIRIE*, Flying Books, Eagan, MN, 1982.

PLANCK, CHARLES E. *WOMEN WITH WINGS*, HARPER AND BROTHERS, NEW YORK AND LONDON, 1942.

REITSCH, HANNA. *FLYING IS MY LIFE*, TRANSLATED BY LAWRENCE WILSON, G.P. PUTNAM'S SONS, NY, 1954.

ROSS, MARK C. *DANGEROUS BEAUTY, LIFE AND DEATH IN AFRICA*; TRUE STORIES FROM A SAFARI GUIDE, HYPERION, NEW YORK, NY, 2001.

RUSSO, CAROLYN. *WOMEN AND FLIGHT, PORTRAITS OF CONTEMPORARY WOMEN PILOTS*. SMITHSONIAN INSTITUTION, 1997.

SCHMID, S.H. "WES" AND WEAVER, TRUMAN C. *THE GOLDEN AGE OF AIR RACING*, PRE-1940, VOL. 1, EAA AVIATION FOUNDATION, INC., OSHKOSH, WI, 1983.

SCHMID, S.H. "WES" AND WEAVER, TRUMAN C. *THE GOLDEN AGE OF AIR RACING*, PRE-1940, VOL. 2, EAA AVIATION FOUNDATION, INC., OSHKOSH, WI, 1983.

SKELTON, BETTY. *BETTY SKELTON'S "LITTLE STINKER,"* CROSS PRESS, WINTER HAVEN, FLORIDA, 1977.

STREETMAN, JOE W. AND PERL, ADOLPH R. (BUD). *THE LINDBERGHS SOAR IN SAN DIEGO*, STREETMAN AND PERL, 10427 LA MORADA DRIVE, SAN DIEGO, CA, 2000.

TAYLOR, MICHAEL J.H., EDITOR. *JANE'S ENCYCLOPEDIA OF AVIATION*, JANE'S PUBLISHING COMPANY, LTD., LONDON, 1980.

TOWARD, LILIAS M. MABEL BELL, *ALEXANDER'S SILENT PARTNER*, BRETON BOOKS, METHUEN, CANADA, 1984.

VAUGHAN, DAVID KIRK. *ANNE MORROW LINDBERGH*, TWAYNE'S UNITED STATES AUTHORS SERIES, KENNETH E. EBLE, EDITOR, UNIVERSITY OF UTAH, G.K. HALL & CO., BOSTON.1988.

YANNUZZI, DELLA A. *MAE JEMISON, A SPACE BIOGRAPHY*, ENSLOW PUBLISHERS, INC., BERKELEY HEIGHTS, NEW JERSEY, 1998.

COLLECTIONS:

DEWEY, DAWNE, ARCHIVIST. KATHARINE WRIGHT HASKELL, SPECIAL COLLECTIONS AND ARCHIVES, THE WRIGHT STATE UNIVERSITY LIBRARIES, DAYTON, OHIO.

MAGAZINE ARTICLES:

"KINGS EXPLORE GA DURING WORLD FLIGHT," EAA SPORT AVIATION, 2005.

"SCHOOL FOR WILLA," TIME MAGAZINE, "NATIONAL AFFAIRS," 25 SEPTEMBER 1939.

"THE QUEEN OF AIRCRAFT IS A KING," WOMAN PILOT MAGAZINE, APRIL 1998.

ALEXANDER GRAHAM BELL. A BROCHURE, MARITIME TELEGRAPH & TELEPHONE COMPANY LIMITED, BADDECK, NOVA SCOTIA, CANADA.

CRIGLER, PAT. "HARRIET QUIMBY AND CONNIE TOBIAS, WOMEN PILOTS OF YESTERDAY AND TODAY," U.S. AIRWAYS NEWS, 8 AUGUST 2001.

DORCEY, ROSE. "WASP TRIBUTE DEDICATED AT THE HIGHGROUND", AERO-NEWS.NET, 1 AUGUST 2006.

GARY, DEBBIE. "GUIDE TO THE GREAT AIRSHOW ACTS YOU MUST SEE," AIR & SPACE SMITHSONIAN, MAY 2007.

GIAMO, COLONEL CHRIS USAF-RETIRED AND PAULS, COLONEL JIM, USAF-RETIRED. "COAST GUARD AUXILIARY PILOT SPEAKS AT LUNCHEON," MILITARY OFFICER, MILITARY OFFICERS ASSOCIATION OF AMERICA, AUGUST, 2004.

HARDY, JEFF. "A DREAM OF WINGS," MOBILE, ALABAMA REGISTER. DATE UNKNOWN.

HOLDEN, HENRY. "CONNIE TOBIAS, I CAN, IF I TRY," WOMAN PILOT, JANUARY/FEBRUARY 2002.

HOLSTON, KEN. "HONORING HEROES," WARBIRDS, EXPERIMENTAL AIRCRAFT ASSOCIATION, JULY 2003.

JONES, MARY. "CONNIE BOWLIN, COOL, CALM, COLLECTED WARBIRD PILOT," AVIATION FOR WOMEN, MARCH/APRIL 1999.

KING, PAT. "ALASKA 99S CELEBRATE 50 YEARS ENCOURAGING WOMEN TO FLY," ALASKA JOURNAL OF COMMERCE, 12 JANUARY 2004.

LABODA, AMY. "SUCCEED," A SPEECH, REPRODUCED BY PERMISSION FROM THE AUTHOR.

LADD, MICHELLE. "PRINCESS-KICK-A-HOLE-IN-THE-SKY, GOLDEN AGE AEROBATIC ACE," AN ESSAY FOR A CLASS IN AMERICA BETWEEN THE WARS, 11 DECEMBER 1987. MICHELLE IS THE GRANDDAUGHTER OF DOROTHY HESTER.

LANDDECK, KATE. "I COULDN'T BELIEVE MY LUCK!" CARO BAYLEY BOSCA, WASP, WOMAN PILOT MAGAZINE, JULY-AUGUST 2000.

LEONHIRTH, JANENE. "TENNESSEE'S EXPERIMENT: WOMEN AS MILITARY FLIGHT INSTRUCTORS," TENNESSEE HISTORICAL QUARTERLY, VOLUME LI, NUMBER 3, NASHVILLE, TENNESSEE, FALL 1992.

ROBERTS, DAVID. "THE ADVENTURES OF KITTY BANNER," OUTSIDE MAGAZINE, 1982.

ROCHE, JAMES G., SECRETARY OF THE U.S. AIR FORCE; "AN UNBROKEN TRADITION OF EXCELLENCE," REMARKS TO THE WOMEN IN AVIATION, INTERNATIONAL, RENO, NV, 12 MARCH 2004.

SCHNELL, CARAMIE. "HIGH COUNTRY CHARACTER," VAIL TRAIL, COLORADO, 9 SEPTEMBER 2004.

SHEPPARD, LAUREL "SISTER OF FLIGHT," VIA PRIVATE CORRESPONDENCE, LASHPUBS@INFINET.COM.

SLACK, GENE. "TEN WOMEN PILOT INSTRUCTORS," JANUARY 1943, NEWSPAPER CLIPPING, CREDIT DOT SWAIN LEWIS.

TERRAZZANO, LAUREN. "THAT GIRL CAN FLY," NEWSDAY, 14 DECEMBER 2000

THADEN, BILL AND WEBB, PAT THADEN. "LOUISE THADEN: PIONEER AVIATOR," VINTAGE AIRPLANE, VOL. 17, NO. 5, EAA ANTIQUE/CLASSIC DIVISION, OSHKOSH, WISCONSIN, MAY 1989.

Tompkins, Captain Mimi. "Critical Incident Stress Management: Preparing for the Aftermath," The International Society of Women Airline Pilots, 1997.

U.S. Department of Transportation, Federal Highway Administration. "Women In Transportation: Changing America's History," Office of Engineering, HNG-22, Office of Highway Information Management, March 1998.

Wideman, Steve. "Not As Crazy As It Looks," Post Crescent Newspaper, Neenah, WI, 2002.

Websites:

HTTP://AEROFILES.COM/_WACO.HTML

HTTP://AFHRA.MAXWELL.AF.MIL/WWWROOT/RSO/MAJOR_COMMANDS.HTML

HTTP://ALASKAWOMENPILOTS.COM

HTTP://ARCHIVES.CBC.CA

HTTP://ARTICLES.GOURT.COM.EDU/

HTTP://WWW.LINDBERGHFOUNDATION.ORG/HISTORY/AMLBIO.HTML

HTTP://WWW.LL.MIT.EDU/ABOUT/ABOUT.HTML

HTTP://WWW.MAEJEMISON.COM/PROJECTS/PROJECTS.HTML

HTTP://WWW.MILITARY.COM

HTTP://WWW.MNSU.EDU/EMUSEUM/CULTURAL/OLDWORLD/AFRICA/HUTU.HTML

HTTP://WWW.MONOLOGS.NET/ARCHIVES/2005/02/

HTTP://WWW.MUNI.ORG/MERRILLI/PANEOKI.CFM

HTTP://WWW.MUSEUMOFFLIGHT.ORG

HTTP://WWW.MYWISEOWL.COM/ARTICLES/V-1

HTTP://WWW.NAA.AERO/

HTTP://WWW.NASA.GOV/RETURNTOFLIGHT/CREW/

HTTP://WWW.NASM.SI.EDU/RESEARCH

HTTP://WWW.NATIONALAIRTOUR.ORG/

HTTP://WWW.NATIONALAVIATION.ORG

HTTP://WWW.NINETY-NINES.ORG

HTTP://WWW.NPR.ORG

HTTP://WWW.NTSB.GOV

HTTP://WWW.NWHP.ORG/TLP/BIOGRAPHIES/JEMISON/JEMISON-BIO.HTML

HTTP://WWW.NZEDGE.COM/HEROES/BATTEN.HTML

HTTP://WWW.OREGONAERO.COM

HTTP://WWW.OREGONAVIATION.ORG

HTTP://WWW.OUTSIDETHEBELTWAY.COM/ARCHIVES/10987

HTTP://WWW.PATTYWAGSTAFF.COM

HTTP://WWW.PEPSITEAM@AOL.COM

HTTP://WWW.PILOTFRIEND.COM/CENTURY-OF-FLIGHT

HTTP://WWW.PILOTSUNITED.COM

HTTP://WWW.PUBLICSHELTER.COM/FLYGIRLS/PROLOGUE/BETH.HTML

HTTP://WWW.PYLONCLUB.COM/HARMON.HTM

HTTP://WWW.RACEDR.COM

HTTP://WWW.RADIOCLUBOFAMERICA.ORG

HTTP://WWW.RADIO-CLUB-OF-AMERICA.ORG/HISTORY1.HTM

HTTP://WWW.RAJNUSART.COM

HTTP://WWW.RARENEWSPAPERS.COM/VIEWISSUE.ASPX?ID=200194

HTTP://WWW.RCOOPER.OCATCH.COM/EGROVMAS.HTM

HTTP://WWW.RIVERDEEP.NET

HTTP://WWW.RONSARCHIVE.COM/OSHKOSH02

HTTP://WWW.ROTORUANZ.COM/ROTORUANZ/PASSWORD/ABOUT_ROTORUA/HISTORY/ROTORUASTORIES/JEAN_BATTEN.HTM

HTTP://WWW.SAFARIWEB.COM

HTTP://WWW.SAFARIWEB.COM/SAFARIMATE/KWS.HTM

HTTP://WWW.SALLYRIDECAMPS.COM

HTTP://WWW.SCLCWOMENINC.ORG/DMFJ2005.HTML

HTTP://WWW.SI.EDU/ARCHIVES/IHD/VIDEOCATALOG/9545.HTM

HTTP://WWW.SKYGOD.COM

HTTP://WWW.SOUTHWEST.COM

HTTP://WWW.SPACEFLIGHTNOW.COM/SHUTTLE/STS114/050728DOCKING/

HTTP://WWW.STEENAERO.COM

HTTP://WWW.SUSANMAULE.COM/

HTTP://WWW.THUNDERBIRDS.AIRFORCE.COM

HTTP://WWW.TUSKEGEE.EDU/

HTTP://WWW.UH.EDU/ENGINES/EPI1857.HTM

HTTP://WWW.UNGERMARK.SE/LAKEHURST.HTML

HTTP://WWW.USAFTHUNDERBIRDS.COM

HTTP://WWW.USAIRWAYS.COM/ABOUT/PRESS

HTTP://WWW.USATODAY.COM/NEWS/SEPT11/2002-08-12-CLEARSKIES_X.HTM

HTTP://WWW.USCGAUX.ORG/~130/

HTTP://WWW.USNTPS.NAVY.MIL/

HTTP://WWW.WACOAIRMUSEUM.ORG/SPECIAL/JOEMACKEY.HTM

HTTP://WWW.WAI.ORG

HTTP://WWW.WALTER-ROCKETS.I12.COM/WALTER/ME163A.HTM

HTTP://WWW.WARBIRDS-EAA.ORG

HTTP://WWW.WASPWWII.ORG/NEWS/03_05_03.HTM

HTTP://WWW.WEBSWITHWINGS.COM/WCC/HEROINES/MAE.HTML

HTTP://WWW.WINGSOVERKANSAS.COM

HTTP://WWW.WISINFO.COM/POSTCRESCENT/NEWS

HTTP://WWW.WOMEN-IN-AVIATION.COM

HTTP://WWW.WOMENINAVIATION.COM/WILLA.HTML

HTTP://WWW.WOMENMILITARYAVIATORS.ORG/

HTTP://WWW.WORLDNOMAD.NET

HTTP://WWW.ZUNDELSITE.ORG/GERMAN/ARTIKEL/HANNAI.HTML

WOMEN AND SPECIAL MENTION

AIRCRAFT

ORGANIZATIONS, SCHOOLS, PROGRAMS